James Dean Died Here

James Dean Died Here

The Locations of America's Pop Culture Landmarks

Chris Epting

SANTA
MONICA
PRESS

SANTA
MONICA
PRESS

Published by:
Santa Monica Press LLC
P.O. Box 1076
Santa Monica, CA 90406-1076
1-800-784-9553
www.santamonicapress.com
books@santamonicapress.com

Printed in the United States

Santa Monica Press books are available at special quantity discounts when purchased in bulk by corporations, organizations, or groups. Please call our Special Sales department at 1-800-784-9553.

Important Note: Although every effort was made to ensure that the information in this book was correct at the time of going to press, the author and publisher do not assume and hereby disclaim any liability or responsibility to any person or group with respect to any loss, illness, injury, or damage caused by errors, omissions, or any other information found in this book.

ISBN 1-891661-31-0

Library of Congress Cataloging-in-Publication Data

Epting, Chris, 1961-
  James Dean died here : the locations of America's pop culture
landmarks / by Chris Epting.
     p. cm.
  ISBN 1-891661-31-0
 1. Historic sites—United States—Guidebooks. 2. Popular
culture—United States—History. 3. United States—Guidebooks. 4.
United States—History, Local. I. Title.
E159.E68 2003
306'.0973—dc21

                         2003002372

Please visit www.chrisepting.com

Book and cover design by Ohmontherange Design

Front cover image: Don't go looking for this sign on the backroads of Central California — alas, it only exists in cyberspace!

Table of Contents

This book is dedicated with love to my wife, Jean; my son, Charlie; and my daughter, Claire.

"Bringing up a family should be an adventure, not an anxious discipline in which everybody is constantly graded for performance."

—*Milton R. Saperstein*

"Remember . . . as far as anyone knows, we're a nice, normal family."

—*Homer Simpson*

Introduction

I believe that no other country embraces, studies, celebrates, laments, digests, and analyzes pop culture like America. Maybe it's because we virtually invented the modern concept of pop culture—this interesting, sometimes uneven mix of history, current events, and celebrity. But in trying to define "pop culture" in order to create a yardstick for this collection, I still found myself searching for a proper definition of what the term means. Then, buried in an obscure, online encyclopedia, I found this:

"Pop Culture: Those series of activities & events that are more or less equivalent to national identity."

In one simple sentence, it was just what I needed: a frame to hold these hundreds of "tiles" (which is how I have now come to view all of the entries in this book). Some tiles are bigger than others, some more interesting to look at, some more colorful, some more vital, but each one necessary to create a full and complete mosaic. In this case, the mosaic forms the American pop culture experience.

But while that definition helped set a criterion for what I would include in this book, it didn't address the main concept. The purpose of this book is not merely to list the events that helped shape our national identity. Rather, the purpose of this book is to identify the exact places where these events took place, thus allowing one to stand on the spot where pop culture history was made.

Think of all the events that have touched us. The news stories, movies, songs, concerts, and television shows. The tragedies, heroic deeds, controversies, and strange phenomena. The historic events we learned in school, from Columbus to Lincoln to Lindbergh to Kennedy . . . all of the moments that have amazed us, stunned us, entertained us, delighted us, appalled us. The landmarks which shaped our tastes, opinions, and passions.

Some aspects of these events we tend remember more than others. For instance, who was involved. When it happened. What the details might have been. But the one component that seems least available is where exactly did the event occur?

We're taught that Columbus discovered the new world, but just where exactly did he land? Where was Lincoln standing when he delivered the "Gettysburg Address"? Where did Lindbergh take off from on his famous transatlantic flight? Images of the Hindenburg's fiery crash are iconic, but where exactly did it occur? We all can picture Marilyn Monroe's white dress billowing up as she stood over a subway grating. But where exactly was she standing? Where did Buddy Holly crash? Where did Jimi Hendrix burn his guitar? Where did Wilt Chamberlain score 100 points? Does the Brady Bunch house really exist? And where exactly was John F. Kennedy, Jr. standing when he saluted his father's casket? That remote intersection on a desolate stretch of highway where James Dean was killed . . . where the heck is it?

Has the exact spot ever been documented? Is it marked? Can I go stand there if I want to? Has it been turned into a parking lot?

I wrote this book to help answer those questions, and all the others that might arise as one attempts to trace the physical path of pop culture history. After all, I think there are many of us who feel the need to visit these places. It's hard to pinpoint exactly why, but for me it's always been about getting "closer" to the event by gaining the same physical perspective as the subject. Whether the environment has been altered or not, you still get a sense of place. Other people I talk to about this seem to have the same motivation, in some cases coupled with a nostalgic desire to make some sense of a part of their own past.

As I began putting this book together, it became clear that its two most important aspects would be:

1. The criteria in choosing the events.

2. The categorizing of these events.

As for the first aspect, choosing the events, there were two simple questions that I attempted to measure each entry against: Would most people be generally aware of the event or landmark? Would most people be unfamiliar with the exact location?

Naturally, there are exceptions to every rule. I'd like to believe that many of the things I've included are at least semi-familiar to most of you reading this. But I've also included some you probably are not aware of, which I feel are relevant in helping to fill out this pop culture mosaic. For instance, most people are aware of the devastating Chicago fire that happened October 8, 1871, started perhaps by Mrs. O'Leary's cow. So in this book, you'll discover the exact site where that fire originated. But did you know that on that same day, an even more devastating fire occurred in Peshtigo, Wisconsin? It's not surrounded by the myth and lore of the Chicago blaze, but it's an event that (I believe) belongs in a collection like this.

Generally speaking, American historical events (including natural disasters and major tragedies) were fairly easy to choose. Where Washington crossed the Delaware, where the Declaration of Independence was signed, where Francis Scott Key wrote "The Star Spangled Banner," etc., are matters of deep historic record and are natural inclusions in a book like this.

However, when it came to the more subjective choosing of events/landmarks that involved the arts, things got trickier. After all, who is to say which film or concert or television program has earned a place among pop culture icons? In my selection, I tried as hard as I could to not let my own tastes get in the way. I chose movies that I believe have stood the popular test of time (i.e. *Casablanca*) and/or greatly influenced pop culture (i.e. *Saturday Night Fever*). Of course, it also helps when there is an actual public place to go visit, given that most movie sets are closed environments. The same standards applied for television, music, and sports sites. Did the event leave an indelible mark on pop culture? Were many people affected by it? Do people still care about it today?

All of the caveat questions aside, I know there are bound to be some issues not just with what has been left out, but with what I have chosen to include as well. As I have learned in discussing this book with friends, that's the fun of a project like this—it demands a debate fueled by personal taste and dissenting opinion.

As for the categorizing of the locations, many events could easily fit into more than one category. For instance, Marvin Gaye was murdered by his father. It's a crime, but he was a singer.

Crime section? Music section? Where does it belong? What we did (myself and my publisher, Jeffrey Goldman) was to classify each event based on its most definitive element. Thus, Marvin Gaye goes into the Celebrity Deaths and Infamous Celebrity Events chapter. Once again, opinions will no doubt differ as to whether each event is in its most appropriate place. But I can assure, we did the best we could given the eclectic range of information. That's sort of the trademark of American pop culture—the wildly disparate quality of what ends up entering the national consciousness.

So that's about it.

Whether you visit these places or not, I hope you find comfort in simply knowing that they actually do exist, that you could go there if you wanted to. To reflect, to inspect, to gain some new insight, perspective, or appreciation. There are so many anonymous, out of the way spots which have been forever altered after their random brush with history. Some have become national historic landmarks, others have evolved into places for fans to pay homage, and many have been forgotten almost entirely.

But however they exist today, they are real.

So, if you've ever found yourself wondering, "Where exactly did that happen?"

Well, look no further. Because you're about to find out.

Chris Epting

PS—The author and the publisher kindly request that readers respect the sanctity and/or privacy of the locations listed in this book.

Thank you!

Americana: The Weird and the Wonderful

Apple Computer

2066 Crist Drive
Los Altos, California

It was 1975 and the paths of two Bay Area tech-heads, teenagers Steve Jobs and Steve Wozniak, had crossed once again. This time, Wozniak was working on a primitive fore-runner of the personal computer. Hewlett-Packard and Atari showed little interest in the invention, but Jobs thought there was something to the device and insisted that he and Woz start a company.

In 1977, they wound up here in the Jobs family's garage, where Jobs' father removed his car-restoration gear and helped the boys by hauling home a huge wooden workbench that served as their first manufacturing base. The Apple Computer Company was born.

Area 51

Groom Lake, Nevada

Directions: From Las Vegas take I-15 north for 22 miles. At exit 64 take US-93 north. After 85 miles, 12 miles past Alamo, you come to the intersection with Highway 318 on the left. Directly across the road, to your right, you will see the ruins of an old casino. At the intersection, turn left onto Highway 318. After less than a mile turn left again onto Highway 375. At that intersection you will see the "Extraterrestrial Highway" signs. From the beginning of Highway 375 it is about 15 miles to the beginning of Groom Lake Road, 20 miles to the Black Mailbox and 39 miles to Rachel.

Area 51, also known as Groom Lake, is a top-secret military facility about 90 miles north of Las Vegas. The number "51" refers to a 6-by-10-mile block of land, at the center of which resides a large air base the government keeps under heavy wraps. The site was selected in the mid-1950s for testing of the U-2 spyplane due to its remoteness, proximity to existing facilities, and presence of a dry lake bed for landings. Due to all of the government secrecy, the area is a hotbed of UFO interest. The boundary of the base is patrolled by a high-tech security system that can detect movement around the installation.

Another 20 miles down Highway 375 is the Black Mailbox, where a former Area 51 worker led groups to view strange aerial displays above the region in the early 1990s. Visitors from all over the world (this world) have left hastily-scrawled thoughts on the box over the years, making it an interesting landmark in an otherwise barren area.

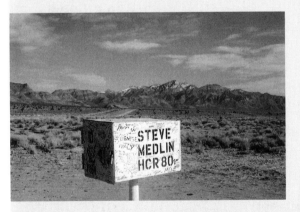

Travel another 19 miles and you'll come to the town of Rachel, Nevada. Dubbed the "UFO Capital of the World," Rachel continues to be a popular destination among UFO fans all over the world, especially those who are attracted to Area 51. This is due to the fact that it's the closest town to the Area 51 region, though "town" seems to be a bit of an overstatement. In Rachel you'll find the Little A'Le'Inn (pronounced "Little Alien"), a casual restaurant and bar that has some fun with its own history, a UFO gift shop, and the Area 51 Research Center.

Arizona Meteor Crater

Located off Interstate 40 at exit 233, 35 miles east of Flagstaff,
20 miles west of Winslow, Arizona
800-289-5898

50,000 years ago, a huge iron-nickel meteorite, hurtling at about 40,000 miles per hour, struck the rocky plain of Northern Arizona with an explosive force greater than 20 million tons of TNT. In less than a few seconds, the meteorite, estimated to have been about 150 feet across and weighing several hundred thousand tons, left a crater 700 feet deep and over 4,000 feet wide. Large blocks of limestone, some the size of small houses, were heaved onto the rim. Flat-lying beds of rock in the crater walls were overturned in fractions of a second and uplifted permanently as much as 150 feet.

Today the crater is 550 feet deep, and 2.4 miles in circumference. Twenty football games could be played simultaneously on its floor, while more than two million spectators could observe from its sloping sides. The topographical terrain of the Arizona Meteor Crater so closely resembles that of the Earth's moon and other planets, that NASA designated it as one of the official training sites for the Apollo Astronauts. The U.S. Government deemed the crater a natural landmark in 1968.

Baby Jessica

3309 Tanner Drive
Midland, Texas

On October 14, 1987, an eighteen-month-old toddler named Jessica McClure fell 22 feet into an abandoned Midland water well that was only eight inches in diameter. For the next three days, rescuers frantically dug a tunnel to reach her while the little girl sang nursery rhymes to herself, called for "Mama," and cried. To keep her company, local police officer Andy Glasscock would call down into the well, "How does a kitten go?" "Meow," Jessica would call back.

Baby Jessica's plight mesmerized the country. CNN covered the story around the clock. When she was finally pulled from the well, the three major networks interrupted their regular programming to cover the moment. Jessica was honored at parades and at a White House ceremony. She was featured on *The Oprah Winfrey Show*, the cover of *People* magazine, and was the subject of a television movie. At the Centennial Plaza in Midland, you'll find a bronze plaque depicting the rescue of Jessica McClure. The address is 105 N. Main; phone is: 915-683-3381.

Bigfoot

About one mile upstream from the confluence of Notice Creek and Bluff Creek
Bluff Creek, California (Humboldt County)
Six Rivers National Forest: 707-442-1721

This remote area (about 38 air miles south of the California/Oregon border and 18 air miles inland from the Pacific Ocean) is in the Six Rivers National Forest. Bigfoot footprints had been found there in prior years, which is why Roger Patterson and Robert Gimlin went out there on horseback on October 20, 1967. They were searching for the creature and, as the world would soon learn, they claimed to have found it.

At first sight of the beast, Patterson's horse reared and knocked him to the ground, but he was able to get his movie camera out and shoot what has become the most famous Bigfoot footage ever recorded. Though it's never been proven to be authentic, Bigfoot aficionado Al Hodgson spoke to Patterson the night the footage was shot, and Al has said that what he heard in his friend's voice felt like nothing but the truth.

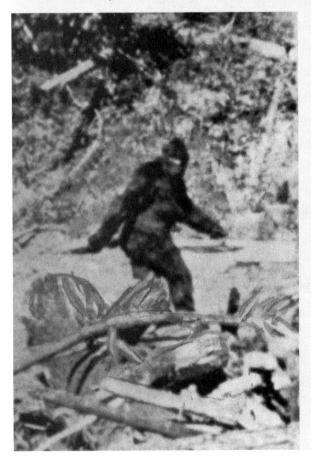

Whatever you believe, there is no denying how compelling the image is of the "Bigfoot" calmly walking off into the woods and looking over his shoulder as the camera rolls. Although other films supposedly showing the creature have been produced, nothing holds a candle to this, the film that first crystallized the myth. Plans are underway to try and erect a marker in the woods identifying the exact spot of the filming.

Bohemian Grove

One mile east of Bohemian Highway; just east of the bridge which leads to Monte Rio,
on the south side of the Russian River
Monte Rio, California

The "secret society" Bohemian Grove is a secluded campground in California's Sonoma County, and is the site of an annual two-week gathering of a highly select, all-male club, whose members have included every Republican president since Calvin Coolidge. Current participants include George Bush, Henry Kissinger, James Baker, and David Rockefeller – a virtual who's who of the most powerful men in business and government. Located in a secluded area 65 miles north of San Francisco, The Grove is owned by the Bohemian Club in San Francisco. Rumor has it that through elaborate stage productions and other entertainment, campers are able to bond with fellow elites.

Branch Davidians

Waco, Texas

Directions: From the Waco Tourist Information Center (I-35 at University Parks Drive) take IH-35 North just across the river to the Lake Brazos exit. Go right on Lake Brazos. Just across from the Holiday Inn is Orchard Lane. Turn left on Orchard Lane and go to Loop 340 where you will turn right. A short distance on the left is FM 2491. Turn left onto that road. You will come to a split in the road, but stay on 2491 which bears to the left. About 5 miles from Loop 340, you will see large wavy metal gates (Double E Ranch Road) on the left (not far from the split). Just beyond that property is a gravel road on the left (Double EE Ranch Road). Turn down that gravel road. The Mount Carmel property is a short distance on the right.

On February 28, 1993, a team of agents from the U.S. Bureau of Alcohol, Tobacco, and Firearms (ATF) launched an assault on the premises of a religious community called Mount Carmel, outside Waco, Texas. The community was occupied by a sect called the Branch Davidians, who were led by a man named Vernon Howell, aka David Koresh. The raid resulted in a shootout in which four ATF agents and six Davidians were killed. This was followed by a 51-day standoff, which ended in an assault on the premises on April 19, 1993, and a fire in which 76 of the occupants died, including many women and children. The circumstances of the assault brought intense criticism of the way government agents handled the situation. Today, the site is scattered with remnants of the tragedy, including several makeshift shrines, tombstone markers, and  a small, freestanding exhibit with information and observations regarding the event.

Buffalo Wings

Anchor Bar
1047 Main Street
Buffalo, New York
716-886-8920

In 1964, Dominic Bellissimo was tending bar at the now famous Anchor Bar Restaurant in Buffalo, New York. Late that evening a group of Dominic's friends arrived at the bar touting a ravenous appetite. Dominic asked his mother, Teressa, to prepare something

for his friends to eat. At about midnight, Teressa brought out two plates she had prepared in the kitchen and placed them on the bar. They looked like chicken wings, a part of the chicken that usually went into the stock pot for soup. Teressa had deep fried the wings and flavored them with a secret sauce.

The wings were an instant hit and it didn't take long for people to flock to the bar to experience this new eating sensation. From that point on, Buffalo Wings became a regular part of the menu at the Anchor Bar. Today, the original restaurant is internationally famous and a tourist destination in Buffalo that serves up over a thousand pounds of wings each day to the likes of famous movie stars, professional athletes, political leaders, and thousands of customers who seek the unique and great taste of their Original Buffalo Wings.

Cabbage Patch Dolls

Baby Land General Hospital
73 West Underwood Street, Cleveland, Georgia
706-865-2171

In 1979, Baby Land General Hospital in Cleveland, Georgia began producing Cabbage Patch dolls. Designed by sculptor Xavier Roberts, the unusual dolls had odd, round faces and tiny, pudgy arms. The eyes were close set, and their hair was made of yarn. Each doll was

unique unto itself, making each original "Cabbage Patch Kid" a one-of-a-kind. The dolls became insanely popular in the '80s, but the fad has since died down. Even so, you can still experience the "magic' here where they were "born" in this "hospital" where sales personnel dress in maternity ward outfits, and the dolls are "up for adoption" and not just for "sale."

Clinton, Bill/Paula Jones

The Excelsior Hotel
3 Statehouse Plaza, Little Rock, Arkansas
501-375-5000

On May 3, 1991, this hotel was the site of a meeting of state employees. In the ballroom amid the drinking and loud talk was a clerical worker named Paula Corbin. At about 2:30 P.M., the 46-year old Governor of Arkansas, Bill Clinton, entered the fray. Clinton, who had then been Governor for 12 years, had with him his usual entourage. Noticing Paula and her associate Pamela Blackard, Clinton allegedly told trooper Danny Lee Ferguson to secure a hotel suite for him for about an hour as he needed to make some important calls.

Clinton retired to the room; meanwhile, Ferguson suggested to Paula that she head up to the suite because the Governor wanted to see her. Paula went to the room, and as the world would soon learn, *something* took place between her and the soon-to-be President. Corbin accused Clinton (after he became President) of sexual harassment, creating a mega-scandal which further crystallized Clinton's reputation as a skirt-chasing good old boy. (Clinton and has lawyers finally reached a financial settlement with Jones, though he would admit no wrongdoing.)

The Collyer Brothers

2078 Fifth Avenue, Harlem, New York

On March 21, 1947, the 122nd Street police station in New York City received a call from a man claiming that there was a dead body at 2078 Fifth Avenue. The police knew of the house, a decaying, three-story brownstone mansion. They also were aware of the occupants, Langley and Homer Collyer, two elderly, eccentric, recluse brothers.

So the day after the call, police broke into the second-floor bedroom, and what they found stunned them. The house was crammed from floor to ceiling with literally thousands of objects—mountains of newspapers and magazines, 14 grand pianos, two organs, a clavichord, human medical specimens preserved in a glass jars, the chassis of a Model-T Ford, thousands of medical and engineering books, weapons and much more useless junk. It actually took them several hours to cross the few feet to where the dead body of Homer lay. (The autopsy revealed that he had died of a heart attack.)

Three weeks later, after sifting through an estimated 136 tons of stuff, Langley's body was also discovered. He had suffocated under a cascade of garbage that fell upon him after he had sprung one of his own burglar traps. Condemned as a health and fire hazard, the house at number 2078 Fifth Avenue where these two paranoid neurotics lived was later razed to the ground and is now a parking lot.

Cooper, D.B.

Portland International Airport
Northwest Airlines
Gate 52
7000 NE Airport Way
Portland, Oregon

On November 24, 1971, Dan Cooper boarded a Northwest Airlines flight from Portland to Seattle, demanded and received a $200,000 ransom, and on the return flight parachuted into the forest. He has never been seen again. The disappearance of Dan "D.B." Cooper is one of the great unsolved mysteries of the 20th century.

It happened on Thanksgiving Eve at the Portland International Airport (PIA) when a smartly dressed, middle aged man calling himself Dan Cooper purchased a one-way ticket on flight 305 to the Seattle-Tacoma (Sea-Tac) airport with a $20 bill. Just past four in the afternoon, Cooper passed most of the other 36 passengers and sat in the back of Capt. William Scott's Boeing 727. He had row 18 to himself as the plane was only a quarter full. Once aloft he threatened to blow up the plane and demanded $200,000 and four parachutes.

After the plane landed at Seattle-Tacoma Airport and his demands were met, Cooper ordered the 727 to take off and head for Mexico. He jumped from the rear of the plane somewhere over Washington state, taking the cash with him. Despite exhaustive searches, Cooper's body was never found and his whereabouts are unknown. The actual Boeing 727-051 used by Northwest that day was flown for one last time to the scrap yard in 1993 where it was destroyed.

Disney, Walt

12174 Euclid Street
(south of Chapman Avenue, in the Stanley Ranch Museum)
Anaheim, California
714-530-8871

From 1923 to 1926, Walt Disney worked within this garage-like structure, creating some of his first animated works. In 1982, the garage was removed from its original location in Los Angeles' Silverlake district and put into storage, eventually making it here to this museum featuring antique buildings. They moved the garage to its present location because of its proximity to Disneyland. Be advised however, the museum is open just one day a month, so be sure to call for the schedule.

Father's Day

Central United Methodist Church
301 Fairmont Avenue, Fairmont, West Virginia
304-366-3351

On December 6, 1907, a West Virginia mine explosion killed more than 360 men, 210 of whom were fathers. A local woman named Mrs. Charles (Grace) Clayton approached her pastor, the Reverend Webb, about a special day to honor fathers. Rev. Webb agreed it would be a good idea. To that end, he held a special mass to honor all fathers here at this church on July 5, 1908, and it is generally considered to be the first formal celebration of Father's Day. Over the years, the holiday

continued to gain popularity and was finally officially established by President Nixon in 1972.

Fiscus, Kathy

San Marino High School
2701 Huntington Drive, San Marino, California
626-299-7020

On April 9, 1949, in San Marino, California, 3-year-old Kathy Fiscus was playing in a field overgrown with weeds when she fell 90 feet down a 14-inch-wide abandoned well. Hearing her cry, her parents immediately called the police and firemen, who in turn summoned well-diggers and heavy equipment operators to dig a shaft from which Kathy could be rescued. Upon hearing of the growing rescue effort over the radio, many other people began to gather in hopes of helping to rescue the little girl.

Also at the scene, newfangled trucks carrying live television equipment arrived so they could begin broadcasting from the rescue sight. Only about 20,000 homes had TV sets in Los Angeles County back then, and this painstaking event became one of the first news stories to receive live coverage. Outside of Southern California, in bars and in homes all across the country, people crowded around sets, becoming fixated on this tortuous situation. Of the 50 hours that rescuers spent trying to rescue Kathy, more than 27 hours aired live on Los Angeles television.

On April 11, rescuers succeeded in reaching the little girl, but it was too late: Kathy Fiscus had died. The well's location is now the upper sports field of San Marino High School, entered from Robles Avenue, 1 1/2 blocks east of Sierra Madre Blvd., north of Huntington Drive, and two miles south of the 210 Freeway.

Fountain of Youth

11 Magnolia Avenue
(off San Marco Avenue, N.)
St. Augustine, Florida
800-356-8222

On April 3, 1513, Ponce de Leon discovered what he considered to be the fabled Fountain of Youth. This archeological park contains foundations and artifacts of the first St. Augustine mission and colony, plus, Ponce de Leon marked the spot where the spring was found by leaving a stone cross in the ground. The cross consists of 27 stone slabs—15 in the staff and 13 in the beam—to indicate the year of his visit, 1513.

The cross remains in its original place, preserved along with the spring in a building that includes a diorama depicting the arrival of the Spanish and a Timucua village scene. The spring still flows and visitors are invited to sample the waters.

Gable, Clark/Carole Lombard

The Oatman Hotel
181 Main Street
Oatman, Arizona
928-768-4408

The Oatman Hotel, built in 1902, is the oldest two-story adobe structure in Mojave County and has housed many miners, movie stars, politicians, and assorted scoundrels. The town was used as the location for several movies such as *How The West Was Won*, *Foxfire*, and *Edge of Eternity*.

But it was Clark Gable and Carol Lombard's honeymoon on March 18, 1939 that made the place really famous. They had been married earlier that day in Kingman, Arizona and stopped here along old Route 66 on their way back to Hollywood. Gable returned here often to play poker with the local miners and enjoy the solitude of the desert. The hotel has 10 rooms available for a $35 donation for a night's stay – except for the honeymoon suite where the famous couple spent their wedding night. That one costs $55.

Groundhog Day

Gobblers Knob
(one-and-a-half miles from downtown Punxsutawney on Woodland Avenue Extension)

Chamber of Commerce
124 West Mahoning Street, Punxsutawney, Pennsylvania
800-752-PHIL

Groundhog Day, February 2nd, is a popular tradition in the United States. It is the day that the Groundhog comes out of his hole after a long winter sleep to look for his shadow. If he sees it, he regards it as an omen of six more weeks of bad weather and returns to

his hole. This is the charming little town where it all happens, including the momentous ceremony held each year at "Gobblers Knob." (It also inspired the 1993 comedy smash *Groundhog Day* starring Bill Murray and Andie McDowell.) *The Punxsutawney Spirit* newspaper is credited with printing the news of the first observance in 1886 (one year before the first legendary trek to Gobbler's Knob): "Today is groundhog day, and up to the time of going to press the beast has not seen his shadow."

Hamburger

Louis' Lunch
261-263 Crown Street, New Haven, Connecticut
203-562-5507

One day in the year 1900 a man dashed into a small New Haven luncheonette and asked for a quick meal that he could eat on the run. Louis Lassen, the establishment's owner, hurriedly sandwiched a broiled beef patty between two slices of bread and sent the customer on his way, so the story goes, with America's first hamburger. The tiny

eatery that made such a big impact on the eating habits of an entire nation was, of course, Louis' Lunch. Today, Louis' grandson, Ken, carries on the family tradition: hamburgers that have changed little from their historic prototype are still the specialty of the house. Each one is made from beef ground fresh each day, broiled vertically in the original cast iron grill and served between two slices of toast. Cheese, tomato, and onion are the only acceptable garnish—no true connoisseur would consider corrupting the classic taste with mustard or ketchup.

Hands Across America

Intersection of Cleveland Street and Highway 51
Ripley, Tennessee

On May 25, 1986, over five million Americans united in Hands Across America, another grand-scale effort to raise money for the hungry and homeless people in the United States. At the appointed hour, participants grabbed hands and formed a nearly uninterrupted human chain across sixteen states and the District of Columbia. Spokesperson Ken Kragen, who had previously helped mastermind the "We Are the World" hunger-relief effort, addressed the crowd gathered on the southern tip of Manhattan. (In Washington, D.C., President Ronald Reagan lent a hand to the charity event.) Today, the center of the chain is marked in this small town next to a roadside fruit stand.

Hart, Gary/Donna Rice

517 6th Street, S.E.
Washington, DC

Back in May of 1987, Gary Hart looked to be on his way to winning the Democratic Presidential Primary. However, rumors abounded of his marital infidelity. To combat the stories, he personally challenged the press to follow him, and reporters from the *Miami Herald* took him up on it. Soon after, they caught model Donna Rice in what was then Hart's townhouse, thus ending Hart's bid for president. Later, the pair would be infamously photographed aboard the good ship *Monkey Business* in Bimini.

Heaven's Gate

18241 Colina Norte
Rancho Santa Fe, California

On March 26, 1997, 39 rotting corpses were found in a home in this wealthy suburb of San Diego. Wearing purple shrouds, black outfits, and Nike sneakers, the dead were members of the Heaven's Gate cult. Following the preachings of their bizarre leader,

Marshall Applewhite, they had believed that a UFO was waiting in the tail of the comet Halle-Bopp to take them to a better place, and so they committed suicide. Before killing themselves, the cult members had their last meal at the Marie Callender's located at 5980 Avenida Encinas in Carlsbad. All 39 members ordered the same thing—turkey pot pie. In June 1999, the house was sold, demolished, and today a new one sits in its place.

Hewlett Packard

367 Addison Avenue
Palo Alto, California

The HP Garage is known as the birthplace of Silicon Valley. It all began here in Palo Alto, California, where Stanford University classmates Bill Hewlett and Dave Packard founded HP in 1939. The company's first product, built in this Palo Alto garage, was an audio oscillator—an electronic test instrument used by sound engineers. The home is now a private residence, and is not open to the public.

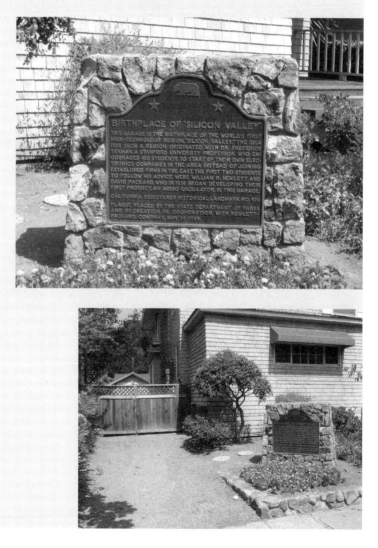

Houdini, Harry

Knickerbocker Hotel
1714 Ivar Avenue (at Hollywood Boulevard)
Hollywood, California

In addition to being a master escape artist, Harry Houdini was known for his crusade to debunk spiritualists, psychics, and others who claimed they could contact the dead. He even wrote a book on the subject exposing many of their techniques, *A Magician Among the Spirits*.

However, as has become legend, just before he died on October 31, 1926, he promised his wife Beatrice that if there were any possible way for him to reach her from the afterlife, he would give her a sign on the anniversary of his death. So, on Halloween night, 1927, Beatrice held a séance at the Knickerbocker Hotel. But the séance did not produce any tangible results (and neither did the yearly Halloween séances she would go on to hold over the following decade).

In addition to the Houdini séance, the Knickerbocker is also the place where Marilyn Monroe honeymooned with Joe Dimaggio in January of 1954, where Elvis Presley stayed in 1956 while shooting *Love Me Tender* (suite 1016), and it was supposedly part of what inspired Presley to co-write "Heartbreak Hotel." On March 3, 1966, William Frawley (Fred Mertz on *I Love Lucy*) died of a heart attack on the sidewalk in front of the hotel (he had lived there for years). The Knickerbocker is now a senior citizen's home.

Howl

110 Montgomery Street (at Broadway)
San Francisco, California

In 1955, poet Allen Ginsberg lived in a furnished room in this building. Many believe that it was here that he wrote his seminal, run-on classic poem, "Howl" (starting with the ominous phrasing, "I saw the best minds of my generation destroyed by madness . . ."). This became the most famous poem of the Beat movement, and thus helped launch Ginsberg as one of the primary counter-culture spokepeople of his generation (his career was fueled by other works such as "Kaddish" and "America"). Ginsberg died in 1997.

Keller, Helen

Ivy Green
300 West North Commons
Tuscumbia, Alabama
256-383-4066

This is the home made famous by the inspirational Helen Keller, who was left both blind and deaf after suffering from an undiagnosed illness (possibly scarlet fever or meningitis) when she was only 19 months old. Keller was born in this house built by her grandparents in 1820, and today it is kept much the way as it was when she grew up here. The small birthplace cottage eventually became the living quarters for Keller and her teacher, Annie Sullivan, whose huge teaching strides with Keller began by simply spelling out the word "W-a-t-e-r" in Keller's hand as she pumped water on it. (The famous water pump is also here on the grounds, made mythical in the film *The Miracle Worker*.) Keller went on to become a vital American force, helping to champion the cause of the blind throughout the world. In 1964, she earned the Presidential Medal of Freedom, the nation's highest civilian award.

Kennedy, Jr., John F.

Cathedral of St. Matthew the Apostle

1725 Rhode Island Avenue
Washington, D.C.

It is one of the most memorable images in U.S. history: Three-year old John F. Kennedy, Jr., standing in front of both his mother, Jacqueline, and his uncle, Robert, saluting the casket of his assassinated father, President John F. Kennedy. It took place on November 25, 1963, as the funeral procession passed outside St. Matthew's Cathedral in Washington, D.C. Today, where the child stood near the front doors of the cathedral remains virtually unchanged.

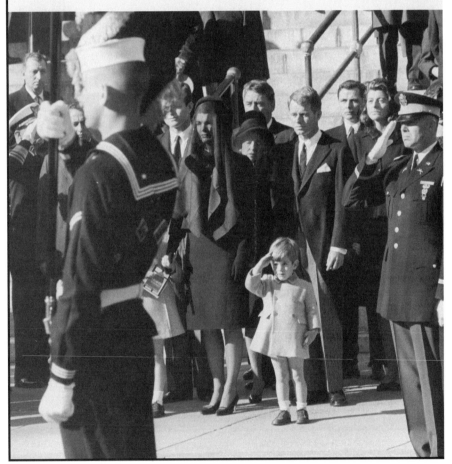

Kennedy, Jr., John F.

The First African Baptist Church

Cumberland Island (off the coast of Georgia)
Saint Mary's, Georgia
912-882-4335

It was on this remote Georgia Island that John F. Kennedy, Jr. married Carolyn Bessette on September 21, 1996. The small, ultra-secret wedding began just after sunset in a Roman Catholic ceremony at this Baptist church which was built by freed slaves after the Civil War. Cumberland Island National Seashore is north of the city of St. Mary's. National Park Service visitor centers are located at the Sea Camp and Dungeness docks. A National Park Service passenger ferry provides access to the island from St. Mary's.

J.F.K., Jr.'s Apartment

20 North Moore Street
New York, New York

This is the fashionable loft in Tri-Beca where the married couple lived (on the 10th floor). For weeks after their deaths, it became a shrine where thousands gathered to mourn (and leave flowers). Kennedy had led a successful fight to stop a developer from opening a movie theater complex across the street, due to the crowds it would have drawn to the normally quiet area. Lauren Bessette, Carolyn's sister, who also died in the plane crash, lived just two blocks away, on White Street and 6th Avenue.

Essex County Airport

125 Passaic Avenue
Fairfield, New Jersey
973-575-0952

This is where John F. Kennedy, Jr.'s single-engine Piper Saratoga II HP took off from on Friday, July 16, at about 8:30 P.M. They departed from Runway 22, and the plane flew about 62 minutes in the air before crashing. They were headed to Massachusetts for the wedding of Rory, one of Bobby and Ethel Kennedy's children. The plan was to drop Lauren off in Martha's Vineyard, and then continue on to Hyannis, where the wedding was to take place on Saturday the 17th.

Kentucky Fried Chicken

Harland Sanders Cafe & Museum
1441 Gardiner Lane
Louisville, Kentucky
606-528-2163

This was where the Colonel, Harland Sanders, developed his famous secret recipe for Kentucky Fried Chicken back in the 1940s. Today, you can dine in the restored restaurant, tour the Colonel's kitchen, and see artifacts and memorabilia. The museum features the colonel's office and kitchen where he experimented with pressure frying and created the recipe for his fried chicken with 11 herbs and spices.

The world-famous secret recipe remains locked in a safe in Louisville. Only a handful of people know the exact details, and they have all been made to sign strict confidentiality contracts.

Killer Bees

Hidalgo, Texas
Chamber of Commerce: 956-843-2734

Killer Bees attack to defend their hives, and have been involved in reported cases which left more than 700 people dead (though none in the U.S.) since their northward migration from Brazil began in the 1950s.

The first of the aggressive insects—called Africanized honeybees—were found in the United States on October 15, 1990 just outside the City of Hidalgo. After that, Hidalgo became the home of "The World's Largest Killer Bee" a statue built 20 feet long and 10 feet high to commemorate the first colony of "Killer Bees" discovered in the city.

McDonald's

1398 N. E Street (at 14th Street)
San Bernardino, California
909-885-6324

Despite several other claims, this is where the hamburger empire truly started in 1940. Brothers Maurice and Richard McDonald (pre-Ray Kroc) opened a restaurant on this site. Though the place served ribs and pork sandwiches, within eight years it reopened as McDonald's Hamburger with the famous paper-wrapped burgers.

Although the original is gone (the headquarters of the Juan Pollo chicken restaurant chain sits here now), there is a nice little museum on the site that's free to the public. Crammed with thousands of McDonald's items, it'll make you long for the days when the menu was simpler and more charming.

Note: The oldest functioning McDonald's is in Downey, California. It's 44-years-old and is the last one with a red-and-white striped tile exterior. After opening in 1953, it immediately become the standard for the fast food franchises across the country. The building and its 60-foot-high neon sign with "Speedee the Chef" are eligible for listing on the National Register of Historic Places. It's located at 10207 Lakewood Boulevard (at Florence Avenue).

Mickey Mouse

2725 Hyperion Avenue (at Griffith Park Boulevard)
Los Angeles, California (Silverlake District)

Though it seems now that Walt Disney's partner Ub Iwerks and not Disney himself actually created and animated Mickey Mouse, this is the spot where it all happened in 1928. Disney had opened his first studio here in 1926, and it was also here in the mid-1930s that Disney created the first feature-length cartoon, *Snow White and the Seven Dwarfs*. In fact, the Tudor-style cottages that inspired the look of the dwarfs' home can still be seen around the corner at 2906-12 Griffith Park Boulevard. Though the current site is occupied by a market, a light pole on the sidewalk in the parking lot holds a sign that marks the site as the approximate entrance to the Disney studio.

Monroe, Marilyn

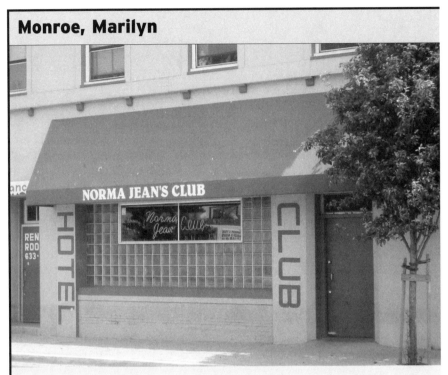

Franco Hotel

10639 Merritt Street
Castroville, California
831-633-2090

This small, central California town is known as "The Artichoke Center of the World," and in February of 1948 it became an interesting footnote in the career of the budding starlet. Having just changed her name from Norma Jean Baker to Marilyn Monroe, the actress had traveled to nearby Salinas for a jewelry store promotion. A local, enterprising artichoke grower seized the opportunity and had her transported to Castroville for a trumped up "crowning" as that year's Artichoke Queen.

The "crowning" ceremony took place at the headquarters of the California Artichoke and Vegetable Growers; Monroe was then shuttled off to the Franco Hotel for a luncheon. Today, the headquarters at the corner of Wood and Del Monte Streets still remains (though it's just a storage building now), and the Franco Hotel is called Franco's Restaurant. Her legacy is intact at the restaurant though, as evidenced by the "Norma Jean's Club" they still run there.

Monroe, Marilyn

Nude Calendar

736 N. Seward Avenue
Hollywood, California

The nude photos of the 22-year old beauty set against red velvet became legendary. Shot at this address by Tom Kelley, the gorgeous out-of-work actress was paid fifty dollars for her modeling (she told the Kelley she would use the money to make an installment on her car). Millions of calendars later, the shots remain some of Monroe's most classic, definitive images.

Seven Year Itch

Subway Grating
Northwest Corner of 52nd Street and Lexington Avenue
New York, New York

It's one of the most enduring, iconic scenes in Hollywood history. More a publicity stunt than a vital scene in Billy Wilder's 1955 comedy *Seven Year Itch*, the press had lots of advance notice the night this event took place. That's why over 2,000 people crowded the street in front of the old Trans-Lux movie theatre (where Monroe and co-star Tom Ewell emerge from in the actual movie) to ogle Marilyn as she posed suggestively over the subway grating in a sheer white dress (close-ups of her legs were later re-shot in Hollywood). Monroe's then-husband Joe DiMaggio was supposedly furious at the stunt; their marriage dissolved soon after. The Tran-Lux theater is no longer there, but the subway grating remains in the identical spot where Monroe posed on it.

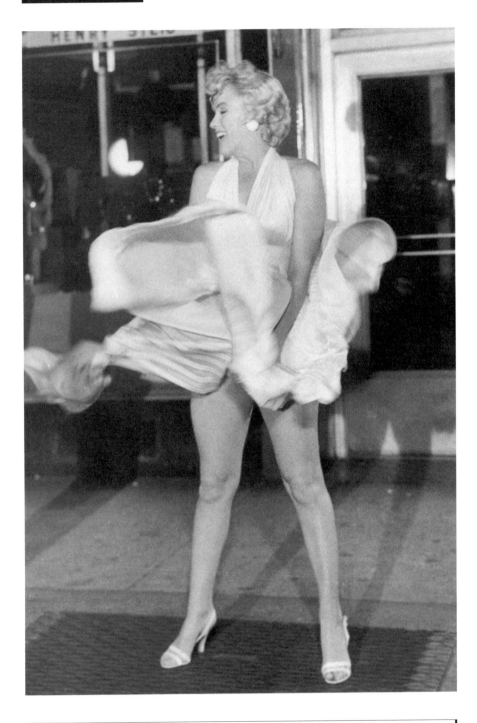

Monroe, Marilyn

Madison Square Garden

50th Street and Eighth Avenue, New York, New York

It was Marilyn's final public (and perhaps most famous) appearance. It happened May 19th, 1962 at the old Madison Square Garden in New York. The event was a massive birthday celebration for President John F. Kennedy, and emcee Peter Lawford introduced her as "the late Marilyn Monroe." In her now-famous sequined, backless gown, the President's (alleged) girlfriend crooned to him a sultry, coy version of "Happy Birthday." It's become one of the most telling clips of the century, a moment when Monroe, although near the end of her rope, still managed to captivate, tease and beguile on a level that's still considered jaw-dropping. Kennedy's comments after the rendition? "I can now retire from politics after having 'Happy Birthday' being sung to me in such a sweet and wholesome manner." An office building now occupies the site.

Monroe and J.F.K.'s Love Nest

625 Beach Road, Pacific Coast Highway, Santa Monica, California

Actor Peter Lawford's beach home is where Marilyn Monroe Monroe and President John F. Kennedy allegedly carried on their secret affair in the early 1960s. Essentially a crash pad for all of Lawford's Hollywood pals (including Sinatra and the rest of the Rat Pack), he allowed his president/brother-in-law full use of the place (and Bobby Kennedy, too) whenever he was in town. Monroe called Lawford here that fateful last night just before she committed suicide.

Monroe's Suicide

12305 Fifth Helena Drive, Brentwood, California

On the night of August 4, 1962, not long after she'd been fired from the film *Something's Got to Give*, Marilyn Monroe died in this three-bedroom bungalow, which she had purchased with borrowed money early in 1962. Dr. Hyman Engelberg, who gave Monroe 50 Nembutal tranquilizers on the morning of the 4th, was called on the morning of the 5th and pronounced the star dead. Coroner Thomas Noguchi ruled Monroe's death a suicide by intentional drug overdose. Although Monroe had done several photo shoots in the months before her death, she had refused to be photographed inside the Brentwood house, saying, "I don't want everybody to see exactly where I live."

Mother's Day

The International Mother's Day Shrine
Andrews Methodist Episcopal Church
11 East Main Street
Grafton, West Virginia
304-265-1589

The Mother's Day Shrine is located in an old church (originally known as the Andrews Methodist Episcopal Church) on Main Street of this small West Virginia town. It commemorates the first celebration of Mother's Day, which took place here back in May of 1908. The holiday was started by local resident Anna Jarvis, who historians say never enjoyed motherhood herself. President Wilson made it a national holiday in 1914, probably to whip up "Let's defend our mothers from the Hun" sentiments during the pre-World War I build-up.

The "Mothman" Bridge

Spanning the Ohio River between Point Pleasant and Kanauga
Point Pleasant, West Virginia

At approximately 5:04 P.M. on December 15, 1967, the Silver Bridge collapsed and 46 people lost their lives. What made this horrific event even more peculiar were the odd sightings between November 1966 and December 1967 of a creature that became known as "Mothman." Most of the sightings took place in the "TNT Area" near the town of Point Pleasant, and they involved a creature described as resembling a "giant butterfly," a "brown human being" fly, and a "Seven foot tall man with big wings folded against its back." The creature also supposedly had huge, glowing red eyes that looked like "automobile reflectors."

The TNT Area, which became ground zero for "Mothman" sightings (as the press dubbed him), was a large tract of land with small concrete "igloos" dotting the landscape (originally used during World War II to store ammunition). Interestingly, the sightings ended after the horrible day that the Silver Bridge collapsed. People began to speculate that the Mothman was somehow responsible for the bridge's collapse, due to some cryptic messages it was said to have left behind. Today, a plaque can be found near the entrance of the bridge.

The Roswell Incident

The Old J.B. Foster Ranch
Approximately 75 miles northwest of Roswell, New Mexico

Directions: From Corona, New Mexico, go east on NM 247. Just past Mile Marker 17, turn right at the Corona Compressor Station sign. The site is about 16 miles southeast of the turnoff. It is on Bureau of Land Management property, which is open to the public, but reaching the site requires passing through private ranch land, which is fenced and gated.

On the night of July 2, 1947 something crashed into the desert outside of Roswell, New Mexico. The first announcement made by the military was that a flying saucer had crashed. Quickly after this first announcement the story was changed—what was thought to have been a flying saucer was in reality a weather balloon.

Almost 60 years later, people are still asking what rancher Mac Brazel and his 8-year-old son, Vernon, found seven or eight miles from the house on the J.B. Foster ranch. Was the large area of bright wreckage (comprised of rubber strips, tinfoil, tough paper, and sticks) the result of a spaceship? Spy balloon? Weather apparatus? We may never know exactly what happened that night, but we do know that no other UFO event has fueled our collective imaginations more than the "Roswell Incident." For more information, you might want to visit the International UFO Museum and Research Center at 114 North Main Street, Roswell, New Mexico.

Schwab's Drugstore

8000 Sunset Boulevard, Hollywood, California

A Virgin Megastore sits on the same spot where the legendary Schwab's Pharmacy once stood. In the movie *Sunset Boulevard*, William Holden's character calls Schwab's Drug Store "headquarters; a combination office, coffee klatch, and waiting room" for Hollywood writers.

F. Scott Fitzgerald (author of *The Great Gatsby*) had a heart attack here in 1940 while buying a pack of cigarettes. Songwriter Harold Arlen wrote "Over the Rainbow" (from *The Wizard of Oz*) by the light of the Schwab's neon sign. Charlie Chaplin and Harold Lloyd used to play pinball in the back room. But the biggest tale of all regarding Schwab's was that it was where starlet Lana Turner was discovered while sitting at the counter. However, that one is not true. Turner, "The Sweater Girl," was actually discovered at the Top Hat Malt Shop, across from Hollywood High.

The South Family

Ghost Mountain
Anza-Borrego Desert
60 miles east of Julian, California

Directions from Julian: Drive east on SR 78 for 12 miles. Then head south on Road S2 for 6 miles to the turn-off on the left for Blair Valley Camp. Drive 1.4 miles, bearing right at the fork. Drive 1.6 miles, bearing right again. Drive 1/2 mile to Marshal South Home Trailhead. A trail map is available at Anza-Borrego Desert State Park, 760-767-5311. It's an easy hike to the site, approximately 1 1/2 miles.

During the depression in 1932, writer Marshal South decided to drop out of society. Driving east from San Diego, he and his wife Tanya stopped at Ghost Mountain in the beautiful but rugged Anza-Borrego Desert. South decided to settle and raise a family here with no modern conveniences like electricity or running water. South christened their new home, "Yacquitepec," and he crafted a home from mud, wood, and old metal. Soon, the Souths had three children, Rider, Rudyard and Victoria. The Souths remained on Ghost Mountain for 14 years, with Marshal penning stories of their collective lives for *Desert Magazine*. People all over the country were fascinated by this family, but the Utopia ended in September 1945 when the U.S. Navy began using the area as a gunnery range, forcing the South family to leave their mountain homestead. They came back a year later, but the dream was nearing the end. Within a few months, Marshal and Tanya South were separated and the family came down from the mountain. Marshal died in October 1948, leaving Tanya to raise the kids. Today, the children are all still alive, though they all have refused to talk much about their upbringing. The ruins of "Yacquitepec" remain for other families to explore.

Spago

1114 Horn Avenue (just above Sunset Boulevard)
West Hollywood, California

Wolfgang Puck's landmark Hollywood restaurant was, for years, the place to be for the world's biggest celebrities. This was especially true on Oscar Night, when super agent "Swifty" Lazar would hold his annual post-Oscar party here, and just about every movie star in town waited for an invitation. Though "Swifty" died in 1994, Spago remained a star magnet on Oscar Night until the time it closed in 2001. Today, the next-generation Spago is located in Beverly Hills, and remains one of the town's most notable restaurants.

The Spruce Goose

1126 Queens Highway
Long Beach, California
562-435-3511

In May 1942, Howard Hughes began to build the world's largest airplane, or what he called at the time "an unsinkable liberty ship." Hughes Flying Boat was designed to carry 700 troops. Ultimately, Hughes spent $7 million of his own money on the project, while the U.S. Government spent $17 million. Many people said that it would never get off the ground, but on November 2, 1947, they were proved wrong. The giant plane, affectionately called the "Spruce Goose," whose wing span was 320 feet, lifted off for a one-mile flight across the Long Beach Harbor. The plane was never to fly again. For years, the plane could be seen inside of a still-standing dome in Long Beach next to the Queen Mary, but in late 1992 and early 1993, it was moved to the Evergreen Aviation Museum, situated in Oregon's Willamette Valley. Address: 3685 NE Three Mile Lane, McMinnville, Oregon. Phone: 503-434-4180.

Studio 54

254 West 54th Street
New York, New York
212-517-4065

On April 26, 1977 the most well known Disco of all-time opened up its doors at this site. It quickly became the symbol of the anything-goes, completely hedonistic, late 1970's disco era in New York. Opened by Steve Rubell (who died of hepatitis in 1989) and Ian Shrager (who went on to make a fortune in the hotel business), the club enjoyed huge notoriety for several years until 1979 when an IRS bust put the two away for several years (thus ending the short life of the jet-setter's haven.) Today, part of the club has been re-opened as Upstairs at Studio 54 (which exists in the former, infamous upstairs VIP room from the old days).

Tube Bar Tapes

12 Tube Concourse East, Jersey City, New Jersey

"Is Ben Dover there?" Long before "The Jerky Boys" there was John Elmo and Jim Davidson, who had started calling an old-time Jersey bar (The Tube Bar) in about 1975. They'd harass 85-year-old bartender Louis "Red" Deutsch by asking to speak with patrons like "Al Kikyoras," "Ben Dover," etc. Red would "page" the names out loud to the bar until eventually he realized he was being yanked. Then, Red (in a torn, raspy, sandpaper voice) would assail his callers, unleashing a flurry of threatening profanity that would make a dockworker blush. The pair taped their exploits and throughout the 1980s, these cassettes made their way up through the underground and filtered through colleges, clubs, and house parties to achieve legendary status. Supposedly, Matt Groenig, the creator of *The Simpsons*, created "Mo," the tavern owner character, after being inspired by these tapes.

Wabash

Chamber of Commerce
111 South Wabash Street, Wabash, Indiana
260-563-1168

On March 31, 1880, Wabash became the first electrically lighted city in the world. As a test, Wabash had purchased four huge lights from the Brush Electric Light Company of Cleveland, Ohio. A threshing machine steam engine was used to generate the electricity needed to create the light, and the four lights were mounted atop the still-standing county courthouse. The switch was thrown at 8:00 P.M. as the courthouse clock started ringing. The test was a success – brush electric lights could in fact efficiently light a large outdoor area. One of the original lights is on exhibition in the county courthouse.

Walden Pond

915 Walden Street, Concord, Massachusetts
978-369-3254

Henry David Thoreau lived at Walden Pond from July 1845 to September 1847. His experience there inspired the book *Walden*, which is generally credited with helping to create awareness and respect for the natural environment. Because of Thoreau's legacy, Walden Pond has been designated a National Historic Landmark and is considered the birthplace of the conservation movement. The Reservation encompasses 333 acres surrounding the pond, which is a 103 foot deep glacial kettle hole pond. 2280 acres of mostly undeveloped woods, called "Walden Woods" surrounds the pond.

War of the Worlds

CBS Radio (former location)
485 Madison Avenue
New York, New York

On October 30, 1938, CBS Radio was broadcasting the music of Ramon Raquello and his orchestra live from the Meridian Room at the Park Plaza in New York City. Suddenly, a reporter interrupted: Astronomers had just detected suspicious movement on the surface of Mars. Soon, another interruption: A meteor had landed on a farm near Grovers Mill, New Jersey. A reporter supposedly was on the scene, describing the events; listeners learned that a spaceship bearing a tentacled creature was shooting humans with a deadly laser beam. The broadcast then changed over to full coverage of this ominous event. By the time the night was over, however, most of the audience had learned that the news broadcast was entirely fictitious. It was simply the regular radio show featuring Orson Welles and the Mercury Theatre, and that week, in honor of Halloween, they had decided to stage a highly dramatized and updated version of H.G. Wells' story, "War of the Worlds."

Though the popular version holds that the nation was in dire panic from this episode, that's probably more of a hoax than the broadcast itself, which was never intended to fool anyone. At four separate points during the program, it was clearly stated that what people were hearing was a play. The notion that millions of people panicked was the result of an overzealous media fanning the flames of the show in the days following its broadcast.

Wright, Frank Lloyd

951 Chicago Avenue
Oak Park, Illinois
708-848-1976

The famed architect Frank Lloyd Wright added this studio to his home in 1898. The complex served as Wright's primary work center in the years that launched his career, 1889 to 1909. Here, among other things, he developed the Prairie style of architecture. The house is open to the public as a historic museum, and the building has been restored to what it would have been like the last year Wright worked and lived here (1909).

The surrounding neighborhood is filled with classic examples of the architect's work, and makes for a wonderful walking tour. Wright designed and built this house in his early twenties, and the buildings were restored between 1976 and 1986 by the Restoration Committee of the Frank Lloyd Wright Home and Studio Foundation.

History and Tragedy

American Flag

Betsy Ross House
239 Arch Street, Philadelphia, Pennsylvania 19106
215-686-1252

History says that Betsy Ross made the first American flag after a visit in June 1776 by George Washington, Robert Morris, and her husband's uncle, George Ross. Supposedly, she demonstrated how to cut a 5-pointed star with a single clip of the scissors, if the fabric were folded correctly. However, this story was not told until 1870 by Betsy's grandson, and many scholars believe that while Betsy probably didn't make the first flag, she was indeed a professional flagmaker. Her house, now a museum, remains one of Philadelphia's most visited landmarks.

The Boston Massacre

Devonshire and State Street, Boston, Massachusetts

In front of the Old State House, a circle of cobblestones commemorates the Boston Massacre. It was here on March 5, 1770, that a minor dispute between a wigmaker's young apprentice and a British sentry turned into a riot. The relief soldiers that came to the aid of the British were met by an angry crowd of colonists who hurled snowballs,

rocks, clubs, and insults. The soldiers fired into the crowd and killed five colonists. Samuel Adams and other patriots called the event a "massacre," thus helping to sow the seeds of resentment towards the British that would culminate in the American Revolution.

Burr, Aaron/Alexander Hamilton

Southern end of Hamilton Park
Boulevard East (atop the Palisades, directly across from Manhattan)
Weehawken, New Jersey

At dawn on the morning of July 11, 1804, political antagonists and personal enemies Alexander Hamilton and Aaron Burr met in this small park on the heights of Weehawken, New Jersey to settle their longstanding differences with a duel. The participants fired their pistols in close succession. Burr's shot met its target immediately, fatally wounding Hamilton and leading to his death the following day. Burr escaped unharmed.

This tragic incident reflected the depth of animosity aroused by the first emergence of the nation's political party system. Both of these men were active leaders in New York. Burr was a Republican, and Hamilton was leader of the opposing Federalist party. They had become political and personal enemies over a variety of run-ins, but it was the 1804 New York Gubernatorial campaign that forced the duel. Hamilton had opposed Burr's closely fought bid for the post and it was on the heels of this narrow defeat that Burr challenged Hamilton to a duel. The actual rock where Hamilton lay after being shot is marked by a plaque at the site.

Challenger

Cape Canaveral, NASA Kennedy Space Center, Florida
321-867-5000   (321-867-4636 for recorded launch information)

On January 28, 1986 America was shocked by the destruction of the space shuttle Challenger, and the death of its seven crew members (including Christa McAuliffe, America's first teacher to fly in space). Following an exhaustive examination of the accident by a presidential commission spearheaded by William P. Rogers, NASA was widely criticized for suppressing key information about the safety of the O-ring seals on the solid rocket boosters.

In the wake of the tragedy, President Reagan made his famous memorial speech (written by Peggy Noonan) with the now-classic closing line, "We will never forget them, nor the last time we saw them, this morning, as they prepared for the journey and waved goodbye and slipped the surly bonds of earth to touch the face of God."

Chappaquiddick

Dike Bridge
Chappaquiddick Island, Martha's Vineyard, Massachusetts

Shortly before midnight on July 18, 1969, Ted Kennedy was involved in a horrible car accident. He had been driving back from a party on Chappaquiddick, Massachusetts, and had driven off the edge of this bridge. Luckily, he was not severely injured; however, Mary Jo Kopechne, a woman who was in his car, was killed. She was a 29-year-old blond secretary in Washington, D.C., who worked for

Senator Robert F. Kennedy and Senator George Smathers. Ted Kennedy's wife was home with their children and had not attended the party.

The accident was not reported until eight hours after the car had sunk to the bottom of the river. On the following Monday, Kennedy was charged for leaving the scene of the accident. Kennedy, who was 37 at the time, said that he was simply in shock, and that was why he had not called the police. Despite his endless denials, this one incident would continue to haunt Kennedy for the remainder of his political career.

The Civil War

Fort Sumter

1214 Middle Street
Sullivan's Island, South Carolina

The first engagement of the Civil War took place at Fort Sumter on April 12 and 13, 1861. After 34 hours of fighting, the Union surrendered the fort to the Confederates. From 1863 to 1865, the Confederates at Fort Sumter withstood a 22-month siege by Union forces. During this time, most of the fort was reduced to brick rubble. Fort Sumter became a national monument in 1948. Fort Sumter, located 3.3 miles southeast of Charleston, sits on a man-made island of 2.4 acres near the inlet of Charleston Harbor. Visitors arrive at Fort Sumter via concessioner tour boats operated by Fort Sumter Tours, Inc.: 843-881-7337.

The Battle at Antietam

Washington County Convention & Visitors Bureau
Elizabeth Hager Center
Hagerstown, Maryland (1 mile north of Sharpsburg, Maryland, on Route 65)
301-791-3246   888-257-2600

This is the battle that sealed the fate of the Confederacy. Established by Act of Congress on August 30, 1890, this Civil War site marks the end of General Robert E. Lee's first invasion of the North in September 1862. The battle claimed more than 23,000 men killed, wounded, and missing in one single day, September 17, 1862, and led to Lincoln's issuance of the Emancipation Proclamation. It is generally regarded to be the bloodiest single day battle in U.S. history.

The Civil War

Gettysburg Address

35 Carlisle Street
Gettysburg, Pennsylvania
717-334-6274

Gettysburg, Pennsylvania is the site of one of the most famous speeches in American history. Located 50 miles northwest of Baltimore, the small town of Gettysburg was the site of the largest Civil War battle ever waged in the Western Hemisphere. The Soldiers' National Cemetery at Gettysburg (which contains more than 7,000 interments including over 3,500 from the Civil War) was where President Abraham Lincoln delivered his immortal Gettysburg Address on November 19, 1863. A statue marks the exact place where Lincoln stood.

General Lee Surrenders to Grant

Appomattox Court House National Historical Park
Appomattox, Virginia
804-352-8987

Directions: The Visitor Center is in the reconstructed courthouse building on VA 24, 13 miles northeast of the town of Appomattox, Virginia.

The McLean home in the village of Appomattox Court House, Virginia was used on April 9, 1865 for the surrender meeting between General Robert E. Lee, C.S.A. and Lt. General Ulysses S. Grant, U.S.A. The house was also used on April 10th for the Surrender Commissioners meeting, and over the next few days as the Headquarters of Major General John Gibbon, U.S.A. The site includes the McLean home (surrender site) and the village of Appomattox Court House, Virginia, the former county seat for Appomattox County. The site also contains the home and burial place of Joel Sweeney – the man who made the modern five-string banjo popular.

Cocoanut Grove

200 Stuart Street
Boston, Massachusetts

One of the deadliest fires in the nation's history occurred here in the Bay Village area of Boston. The blaze at the Cocoanut Grove, a nightclub located where the 57 Restaurant & Bar now stands on Stuart Street, killed 492 people on the night of November 28, 1942. The club was packed with approximately 1,000 occupants, many of whom were people preparing to go overseas on military duty. There were also a lot of college football fans who were in the club celebrating Holy Cross's upset victory that afternoon over the heavily favored Boston College.

A lighted match used by an employee who was changing a light bulb has been considered the possible cause for this tragic fire. The fire started in the basement of the one-story building, in an newly opened area of the club called the Melody Lounge shortly after 10 p.m. Authorities estimated that possibly 300 of those killed could have been saved had the two revolving doors at the main entrance been built to swing outward. The Cocoanut Grove fire prompted major efforts in the field of fire prevention and control for nightclubs and other related places of public assembly.

The Collinwood School Fire

410 East 152nd Street (at Lucknow Avenue)
Cleveland, Ohio

There's a memorial marker here to the 172 children and two teachers who died in America's deadliest school accident. The Collinwood School fire occurred on March 4, 1908 at the Lakeview Elementary school. The fire began shortly after 9:00 A.M. when an

overheated steam pipe came in contact with wooden joists. It took just 30 minutes to wreak its full havoc. Tragically, just 194 of 366 students escaped.

Examination of the building, along with eyewitness accounts, proved that the doors opened outward and that the children's failure to escape resulted from their own panic. Tragic as the Collinwood School fire was, it did inspire many more school inspections across the country along with stricter laws regarding disaster escape plans. There's also a monument to the victims at the Lake View Cemetery, 12316 Euclid Avenue, Cleveland. Phone: 216-421-2665.

Columbus, Christopher

San Salvador, Bahamas

For centuries, scholars have debated where Columbus first set foot in the Western Hemisphere – so much so that it's been dubbed the "landfall controversy." Everyone agrees that Columbus arrived on an island in the Bahamas that he named San Salvador (Holy Savior), but many islands have been tossed around as the genuine San Salvador. The three most popular places have been Watlings Island (called San Salvador today), Cat Island, and Grand Turk (which today is no longer part of the Bahamas).

More than 500 years after the fact, there is still no definitive answer, but the general consensus is that Columbus landed on what was known until 1926 as Watlings Island. Today, a crude stone structure on a narrow piece of land between the ocean and the bay marks the spot where Columbus first set foot on the soil of the New World. The landmark features an inscribed marble plaque and a marble ball representing the world. Additionally, a monument rests on the floor of the ocean where it is believed Columbus dropped anchor on October 12, 1492.

Cook, Captain James

Kealakekua Bay Historical Park
Kona coast of the island of Hawaii, about 12 miles south of Kailua-Kona, along Highway 11 near the town of Napoopoo
808-974-6200

When Captain James Cook sailed into Kealakekua Bay on January 17, 1779, he was on his second visit to the Hawaiian Islands. Cook had first dropped anchor in Kealakekua Bay the year before, after cruising Alaska's coast and failing to find a Northwest Passage from the Atlantic to the Pacific. This was considered the "discovery" of Hawaii.

On February 14, 1779, surrounded by thousands of hostile warriors, Cook was murdered at the water's edge. Supposedly, he was killed over a small launch stolen from his ship, the *Resolution*. Today, a monument to the memory of Captain Cook rests on the shore of Kealakekua Bay. The obelisk sits near the exact spot where Cook was killed.

Custer, General George

Little Bighorn
Exit 510 off I-90
Crow Agency, Montana
406-638-2621

This legendary battlefield is where Lt. Col. George Armstrong Custer led a force of 647 men on June 25th, 1876, against the Lakota, Sioux, and Cheyenne Indians in southeastern Montana. Commonly known as "Custer's Last Stand" and "The Battle at Little Big Horn," it's an event which rose beyond its military significance to the level of myth. Thousands of books, magazine articles, performances in film and theater, paintings, and other artistic expressions have memorialized the Indian warriors' slaughter of Custer's men, and in 1879, the Little Bighorn Battlefield was designated a national cemetery administered by the War Department. In 1881, a memorial was erected on Last Stand Hill, over the mass grave of the Seventh Cavalry soldiers, U.S. Indian Scouts, and other personnel killed in battle. Today, it's a popular tourist attraction.

Declaration of Independence

143 South Third Street, Philadelphia, Pennsylvania
215-597-8974

National Historical Park, located in downtown (called "Center City") Philadelphia, is often referred to as the birthplace of our nation. Here, visitors can see the Liberty Bell, an international symbol of freedom, and Independence Hall, a World Heritage Site where both the Declaration of Independence and the U.S. Constitution were created. A section of the park where Benjamin Franklin's home once stood is dedicated to Franklin's life and accomplishments. Spanning approximately 45 acres, the park has about 20 buildings open to the public.

Edison, Thomas

37 Christie Street
Menlo Park
Edison, New Jersey

The Edison Memorial Tower looms 131 feet and 4 inches above Menlo Park, New Jersey, and it marks the spot where Thomas Alva Edison conceived the first practical incandescent light bulb. But that wasn't all that happened here. For 10 years, Edison toiled over what would eventually total approximately 400 patented ideas before he moved his "Invention Factory" to West Orange, New Jersey. The Tower, which was erected in 1937, is topped by the world's largest working light bulb. It weighs 3 tons and is comprised of 153 single pieces of 2-inch-thick, amber-tinted Pyrex glass.

Edison National Historic Site

Intersection of Main Street and Lakeside Avenue
West Orange, New Jersey
201-736-5050

Though he invented the lightbulb some 20 miles away in Menlo Park, this is also an important spot in the course of Thomas Alva Edison's inventive life. For more than 40 years, the laboratory created by Thomas Alva Edison in West Orange, New Jersey, had enormous impact on the lives of millions of people worldwide. Out of the West Orange laboratories came the motion picture camera, vastly improved phonographs, sound recordings, silent and sound movies, and the nickel-iron alkaline electric storage battery.

The *Edmund Fitzgerald*

Whitefish Point, Michigan
877-SHIPWRECK

When she was first launched, the *Edmund Fitzgerald* was the largest carrier on the Great Lakes, and remained so until 1971. On November 9, 1975 she departed from Superior, Wisconsin (Ford Rouge Dock) with approximately 26,000 tons of ore bound for Detroit. However, the *Edmund Fitzgerald* was lost with her entire crew of 29 men on Lake Superior on November 10, 1975, 17 miles north-northwest of Whitefish Point, Michigan. Whitefish Point is the site of the Whitefish Point Light Station and the Great Lakes Shipwreck Museum. The tragic loss was behind the well-known Gordon Lightfoot song, "The Wreck of the *Edmund Fitzgerald*."

Exxon Valdez Spill

Bligh Reef, Prince William Sound, Alaska

 On March 24, 1989, shortly after midnight, the oil tanker *Exxon Valdez* struck Bligh Reef in Prince William Sound, Alaska, spilling more than 11 million gallons of crude oil. The spill was the largest in U.S. history and tested the abilities of local, national, and industrial organizations to prepare for, and respond to, a disaster of such magnitude. Many factors complicated the cleanup efforts following the spill. The size of the spill and its remote location, accessible only by helicopter and boat, made government and industry efforts difficult and tested existing plans for dealing with such an event.

Following the *Exxon Valdez* spill, Congress passed the Oil Pollution Act of 1990, which required the Coast Guard to strengthen its regulations on oil tank vessels and oil tank owners and operators. Today, tank hulls provide better protection against spills resulting from a similar accident, and communications between vessel captains and vessel traffic centers have improved to make for safer sailing.

Gay Rights Movement

The Stonewall Bar and Club
53 Christopher Street, New York, New York

This is generally considered to be the birthplace of the gay liberation movement because of what happened the night of June 27, 1969. A police inspector and seven officers from the Public Morals Section of the First Division of the New York City Police Department arrived after midnight to look for violations of the alcohol control laws. After checking identifications, they tossed the patrons out while others lingered outside to watch. They were soon joined by passers-by.

The arrival of the police wagons altered the atmosphere of the crowd from passivity to defiance. The first vehicle left without incident, apart from shouts from the crowd. The next individual to emerge from the bar was a woman in male clothing who put up a struggle, which caused the bystanders to take action. The crowd erupted and began throwing cobblestones and bottles. Some officers took refuge in the bar while others turned a fire hose on the crowd. Police reinforcements arrived and soon the streets were cleared. The news spread throughout the day, and the following two nights saw further violent confrontations between the police and gay people. These incidents became known in history as The Stonewall Rebellion, and it sparked a new, highly visible, mass phase of political organization for gay rights.

Golden Spike National Historic Site

32 miles west of Brigham City on State Routes 13 and 83
Promontory Point, Utah
435-471-2209

Completion of the world's first transcontinental railroad was celebrated here where the Central Pacific and Union Pacific Railroads met on May 10, 1869. Golden Spike was designated as a national historic site in nonfederal ownership on April 2, 1957, and authorized for federal ownership and administration by an act of Congress on July 30, 1965.

The Gold Rush

Marshall Gold Discovery State Historic Park
310 Back Street, Coloma, California
530-622-3470

 James W. Marshall discovered gold in 1848 on the South Fork of the American River in the valley the Nisenan Indians knew as "Cullumah." This event led to the greatest mass movement of people in the Western Hemisphere and was the spark that ignited the spectacular growth of the American west during the ensuing decades.

The gold discovery site, located in the still visible tailrace of Sutter's sawmill, in present day Coloma, California, is one of the most significant historic sites in the nation. The park has a museum, with exhibits that tell the story of the Gold Rush, a replica of the sawmill, and a number of historic buildings. Visitors also have the opportunity to try panning for gold in the American River or enjoy a picnic under the trees. The monument and statue placed above Marshall's gravesite (who died in 1885) is California's first historic landmark.

The Great Chicago Fire

558 Dekoven Street (at Jefferson Street—formerly 137 DeKoven Street)
Chicago, Illinois

According to legend, the Great Chicago Fire was started by a cow that belonged to an Irishwoman named Catherine O'Leary. She ran a neighborhood milk business from the barn behind her home, and after carelessly leaving a kerosene lantern in the barn following her evening milking, a cow kicked it over and ignited the hay on the floor. Of course, no proof of this story has ever been offered, but the legend took hold in Chicago and was told around the world.

Regardless of how the fire started though, on Sunday evening, October 8, 1871, Chicago became a city in flames. The blaze burned homes and shops and left 300 people dead and 500,000 people homeless. Firefighters brought the fire under control the next day, but only with the help of a rainstorm. It had been unusually warm and dry that year, and the city's wood buildings burned like matches until finally the rain came down. Today, the site of the fire's origin is ironically occupied by the Chicago Fire Department's Training Academy, and marked with a historic plaque.

Harding, Warren

Palace Hotel
2 New Montgomery Street, San Francisco, California
415-512-1111

Warren G. Harding, the 29th President of the United States, died at the Palace Hotel in San Francisco on August 23, 1923 under circumstances that began as mysterious and were then varnished by rumor in the aftermath of scandals and salacious revelations that surfaced following the president's demise. The ailing president arrived in San Francisco and was taken to the Palace Hotel where he died either of anxiety, a stroke, a heart attack, food poisoning, or from deliberate poisoning by First Lady Florence, fed up with her husband's philandering.

The legend continues that Mrs. Harding's psychic had, on the eve of his nomination, predicted the president would die in office. The fact that Mrs. Harding refused to allow an autopsy of the president contributed to suspicion of her guilt; the official cause of President Harding's death is listed as a stroke. This exquisite hotel makes no special recognition of Harding's death.

The Hartford Circus Fire

Area bounded by Barbour Street, Cleveland Avenue, Hampton Street,
and Kensington Street, Hartford, Connecticut

On July 6, 1944, 8,000 spectators were gathered in Hartford, Connecticut under the Big Top of the world famous Ringling Brothers, Barnum and Bailey Circus. During the show (which in addition to animals featured the legendary Flying Wallendas trapeze act), a tiny fire was ignited on one of the tent's sidewalls. Had it been spotted immediately, it could have been extinguished with a pail of water, but within minutes the small fire became a raging tower of flames that had engulfed the entire tent. In all, 167 people were killed and 487 were injured in what remains the worst single disaster in Hartford's history (it's also the worst disaster in circus history). Tragically, children accounted for the bulk of the casualties. Today, the Stowe Village Housing Project occupies the area where the catastrophic blaze occurred.

Hinckley Fire Museum

106 Old Highway 61, Hinckley, Minnesota
320-384-7338

With the coming of the railroad industry, the lumber industry boomed, and for 20 years Hinckley was a growing, prosperous town with a population of 1,500. But on September 1, 1894, everything changed. In just four hours, a raging fire ended up destroying six towns, and over 400 square miles. Located in a restored railroad depot, this museum commemorates the forest fire that destroyed the town in 1894. Photographs, newspaper accounts, and items from the fire are displayed.

The Hindenburg Crash

Naval Air Engineering Station
Highway 547, Lakehurst, New Jersey
732-323-2620

At 7:25 P.M. on May 6, 1937, the German airship Hindenburg was coming in for a landing at the naval air station at Lakehurst, after its flight across the Atlantic from Germany. On board were 61 crew and 36 passengers. Hundreds of people were at this site to watch the beautiful ship land on this warm spring evening. A radio announcer, Herb Morrison from WLS Chicago,  was describing how gorgeous the ship looked against the night sky. But we all know what happened as it approached the mooring post. Flames appeared near the stern. Within just a few seconds, the craft exploded in a fireball. Falling tail first, it crashed a mere 32 seconds after the flame was first spotted.

Morrison's audio document of the tragedy ("It's burst into flames....Get out of the way, please, oh my, this is terrible, oh my, get out of the way, please...Oh, the humanity and all the passengers!") has since become one of history's most famous recordings. Thirty-six people died in the crash, and while several theories abound as to what happened that night to the Hindenburg, many experts believe that an electrical storm that night sparked the explosion when it came in contact with the highly flammable hydrogen gas. On May 6th of each year, at 7:25 P.M., a memorial service for those who lost their lives in the Hindenburg and all other airship accidents is held on the site.

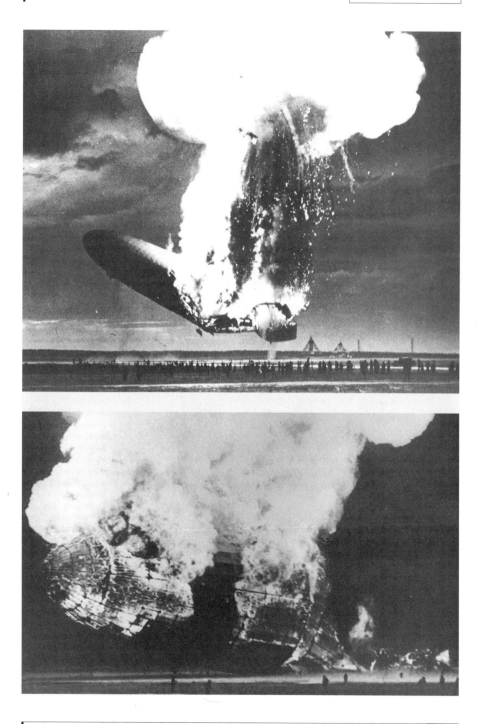

Homestead National Monument

Beatrice, Nebraska

Directions: Homestead National Monument is located in southeastern Nebraska, about 40 miles south of Lincoln. Follow the signs from I-80 at Lincoln. At Beatrice, turn west and follow Nebraska Route 4 for 4 1/2 miles to the park entrance.

The Homestead Act of 1862 was one of the most significant and enduring events in the westward expansion of the United States. By granting 160 acres of free land to claimants, it allowed nearly any man or woman a chance to live the American dream. President Abraham Lincoln signed the Homestead Act of 1862 as the American Civil War entered into its second year. The act declared that any citizen or intended citizen could claim 160 acres – one quarter square mile – of surveyed government land. Claimants had to "improve" the plot with a dwelling and grow crops. After five years, if the original filer was still on the land, it was his property, free and clear.

One of the first takers was Daniel Freeman, a Union scout from Iowa. Freeman persuaded a Brownville, Nebraska land agent to let him sign up shortly after midnight on January 1, 1863, the day the Homestead Act took effect, allowing Freeman him to rejoin his Union Army regiment. The Homestead National Monument is located on the site of Freeman's original land claim.

Hostages/Iran

Stewart International Airport
1035 First Street, New Windsor, New York
845-564-2100

The Iranian Hostage Crisis began on November 4, 1979, when 3,000 militants overran the U.S. Embassy in Teheran and captured 54 embassy staff members. Thirteen hostages were released shortly after, but the remaining 53 were held in secret locations throughout Iran. (This ongoing news story led to the creation of the program *Nightline*.)

In 1980, the death of the Shah in Egypt and the invasion of Iran by Iraq made Iranians more open to resolving the Hostage Crisis. In the United States, the crisis helped Ronald Reagan defeat Jimmy Carter in the presidential election. Just after the election, with the assistance of Algerian intermediaries, successful negotiations with Iran began. On January 20, 1981, the day of President Reagan's inauguration, the hostages were freed after 444 days in Iranian detention. Stewart International Airport is where they first set foot back on American soil.

Hurricane Andrew

Biscayne National Park
9700 SW 328 Street, Homestead, Florida
305-230-7275

Biscayne National Park, Fla., May 20– On Monday, August 24, 1992, at 4:30 A.M., the eye wall of Hurricane Andrew passed over this point before striking Homestead and southern Miami-Dade County.

That's the opening line of text on the marker that rests here, testament to one of the most ferocious storms in U.S. history. On August 17, 1992, Hurricane Andrew became the first tropical storm of the season, and moved rapidly west and northwest during the next few days. By August 22nd it had reached hurricane status. It made landfall on August 24th at approximately 5:00 A.M. By the time it hit land, it was a Category 4 storm, with wind gusts estimated in excess of 175 m.p.h. When all was said and done, Andrew was by far the most expensive natural disaster in history (up to that date), with estimated damages exceeding $20 billion. More than 60 people were killed and approximately 2 million people were evacuated from their homes.

Hurricane Islamorada Monument

Located between the Old State Road 4A Highway and the present U.S. 1,
at mile marker 81.5, across from the library, Islamorada, Florida

The "Hurricane Monument," honors the hundreds of American veterans and local citizens who perished right here in the "Great Hurricane" on Labor Day, September 2, 1935. Islamorada sustained winds of 200 miles per hour and a barometer reading of 26.35 inches for many hours on that fateful holiday; most local buildings and the Florida East Coast Railway were destroyed by what remains the most savage hurricane on record.

Hundreds of World War I veterans who had been camped in the Matecumbe area while working on the construction of U. S. Highway One for the Works Progress Administration (WPA) were killed. The cremated remains of approximately 300 people were placed within the tiled crypt in front of the monument. It was unveiled before a crowd of 5,000 by nine-year-old survivor Fay Marie Parker on Sunday, November 14, 1937.

Johnstown Flood

Johnstown Flood National Memorial
733 Lake Road, South Fork, Pennsylvania
814-495-4643

Johnstown lies at the confluence of the Conemaugh River and Stony Creek; at the time of the flood it was a leading U.S. steelmaking center. But at 3:10 P.M. on May 31, 1889 the old South Fork Dam, a poorly maintained earthfill dam holding a major upstream reservoir, collapsed after heavy rains. It sent a wall of water rushing down the Conemaugh Valley at speeds of 20-40 m.p.h., and a 30-foot wall of water smashed into Johnstown at 4:07 P.M., killing 2,209 people. It remains one of the worst disasters in our nation's history. Today, the historic remnants of South Fork Dam are preserved by the National Park Service. Johnstown Flood National Memorial is located in southwestern Pennsylvania, about 10 miles northeast of Johnstown.

Jones, Casey

Casey Jones State Park
10901 Vaughn Road #1, Vaughn, Mississippi
662-673-9864

On the early morning of April 30, 1900, rushing down the tracks to make up lost time on a run of the "Cannonball Express," engineer Casey Jones approached the station at Vaughan. Three trains were arranging to let the Cannonball pass when an airhose burst on one of the trains, leaving four cars on the mainline.

Oblivious to the mishap, Casey careened through the darkness when, without warning, the lights on the stranded caboose became visible. Casey ordered Sim Webb, his fireman, to jump as he tried desperately to slow his train. At 3:52 A.M., the trains collided and Casey Jones became a legend. A marker identifies the site of the wreck at Vaughan. The town also houses a Casey Jones Museum, in operation since 1979, in an old depot. (Ask for details about how to locate the exact site of the crash within the park—it's 1/2 to 3/4 of a mile north of the current site of the museum.)

Kansas City Hyatt Regency Walkway Collapse

2345 McGee Street
Kansas City, Missouri
816-421-1234

At 7:05 P.M. on July 17, 1981, two 120-foot-long walkways tore loose from their suspension rods, dumping 65 tons of concrete, metal, glass, and dance spectators onto hundreds of people below. That tragic night, 111 persons died, including 18 pairs of husbands and wives. Of the 200 injured, three died weeks or months later, pushing the death toll to 114.

Twenty years later, the Hyatt skywalk tragedy remains the nation's worst structural failure disaster. It triggered multimillion-dollar lawsuits, and focused attention on the importance of treating the psychological scars of rescue workers. Closed during repairs, the Hyatt reopened 75 days later – but without skywalks and without a plaque or other memorial marking what had happened (to date, there is still no memorial or marker).

Kennedy/Nixon Debate

WBBM TV
Studio One
630 North McClurg Court
Chicago, Illinois
312-944-6000

On September 26, 1960, 70 million U.S. viewers tuned in to watch Senator John Kennedy of Massachusetts and Vice President Richard Nixon in the first-ever televised presidential debate, and the first of four televised "Great Debates" between Kennedy and Nixon. It had a decisive impact on the outcome of the 1960 election, and had Kennedy not emerged from that debate as the clearly perceived winner, it is believed he almost certainly would not have gone on to capture the White House later that year. Newscasts emanate from Studio One today, and a plaque in the building's lobby acknowledges the history that took place there.

The Kent State Murders

Prentice Hall Parking Lot
Kent State University, Kent, Ohio

Directions: In Kent, turn right onto State Route 59. Turn right onto Midway Drive. At the stop sign go straight. Prentice Hall is the first building on the right at the top of the hill.

On May 4th, 1970, U.S. National Guardsmen opened fire on students demonstrating against the war in Southeast Asia at Kent State University in Ohio. The National Guard had been sent in to prevent riots and regain control of the campus, but began shooting after some of the students started throwing rocks. More than 60 shots were fired killing four and wounding nine. The Kent State campus was shut down and 20,000 students were sent home.

Within the next two weeks over 500 campuses around the country would close as millions of students took to the streets to protest the Kent State murders and the Cambodian Invasion. Plaques have been laid at the sites in the parking lot and surrounding area where the students were taken down. Neil Young bitterly documented this tragic event in his musical diatribe, "Ohio."

King, Jr., Martin Luther

The Steps at the Lincoln Memorial
Washington, D.C.

"I have a dream that one day this nation will rise up and live out the true meaning of its creed: 'We hold these truths to be self-evident: that all men are created equal.'" Dr. Martin Luther King, Jr. delivered his most famous speech on August 28, 1963 from the steps of the Lincoln Memorial in Washington, D.C. He spoke to an audience of about 250,000 people who were protesting against discrimination. King's strategy of "active nonviolence" (including peaceful marches and sit-ins) had put civil-rights squarely on the national agenda, which gave the moment even more drama.

The speech was also broadcast to millions on television and radio, and printed in many newspapers. Since 1963, King's speech has since become one of the most famous public addresses of 20th-century America.

King's Highway/El Camino Real

Mission at San Juan Bautista
Second and Mariposa Streets, San Juan Bautista, California
831-623-4528

The "King's Highway," or "El Camino Real" was pioneered by Spaniards in the late 1700s when they colonized California in the name of their king. Beginning in 1769 with the founding of a fortress and a Franciscan mission at San Diego, a series of small self-reliant religious colonies was established, each a day's travel apart and linked by El Camino Real.

Overall, El Camino Real linked 21 missions, 2 pueblos and 4 presidios from San Diego to Sonoma. Today, the missions are some of California's most historic, most visited and most interesting landmarks. Though Highway 101 roughly traces El Camino Real and still connects the missions, a small part of the original foot trail forged in the 1700s is preserved here, just behind the mission at San Juan Bautista.

La Brea Tar Pits

Page Museum
5801 Wilshire Boulevard, Los Angeles, California
323-934-PAGE

Rancho La Brea is one of the most important fossil discovery sites in the world, boasting the largest array of extinct Ice Age plants and animals. Much of what has been discovered dates back to between 10,000 and 40,000 years ago, during the last Ice Age, when saber-toothed cats, sloths, camels and mammoths roamed the Los Angeles basin.

The Page Museum features hundreds of beautifully preserved specimens, and their laboratory allows visitors to watch as bones are cleaned and repaired. On the grounds of the museum, life-size replicas of several extinct mammals are featured. What's most amazing is that, unlike any other natural history museums, virtually everything you see at the museum was discovered right at the site.

Legionnaire's Disease

Park Hyatt Hotel at the Bellevue
Broad and Walnut Street
Philadelphia, Pennsylvania
215-893-1234

When 200 members of a war veteran's club called the American Legion became seriously ill during a conference at the Park Hyatt Hotel in 1976, doctors were mystified. What was causing the pneumonia-like disease with its symptoms of fever, chills, aches and pains, cough, diarrhea and abdominal pain? By the time the problem was traced to germs breeding in the hotel's air conditioning system, 34 men were dead and newspaper headlines were talking about a "new" disease – Legionnaire's Disease, named after the club members who became ill. Because of the size and severity of the outbreak, federal, state, and local health authorities launched what was at the time the largest cooperative investigation in history to determine the cause of the outbreak.

Lewis and Clark

National Historic Trail–Site #1
Route 3 (at Poag Road)
Hartford, Illinois
618-251-2680

The famous Lewis and Clark expedition started here in the Wood River/Hartford Clark area, where Camp DuBois was established to train and outfit the explorers. The group settled in Wood River longer than any other stop along their venture, staying from December 12, 1803 to May 15, 1804.

During this period, Corps of Discovery trained the men, helped build unity and discipline and prepared supplies and sharpened survival skills. Inside the 14,000 square foot interpretive center, there are many relevant exhibits, including a 55-foot keelboat replica with full mast and sail. Outside, the Lewis and Clark "Point of Departure" displays 11 concrete pylons, representing each of the 11 states traveled by the Expedition. Individual plaques are mounted on each pylon reviewing the group's fearless activities.

Lincoln, Abraham

Log Cabin
2995 Lincoln Farm Road, Hodgenville, Kentucky
270-358-3137

In the fall of 1808, Thomas and Nancy Lincoln settled on this 348 acre Sinking Spring Farm. Two months later, on February 12, 1809, Abraham Lincoln was born in a one-room log cabin near the Sinking Spring. Here the Lincolns lived and farmed before moving to land a few miles away at Knob Creek. The area was established by Congress on July 17, 1916. An early 19th-century Kentucky cabin, symbolic of the one in which Lincoln was born, is preserved in a memorial building at the site of his birth.

Lindbergh, Charles

The Mall at the Source
1504 Old Country Road, Westbury, New York
516-228-0303

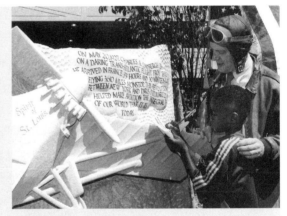

There is some question, even controversy, regarding the exact take-off point of Lindbergh's historic 33 hour, 30 minute nonstop flight to Le Bourget, Paris. There's a stone monument outside Fortunoff's (in The Mall at the Source) in Westbury that supposedly marks the spot. But there's also a metal plaque underneath an escalator at nearby Roosevelt Field Mall claiming that as the point of departure. However, the truth of the matter is that on May 20, 1927, Charles Lindbergh actually took off in the Spirit of St. Louis from the area near the present-day Fortunoff's, where the original Roosevelt Field airstrip used to be, and where the monument is today. The two malls are close to each other, and Lindbergh's plane was stored where Roosevelt Field Mall is located today.

The Louisiana Purchase

Louisiana Purchase State Park
19 miles southeast of Brinkley, Arkansas

Directions: Louisiana Purchase State Park is located near the tri-corner of Monroe, Lee, and Phillips counties, at the end of Arkansas 362 and two miles east of U.S. 49. The small park is a National Historic Landmark, and home to a monument marking the initial point for surveys of the 1803 Louisiana purchase.

Arkansas's 16th state park, Louisiana Purchase, is a National Historic Landmark and home to a monument marking the initial point for surveys of the 1803 Louisiana Purchase. The monument lies within a headwater swamp and can be viewed via an elevated boardwalk that has wayside exhibits. The granite marker, at the end of the park boardwalk, reads in part: "This stone marks the base established November 10, 1815, from which the lands of the Louisiana Purchase were surveyed by United States engineers."

Love Canal

Located in the southeast section of the La Salle area of Niagara Falls, New York

Love Canal first came to international attention during the summer of 1978 when President Jimmy Carter declared a federal emergency here at this infamous former chemical landfill. Love Canal is actually a neighborhood in Niagara Falls, New York. The nickname "Love Canal" came from the last name of William Love, who in 1896 began digging a canal connecting Lake Ontario and Lake Erie, bypassing Niagara Falls in order to serve as a water power conduit. It was never completed, but the Hooker Chemical Company, located west of the canal, had the ingenious idea of turning the uncompleted canal into a dumping ground for the chemical by-products of its manufacturing process.

Once the canal was filled with waste, the land was covered over and sold to the Niagara Falls city school board for $1.00, and a school and subdivision of homes were built right on top of the waste. The chemicals were detected leaking out of the site in 1977, and many health problems were reported. Residents were evacuated after a lengthy fight with the New York State government.

Today, the main dump site is fenced in, and many of the buildings have been bulldozed over and buried in the ground with the waste. The rest of the area is a ghost town of crumbling buildings, a testament to the ruinous power of hazardous waste.

Marconi, Guglielmo

Lecount Hollow Road off Route 6
(Now part of the Cape Cod National Seashore)
Wellfleet, Massachusetts
508-255-3421

On January 19, 1901, the "Father of Radio," 28-year old Guglielmo Marconi, erected his first ever American wireless radio station on this Cape Cod beach. Standing on this sandy bluff, he sent a 54-word greeting from President Theodore Roosevelt across the ocean to England's King Edward VII. Several hours later, the king responded, completing a two-way message. In that moment, Marconi had launched the era of global wireless communications.

In 1920, the station was dismantled and the towers were taken down. While the station is no longer there, in 1953 the Wellfleet Historical Society placed a bronze plaque near the original site commemorating the station. It reads: "Site of the first United States transatlantic wireless telegraph station, built in 1901-1902, Marconi Wireless Telegraph Company of America, predecessor of RCA, transmitted January 19, 1903. The first U.S. transatlantic wireless telegram addressed to Edward VII King of England. By Theodore Roosevelt, president of the United States."

In 1974, an exhibit shelter was built to house a scale model of the wireless station and a bronze bust of Marconi, along with the commemorative plaque dedicated in 1953. It's located on Main Street in the small town of Wellfleet.

Mars Bluff

Mars Bluff, South Carolina
Directions: Take I-20 east past Florence to Mars Bluff. After Francis Marion College, turn right on Mars Bluff Road and proceed about a mile.

On March 11, 1958 a B-47 left Hunter Air Force Base in Georgia for a field maneuver to North Africa. However, it experienced a malfunction of its bomb locking mechanism and inadvertently dropped an atomic bomb on the crossroads named Mars Bluff near Florence, South Carolina. The safety devices prevented a nuclear explosion, but the trigger composed of conventional explosives went off, creating a crater 75 feet across and 35 feet deep, damaging houses as far as a half mile away, knocking cars out of control on a nearby highway, and vaporizing the nuclear material, dispersing a ring of intense plutonium contamination in the surrounding area. The 35-foot crater where Walter Gregg's farmhouse once sat is still there, but it's now covered with a swamp.

The McCarthy Hearings

Senate Caucus Room
Russell Senate Office Building
Located northeast of the Capitol on a site bounded by Constitution Avenue, First
Street, Delaware Avenue, and C Street, N.E., Washington, D.C.

It was in the Senate Caucus Room of this ornate building where the dramatic exchanges were recorded between Sen. Joseph McCarthy and witnesses during the 36-day Army-McCarthy hearings. McCarthy had made a name for himself with his anti-Communist crusade and his highly publicized accusations of communist influence in the U.S. government, including the military.

Television was there to broadcast the drama of McCarthy's attacks and his debate with counsel Joseph Welch, and it was this exposure that helped turn the tide of public opinion

against him. Soon after, McCarthy was censured by his Senate colleagues. (This is also the room where John F. Kennedy announced his candidacy for president; it was used for the televised special investigation into the Watergate scandal in the 1970s and, in the 1980s, it was used for the Senate investigation into the Iran-Contra scandal.)

Mount St. Helens

Mount St. Helens National Volcanic Monument
42218 NE Yale Bridge Road, Amboy, Washington
360-247-3900

Mount St. Helens erupted at 8:32 on the morning of May 18, 1980. After being shaken by an earthquake measuring 5.1 on the Richter scale, the entire north face of this mountain collapsed in a massive avalanche. Nearly 150 square miles of forest was blown over or left dead and standing, and a mushroom-shaped column of ash blacked out the sun. For 9 hours, Mount St. Helens belched tons of ash and debris, dramatically changing the landscape.

In 1982, the 110,000-acre National Volcanic Monument was created, and today, there are three unique areas of Mount St. Helens to explore: Visitor centers on State Highway 504 reveal tremendous views of Mount St. Helens, including the crater, lava dome, and blast zone; Forest Roads 25 and 99 provide access to the vast blown down forest and views of the legendary Spirit Lake; Forest Road 83 passes through lava flows and mudflows from earlier eruptions and provides access to the Climber's Bivouac.

National Anthem

Fort McHenry National Monument and Historic Shrine
2600 E. Fort Avenue, Baltimore, Maryland
410-962-429

This late 18th century star-shaped fort is world famous as the birthplace of the United States' national anthem. It was during a British attack on September 13-14, 1814, that a 35-year-old poet-lawyer, Francis Scott Key, was inspired to write "The Star-Spangled Banner." Key was born on August 1, 1779. By 1805, Key had established a law practice in George-town, Maryland, and, by 1814, had appeared many times before the U.S. Supreme Court.

In August 1814, Key's friend Dr. William Beanes was taken prisoner by the British army soon after its departure from Washington. Key left for Baltimore to obtain the services of Colonel John Skinner, the government's prisoner of war exchange agent. Together they sailed down the bay on a truce ship and met the British fleet. Key successfully negotiated the doctor's release, but was detained with Skinner and Beanes by the British until after the attack on Baltimore. Key's vessel was 8 miles below the fort during the bombardment, under the watchful care of a British warship. It was from this site that he witnessed the British attack on Fort McHenry, after which he wrote the words to "The Star-Spangled Banner."

Northridge Earthquake

Roscoe and Wilbur Avenue
Northridge Meadow Apartments
(actual location was 9565 Reseda Boulevard), Northridge, California

On January 17, 1994, a 6.7 earthquake struck Southern California with a vengeance. Billions of dollars of damage were caused all throughout the Southland, although miraculously, only 57 people were killed. The epicenter was marked at the intersection of Roscoe and Wilbur Avenue in Northridge. A couple of miles away stood the Northridge Meadow Apartments which pancaked during the event, killing 16 people.

The scene became a landmark of the tragedy, and today, the Parc Ridge Apartments have been built in their place.

Nuclear Reaction

Joseph Regenstein Library
University of Chicago
1100 East 57th Street
Chicago, Illinois

The Joseph Regenstein Library stands on the site of the original Stagg Field, the University's athletic field from 1892 to 1967. It was here on December 2, 1942 that Enrico Fermi supervised the design and assembly of an "atomic pile," a code word for a device that in peace time would be known as a "nuclear reactor." The bronze memorial "Nuclear Energy" by famed sculptor Henry Moore is situated on the west edge of the 12-acre site of the library, marking the exact spot where Fermi and other scientists achieved man's first controlled, self-sustaining, nuclear chain reaction.

Oklahoma City Bombing

Alfred P. Murrah Federal Building
Northwest Fifth and Harvey
Oklahoma City, Oklahoma

On April 19, 1995, around 9:03 A.M., just after parents had dropped their children off at day care at the Murrah Federal Building in downtown Oklahoma City, a massive bomb inside a rental truck exploded, blowing half of the nine-story building into oblivion. A stunned nation watched as the bodies of men, women, and children were pulled from the rubble for nearly two weeks. When the smoke cleared, 168 people were dead in the (then) worst terrorist attack on U.S. soil.

Just 90 minutes after the explosion, an Oklahoma Highway Patrol officer pulled over 27-year-old Timothy McVeigh for driving without a license plate. Ultimately, McVeigh was found guilty of the crime and was put to death by lethal injection at 7:14 A.M. on Monday, June 11, 2001. Today, the area is marked by a poignant memorial and monument and recently, a museum dedicated to preserving the memory of the victims and the scope of the loss was opened right next to it.

Parks, Rosa

251 Montgomery Street
Montgomery, Alabama
334-241-8661

On December 1, 1955, forty-three-year-old Rosa Parks boarded a Montgomery, Alabama city bus after finishing work as a tailor's assistant at the Montgomery Fair department store. As black patrons were then required to do, she paid her fare at the front and then re-boarded in the rear of the bus. As the bus became full, the driver soon ordered Parks to give up her seat to a white man who had boarded. Parks refused several times, which prompted the driver to call the police, who then arrested Parks.

This event sparked the bus boycott in Montgomery, which eventually led to the desegregation of buses throughout the United States. In addition, Parks became a recognized figure in the Civil Rights Movement. At the arrest site today, where there used to be just a plaque, there is now the Rosa Parks Library and Museum, built for the woman who was arrested for her courageous stand against bigoted behavior. It's part of the revitalization of downtown Montgomery, and even includes a replica of a bus similar to the one Rosa Parks was sitting on that historic day.

The Peshtigo Fire Museum

400 Oconto Avenue
Peshtigo, Wisconsin
715-582-3244

The Peshtigo fire happened October 8, 1871 – the same day as the Great Chicago Fire. Though the Peshtigo fire had many more casualties than the Chicago fire (800 people perished in Peshtigo), and also did much more damage to the town, it's barely a footnote to this nation's history. The fire started easily because it had been a very dry summer with very little rain. Several small fires sprang up that, when combined, formed a monstrous inferno that was out of control before anybody could stop its destruction. The Peshtigo Fire Museum is in the first church that was built after the fire.

The Pilgrims

West end of Commercial Street
Provincetown, Massachusetts

Contrary to popular belief, Plymouth was not the first place the Pilgrims landed in the New World. They actually first arrived at Provincetown, on the tip of Cape Cod. Although the Pilgrims did not start their colony at Provincetown, they remained in its harbor and explored its shore for a month before moving on to Plymouth, where they established their permanent settlement. Set into a boulder at the center of a little park, the bronze plaque commemorates the first footfall of the Pilgrims onto Cape soil — Provincetown's equivalent of the Plymouth Rock.

Plymouth Rock

Water Street
Plymouth, Massachusetts
508-866-2580

The smallest park in the Massachusetts state forest and park system, Pilgrim Memorial is also the most heavily visited. Nearly one million people a year come from all over the world to visit the town where in 1620 Europeans first made a home in New England. They also, of course, come here to see Plymouth Rock where, tradition tells us, the passengers on the Mayflower first set foot in the New World. This small boulder has become synonymous with the faith, courage and persistence embodied by the men and women who founded the first New England colony. Near the rock, a replica of the Mayflower is anchored at a park that also provides scenic views of Plymouth Harbor.

Pony Express

Pony Express Museum
914 Penn Street, St. Joseph, Missouri
816-279-5059

PONY EXPRESS

St. JOSEPH, MISSOURI to CALIFORNIA
in 10 days or less.

☞ **WANTED** ☜

YOUNG, SKINNY, WIRY FELLOWS
not over eighteen. Must be expert
riders, willing to risk death daily.
Orphans preferred.
Wages $25 per week.

APPLY, **PONY EXPRESS STABLES**
St. JOSEPH, MISSOURI

The purpose of the Pony Express was simple: to provide the fastest mail delivery between St. Joseph, Missouri, and Sacramento, California. The service was active from April 3, 1860, to late October 1861. The Pony Express ran day and night, and 183 men are known to have ridden for the organization during its 18-month existence. As far as what it took to be a rider, here's how one recruitment ad read: "Wanted. Young, skinny, wiry fellows. Not over 18. Must be expert riders. Willing to risk death daily. Orphans preferred."

While most riders were around 20 years old, the youngest was 11, and the oldest was in his mid-40s. Riders were paid $100 per month, and a relay system ensured that each rider got a fresh horse every 10 to 15 miles. Four hundred horses were purchased to stock the Pony Express route – thoroughbreds, mustangs, pintos, and morgans were often used across about 165 stations. The total trail length was almost 2,000 miles, and ran from St. Joseph, Missouri to Sacramento, California, through the present-day states of Kansas, Nebraska, Colorado, Wyoming, Utah, Nevada, and California.

The Red Cross

Clara Barton National Historic Site
5801 Oxford Road, Glen Echo, Maryland
301-492-6245

The Clara Barton National Historic Site commemorates the life of Clara Barton, founder of the American Red Cross. This house in Glen Echo served as her home, headquarters for the American Red Cross and a warehouse for disaster relief supplies. From this house, she organized and directed American Red Cross relief efforts for victims of natural disasters and war. Clara Barton National Historic Site was established in the National Park Service in 1975 and is administered by the George Washington Memorial Parkway.

The Revolutionary War

The Midnight Ride of Paul Revere

Hancock-Clarke House
36 Hancock Street
Lexington, Massachusetts
781-861-0928

This is the home to which Paul Revere rode on his famous "midnight ride" to warn John Hancock and Samuel Adams, "The British are coming!" On the evening of April 18, 1775, John Hancock and Samuel Adams, prominent leaders in the colonial cause, were guests at this residence. Fearing that they might be captured by the British, Dr. Joseph Warren of Boston sent William Dawes and Paul Revere to Lexington with news of the advancing British troops. Arriving separately, they stopped to warn Hancock and Adams, then set off for Concord. Today, few remember Dawes, but Paul Revere's midnight ride has been immortalized by Longfellow.

The Old North Church

193 Salem Street
Boston, Massachusetts
617-523-6676

"One if by land . . . two if by sea." The enduring fame of the Old North Church was inspired by a fleeting moment on the night of April 18, 1775. Robert Newman, the church sexton, hung two lanterns in its steeple to warn that the British troops were arriving "by sea," thereby sending Paul Revere on his famous "midnight ride" to Lexington and Concord to warn Samuel Adams and John Hancock that the British were approaching. Revere's dash on horseback, immortalized by Henry Wadsworth Longfellow's "Paul Revere's Ride," brought out the militia and the shot heard round the world was fired on Lexington Green the following day.

The Revolutionary War

North Bridge

174 Liberty Street
Concord, Massachusetts
978-369-6993

The Old North Bridge, in Concord, Massachusetts, was the site of the first battle between British government soldiers and British colonial rebels, who later became independent Americans. Fought on April 19, 1775, the battle began when government troops, attempting to confiscate weapons from the colonists, found themselves opposed by a determined militia of local farmers. Militia Captain John Parker gave his troops the famous order, "Stand your ground. Don't fire until fired upon. But if they mean to have a war, let it begin here." The "shot heard around the world," as Ralph Waldo Emerson called it in his "Concord Hymn," rang out from this bridge and the American Revolution had begun.

Scopes Trial

The Scopes Trial Museum and Rhea County Courthouse
1475 Market Street, Dayton, Tennessee
423-775-7801

In 1925, John Thomas Scopes, a biology teacher in Dayton, Tennessee, was arrested for the teaching of evolution in schools. The ACLU defended him and America's most famous criminal lawyer, Clarence Darrow, was then enlisted (pro bono) to help Scopes. The prosecution was led by Attorney General A. T. Stewart, and the former presidential candidate William Jennings Bryan.

What would eventually become known as the "Monkey Trial" started on July 11, 1925, and was the first trial in American history to be broadcast via radio to the nation. After Judge John T. Raulston refused to allow scientists to testify about the truth of evolution, Clarence Darrow called William Jennings Bryan to the witness stand and successfully exposed the flaws in Bryan's arguments during the cross-examination. The jury, however, found John Thomas Scopes guilty and the judge fined him $100. This verdict was eventually reversed on appeal as a result of a technicality.

"Sue" the T-Rex

The Cheyenne River Sioux Indian reservation
Near the town of Faith, in the badlands of South Dakota
605-967-2001

The Field Museum
1400 S. Lake Shore Drive, Chicago, Illinois
312-922-9410

The famous middle-age female T-Rex was discovered in 1990 by Sue Hendrickson, who was walking on a Cheyenne River Reservation ranch in South Dakota, owned by Maurice Williams. Sue is the largest, most complete, and best preserved Tyrannosaurus rex, and was purchased by The Field Museum at public auction in 1997 with generous financial support from McDonald's Corporation, Walt Disney World Resort, and private individuals.

Today, the actual skeleton is on display (not a plastic model or a plaster cast). Sue stands 13 feet high at the hips and 42 feet long from head to tail. One of the only pieces of Sue that is not mounted is her 5-foot-long skull, which is too heavy to be placed on the steel armature that holds together her more than 200 fossilized bones. In its place, the Museum has installed a cast replica. Sue's real skull is on display in an exhibit on the second-floor balcony at the museum overlooking Stanley Field Hall.

Telephone

The Verizon building
Post Office Square
185 Franklin Street, Boston, Massachusetts

On March 10, 1876, Alexander Graham Bell transmitted actual speech for the first time in history. Sitting in one room, he spoke into the phone to his assistant Mr. Watson in another room, uttering the now famous words: "Mr. Watson, come here. I need you."

Watson heard Bell's voice through the wire, realized he had just received the first telephone call, and quickly went to answer it. Bell soon introduced the telephone to the world at the Centennial Exhibition in Philadelphia. This room where Alexander Graham Bell invented the telephone is just off the lobby of the Verizon Building. Originally on Court Street, the attic was disassembled when its building was torn down in 1959 and reassembled here.

Three Mile Island

Harrisburg, Pennsylvania

Directions: The Three Mile Island Nuclear Generating Station is approximately 10 miles South-Southeast of Harrisburg, Pennsylvania. Most commonly it is reported to be in Middletown, but it is actually in Londonderry Township on the Susquehanna River.

The infamous incident at Three Mile Island began with a small mechanical problem – and ended as the worst accident in the history of American nuclear power. The nuclear power plant's cooling towers still loom over the farms and small towns that line Pennsylvania's Susquehanna River. Back in the 1970s, they were symbols of progress. But that all changed on March 28, 1979, when a small valve stuck open, cooling water escaped, and the reactor core of TMI's Unit 2 began to melt. At the time, nobody seemed to know what was going on.

Though workers spent years cleaning up the accident, how much radiation escaped is still open to debate. The partial meltdown prompted the evacuation of about 140,000 people from the Harrisburg area. Ironically (and somewhat eerily), the accident happened just eleven days after the chilling reactor-disaster film *The China Syndrome* opened.

USS Olympia

Penn's Landing
Independence Seaport Museum, 211 South Columbus Boulevard and Walnut Street
Philadelphia, Pennsylvania
215-925-5439

"You may fire when you are ready, Gridley." Thus Commodore Dewey ignited the 1898 Battle of Manila Bay from the bridge of the *Olympia* (as he addressed Captain Charles V. Gridley). Seven-and-a-half hours later the Spanish fleet in the Philippines had been destroyed and the U.S. had arrived as an imperial power. The *Olympia*, built in 1892, was one of America's first steel ships. She became the flagship of the North Atlantic Squadron, and protected American interests in many foreign countries. The *Olympia's* last assignment was bringing the body of the Unknown Soldier back from Europe in 1921.

Washington, George

Washington Crossing, Pennsylvania
215-493-4076

Directions: The park is located at Washington Crossing on PA Route 32 just a few miles north of I-95, and seven miles south of New Hope, Pennsylvania. The 500 acres of Washington Crossing Historic Park are divided into two areas. The Thompson's Mill section is 1.5 miles southeast of New Hope on Route 32. The McConkey's Ferry section, 5 miles farther south, is the location of the park's Visitor Center.

On December 25, 1776, Washington's 2,400 troops gathered at McConkey Ferry, now called Washington Crossing. As night fell, the long boat crossing began. As dawn broke, the troops surprised the Hessian mercenaries, who quickly surrendered. Washington Crossing Historic Park was founded in 1917 to preserve this site from which the Continental Army crossed the Delaware. A stone plaque signifies the place where George Washington crossed the river. Nearby is a statue of Washington and his men in their boat. The monument reads: "Near this

spot, Washington crossed the Delaware on Christmas night 1776, the eve of the Battle of Trenton. Erected 1895, Bucks County Historical Society."

World War II

Japanese Internment Camp

Manzanar National Historic Site
Independence, California
760-878-2932

Directions: Just off of U.S. Highway 395, 12 miles north of Lone Pine, California, and 5 miles south of Independence, California.

The American internment of Japanese during World War II is one of the black eyes of American history. On February 19, 1942, President Roosevelt signed Executive Order 9066, which called for the forcible internment of 120,000 Japanese-Americans. The Manzanar War Relocation Center was one of ten camps at which Japanese-American citizens and resident Japanese aliens were interned during the war. Located at the foot of the imposing Sierra Nevada in eastern California's Owens Valley, Manzanar has been identified as the best preserved of these camps (though remnants of others still survive).

The U.S. Mainland is Attacked by the Japanese

Ellwood Oil Field (Access not available)
Goleta, California (12 miles northwest of Santa Barbara)

December 7, 1941, is a "date that will live in infamy," but few people will remember February 23, 1942, the date the Japanese attacked the U.S. mainland. A Japanese submarine fired 25 shells at an oil refinery at the edge of Ellwood Oil Field, twelve miles northwest of Santa Barbara. One shell actually hit on the rigging, causing minor damage. (President Roosevelt was giving a fireside chat at the time of the attack.)

On its face, the shelling of Ellwood beach February 23, 1942, was not a major event of the war. It injured no one and did a mere $500 damage to a shed and catwalk belonging to the Barnsdall-Rio Grande Oil Co. Yet, for a country still recovering from the brutal Pearl Harbor attack just two months before, the 5-inch shells were enough to scare many into the belief that Japan could wage war on mainland American soil. After all, this was the first enemy attack on U.S. shores since the War of 1812. The attack also quickened the rounding up of Japanese-Americans in internment camps for the remainder of the war, a move Franklin D. Roosevelt had authorized just four days earlier.

World War II

The Japanese Bomb Oregon

North Bank Chetco River Road and Highway 101
Mt. Emily, Brookings, Oregon

In the uninhabited mountains east of Brookings, Oregon, you can hike a trail and see where a Japanese bomb landed on September 9, 1942 during World War II. The idea had

been conceived by the Japanese imperial general staff, still smarting from General Jimmy Doolittle's Tokyo raid. To retaliate, the Japanese hatched a plan to set the Oregon forests afire; they expected that the flames would spread to the cities and panic the entire West Coast. However, three of the bombs were duds; the fourth started a small blaze that was quickly spotted and doused by forest rangers.

There's an Oregon State Historic Marker where North Bank Chetco River Road meets Highway 101 (and directions there about how to reach the exact bombing site up the mountain, where a plaque sits at the site where one of the bombs hit). Interestingly, the pilot of the Japanese bomber, Nobuo Fujita, was invited to Brookings 20 years after the war as a sign of peace, and 30 years later he returned again to plant a commemorative redwood at the bombsite. When he died in 1997, he had just been named an honorary citizen of Brookings by the city council.

The Enola Gay

Tinian Airport on Tinian Island
(Part of the Northern Mariana Island chain in the western North Pacific)

Tinian (a U.S. territory) lies north of Guam on the eastern edge of the Philippine Sea, and was one of the primary staging areas for U.S. Pacific air operations during World War II. (Tinian Island airport is toward the southeast side of the island.)

Though little remains of what was once one of the world's busiest airports, a visitor to Tinian's North Field can pause at one of modern history's most somber locations. It is the site where the atomic bombs nicknamed *Fat Man* and *Little Boy* underwent final assembly and were then loaded onto the B-29 bombers – including the *Enola Gay* – that carried them to Hiroshima and Nagasaki.

Though the bomb pits are now home to plumeria and coconut trees, a plaque on one of the pits reads: "Atomic Bomb Loading Pit." The bomber, piloted by Colonel Paul W. Tibetts, Jr., was loaded late in the afternoon of August 5, 1945, and at 2:45 A.M. the following morning it took off on its mission.

World War II

Atomic Bomb Test Site

Trinity Site
110 miles south of Albuquerque between the Oscura mountains on the east
and the San Mateo mountains on the west, about 60 miles northwest of
Alamogordo, New Mexico
800-826-0294

Trinity Site is where the first atomic bomb was tested at 5:29:45 A.M. on July 16, 1945. It is estimated that 100-250 tons of sand vaporized by the blast went up in the cloud following the explosion. The 19-kiloton explosion not only led to a quick end to the war in the Pacific but also ushered the world into the atomic age. A triangular-shaped monument at Trinity Site on White Sands Missile Range marks ground zero.

The 51,500-acre area was declared a national historic landmark in 1975. The landmark includes base camp, where the scientists and support group lived; ground zero, where the bomb was placed for the explosion; and the McDonald ranch house, where the plutonium core to the bomb was assembled. Visitors to a Trinity Site Open House see ground zero and the McDonald ranch house. In addition, one of the old instrumentation bunkers is visible beside the road just west of ground zero. Note: The site is only open to the public twice a year—on the first Saturday in April and the first Saturday in October.

World War II

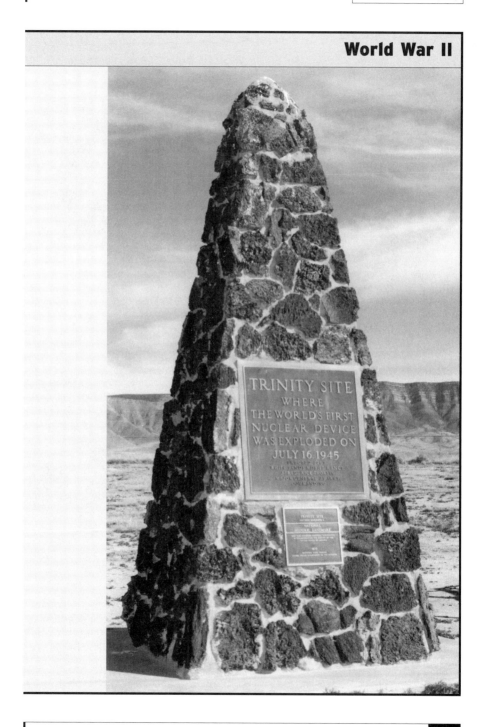

Wreck of Old '97

**Memorial is located west of Danville on Riverside Drive (U.S. 58) between Locust Lane and North Main Street at the train crash site
Danville, Virginia**

On September 27, 1903, the mail-and-express train No. 97 vaulted off the Stillhouse Trestle in Danville, Virginia, killing 11 people aboard and inspiring "The Ballad of the Wreck of the Old 97," one of the most famous country songs of all time. The song, whose authorship became a source of controversy and led to an extended legal battle, became the first single in U.S. history to sell 1 million copies after it was recorded by light-opera singer Vernon Dalhart.

Wright Brothers

**Wright Brothers National Memorial
National Park Service
1401 National Park Drive, Manteo, North Carolina
252-441-7430**

The first successful sustained powered flights in a heavier-than-air machine were made here by Wilbur and Orville Wright on December 17, 1903. A 60-foot granite monument dedicated in 1932 is perched atop 90-foot tall Kill Devil Hill commemorating the achievement of these two visionaries from Dayton, Ohio. Also placed in this park is "The First Flight Lift-off Commemoration Boulder." The granite marker was placed at the approximate site of the revolutionary 1903 liftoff and the text

reads: "The first successful flight of an airplane was made from this spot by Orville Wright December 17, 1903 in a machine designed and built by Wilbur and Orville Wright. This tablet was erected by the National Aeronautic Association of the U.S.A. December 17, 1928 to commemorate the 25th anniversary of this event."

Yeager, Chuck

Edwards Air Force Base
Located on the western edge of the Mojave Desert, about 90
miles north of Los Angeles
661-277-351

Directions: From Los Angeles, take the Rosamond exit off the Antelope Valley Freeway (State Highway 14) and travel east on Rosamond Boulevard into the base. Edwards can also be reached via Highway 58 near North Edwards and via 120th Street from Lancaster.

In 1947, flight instructor and test pilot Chuck Yeager was chosen from several volunteers to test-fly the secret, experimental X-1 aircraft, built by the Bell Aircraft Company. The Bell X-1 was designed to test human pilots and fixed wing aircraft against the severe stresses of flight close to the speed of sound, and to see if a straight-wing plane could fly faster than the speed of sound (approximately 760 mph, in air at sea level). No one knew if a pilot could safely control a plane under the effects of the shock waves produced as the plane's speed neared Mach 1.

On October 14, 1947, after taking off from Muroc air Base (now called Edwards), Yeager rode the X-1, attached to the belly of a B-29 bomber, to an altitude of 25,000 feet. After releasing from the B-29, he rocketed to an altitude of 40,000 feet. He became the first person to break the sound barrier, safely taking the X-1 to a speed of 662 m.p.h.

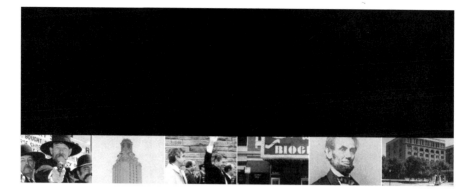

Crime, Murder, and Assassination

Abbot, Jack Henry

BiniBon Restaurant (now the Madras Café)
79 Second Avenue
New York, New York
212-254-8002

Jack Henry Abbott spent nearly 50 of his 58 years in custody. In 1977, while doing time for bank robbery and killing a fellow inmate, he wrote novelist Norman Mailer with an offer to share his insights into "violent men." Mailer jumped at the chance and they struck up a correspondence that ultimately resulted in the book, *In the Belly of the Beast*. Mailer helped get the book published and tried to get Abbott released from jail, saying to the parole board that "Mr. Abbott has the makings of a powerful and important writer."

Mailer ultimately succeeded in freeing the murderer, and in July 1981 (just six weeks after leaving prison), the writer's protégé knifed and killed waiter and aspiring actor Richard Adan outside this restaurant. Mailer was roundly criticized for his infatuation and sponsorship of this notorious "fellow artist." On February 10th, 2002, Jack Henry Abbott took his own life at Wende Correctional Facility in Alden, N.Y.

Bakley, Bonnie Lee

Vitello's Italian Restaurant
4349 Tujunga Avenue, Studio City, California

This is where actor Robert Blake ate with his soon-to-be-widow Bonnie Lee Bakley on Friday, May 4, 2001. It was a favorite haunt of Blake's, the actor who played TV cop "Baretta" back in the 1970s. (According to the restaurant's owner, he ate here twice a week, and even had an item on the menu named after him, "Fusilli a la Robert Blake".)

At about 9:40 P.M., someone shot Blake's wife, while she sat in their black sports car. It was parked on Woodbridge Street, a block and a half away from the restaurant.

According to Blake, he had briefly returned to Vitello's to retrieve a gun he had left behind, and when he returned to the car, he found Bonnie Lee dying from a gun-shot to her head. He ran to a nearby house (of director Sean Stanek) for help and the police were called. At the time of this writing, Blake is being held in prison without bail on charges of committing the murder.

Berkowitz, David/Son of Sam

42 Pine Street (originally 35 Pine Street)
Yonkers, New York

The summer of 1977 was a terrifying one for New Yorkers, thanks to David Berkowitz (AKA the "Son of Sam"). Berkowitz, a chubby, bookish loner, prowled the streets of New York looking for attractive young women to kill with his .44-caliber pistol. The first shooting occurred in early 1976. By the next summer, the city would literally be paralyzed with fear and the night streets would be empty. Police unleashed the largest manhunt in city history to try and stop the killer (whose nickname came from one of the taunting notes he began sending local reporters).

Finally, on August 10, 1977 residents got the news they were waiting to hear. "Police have captured a man whom they believe to be the Son of Sam." David Berkowitz, a then 24 year-old Yonkers postal worker, confessed to a year-long rampage of eight shooting attacks in Queens, the Bronx, and Brooklyn after being arrested in front of this nondescript apartment building. The attacks left a toll of six young people dead and seven others wounded. A trial was avoided as Berkowitz pleaded guilty and he was sentenced to life.

"Black Dahlia"

3925 South Norton Avenue (just south of 39th Street)
South Central Los Angeles, California

The once undeveloped area where the horribly mutilated body of "The Black Dahlia" (aspiring 22-year old actress Elizabeth Short) was found cut in half on January 15, 1947 is now a residential neighborhood. For a long time the most infamous murder case in the history of Hollywood, the body was found two blocks east of where the Baldwin Hills-Crenshaw Plaza mall is today. The grisly murder inspired the James Elroy best-seller, *The Black Dahlia*, and several movies, most notably 1981's *True Confessions*.

Bobbit, John Wayne and Lorena

Maplewood Drive off Centreville Road (Route 28)
(The apartment complex across from the street from the Maplewood
Plaza shopping center)
Manassas, Virginia

John Wayne Bobbit made national headlines when his wife, Lorena, maimed him on grounds of cheating, abuse, forcing her to get an abortion, and other despicable acts. (His organ was recovered from the scene and re-attached.) He later appeared in an adult film of his own life in order to help pay his medical (a nine-hour operation) and legal bills. In two separate trials, Lorena was found innocent by reason of insanity, while John Wayne was acquitted of sexually assaulting his wife.

Bonnie and Clyde

Route 154, just south of Gibsland, Louisiana

Directions: From Shreveport, take the I-20 about 45 miles to the Gibsland/Athens exit, which puts you on Route 154. The marker is about eight miles after you pass the small town of Gibsland.

On Wednesday, May 23, 1934, six officers acting on a tip laid in wait for outlaw Clyde Barrow and his companion in crime, Bonnie Parker. Bonnie and Clyde were accused of killing 12 innocent people, and the entire country had been searching for them. As they approached the ambush spot, the police shouted a warning. The outlaws drew their guns, but in moments they were riddled with over 50 bullets.

Many believe that had they not been glamorized by the 1967 film *Bonnie and Clyde*, they would have remained what they were—obscure, petty, cold-blooded killers. A stone marker sits at the exact spot where it happened. On the weekend closest to May 23, the town of Gibsland stages a Bonnie and Clyde Festival (318-843-6141). Incidentally, the 1934 Ford in which Bonnie and Clyde were killed is on display in Primm, Nevada at Whiskey Pete's Casino. In 1997, Whiskey Pete's paid $85,000 for the light blue, bullet-ridden, bloodstained shirt that Barrow was wearing when he was killed. The shirt is also on display in the casino.

Borden, Lizzie

92 Second Street, Fall River, Massachusetts
508-675-7333

Lizzie Borden took an axe
and gave her Mother 40 whacks.
When she saw what she had done
She gave her Father forty-one.

On the morning of August 4, 1892, Lizzie Borden murdered her stepmother with an axe in the Borden's family house. Abby Borden's body was found in the guest room between the bed and bureau. Soon after, Lizzie axed her father, Andrew Borden, to death.

While there is little doubt that Lizzie committed the crime, she was acquitted at trial due to a lack of evidence. Although ostracized by the community, Lizzie lived in the house until she died on June 1, 1927. After her death, the house remained a private residence for several decades before being converted into a bed and breakfast. Guests are allowed to view the murder scene and can sleep in Lizzie and her sister Emma's bedrooms, Abby and Andrew's bedrooms, or the guest room where Abby was killed.

Boston Strangler

79 Gainsborough Street, Back Bay, Boston, Massachusetts

On October 27, 1964, a man entered a young woman's home at this address, posing as a detective. He tied the woman to her bed, sexually assaulted her, and then suddenly left, saying "I'm sorry" as he went. The woman's description to the police led to his identification as Albert De Salvo. After his photo was published, many other women came forward to identify him as their attacker, too.

At this point, De Salvo was not a suspect in the string of strangling crimes that had taken place over the previous two years. But several months later, while being held on a separate rape charge, DeSalvo confessed in great detail to his activities as the Boston Strangler. However, there was no evidence to substantiate his confession, so he stood trial for a series of earlier, unrelated crimes of robbery and sexual offenses. He was sent to prison for life in 1967, only to be murdered six years later while in his cell.

Brando, Christian

12900 Mulholland Drive, Hollywood Hills, California

This is the house of actor Marlon Brando, and also where his son, Christian Brando, shot and killed his half-sister's lover, Dag Drollet, in May of 1990. According to Brando, his sister Cheyenne said Drollet had been beating her. A fight between the two men then broke out, and Brando claimed that in the heat of the moment, an accidental shooting occurred. Brando was convicted and sentenced to 10 years in prison. His half-sister, Cheyenne, committed suicide in Tahiti in 1995. After his early release from prison in January of 1996, "The Godfather's" son returned home to his father's estate.

Brinks Heist

165 Prince Street, Boston, Massachusetts

Shortly before 7:30 P.M. on the evening of January 17, 1950, a group of armed, masked men emerged from the Brinks offices in Boston, Massachusetts, dragging bags containing $1,218,211.29 in cash and $1,557,183.83 in checks, money orders, and other securities. These men had just committed the "crime of the century." As the robbers sped from the scene, a Brinks employee telephoned the Boston Police Department. Minutes later, police arrived at the Brinks building, and Special Agents of the FBI quickly joined in the investigation.

It was the biggest cash haul in history, and it would take six years and the combined investigative efforts of the Boston police and the FBI (not to mention the help of local police departments across the country), to solve the case. At the time, the Brinks offices were located in the North Terminal Garage Building in the North End of Boston — the building still stands today.

Bundy, Ted

Chi Omega Sorority House
661 West Jefferson Street
Tallahassee, Florida

Though there were many ghoulish scenes in Ted Bundy's history, this was the final eruption – the end of Bundy's infamous six-state murder spree. He had escaped from a Colorado jail, headed to Florida, and in January, 1978, broke into Chi Omega and killed four young women while they slept. A month later, he killed a 12-year old girl after taking her from outside her school in Lake City, Florida.

It may never be known exactly how many people Bundy actually murdered, though authorities believe the number to be around 36. From 1973–1978, the clean-cut, charming killer eluded arrest as he went from state to state. But his luck ran out in Pensacola, Florida when he picked a fight with a cop who had pulled him over on a routine traffic stop (Bundy was driving a stolen car), thus ending his career as a killer. Eleven years later, he was executed by the state of Florida in the electric chair.

Cassidy, Butch

Montpelier Bank Building
833 Washington Street
Montpelier, Idaho
800-448-2327 (Visitors Bureau)

This building housed the original "Bank of Montpelier" and is the site of a famous Butch Cassidy bank robbery. On August 13, 1896, Butch, Elza Lay, and Bob Meeks arrived at the bank just before closing time, and tied up their horses at the hitching rack across the street. Cassidy and Lay left Meeks to watch, they entered the bank, and forced the employees up against the wall. Lay kept guns on the bank staff while Cassidy quickly scooped money into a gunny sack.

Cassidy left the bank first with the money. He walked nonchalantly across the street, got on his horse and rode slowly away. Meeks moved across the street with the remaining horses and left Lay's horse standing in front of the bank as he rode away. Finally, Lay left the bank in haste. Cassidy was never brought to trial. Today, the site is occupied by the Mountain Litho printing company, run by a nice man named Kent Bunn. He knows all the history of the place if you have any more questions.

Castellano, Paul

Sparks Steakhouse
210 East 46th Street
New York, New York
212-687-4855

On February 25, 1985, Paul Castellano was arrested along with several other crime family bosses in what became known as the "Commission Case." Evidently, Castellano planned to rat on the Gambino family, which prompted John Gotti to seek his murder. Using an insider close to Castellano, Gotti arranged for Castellano to meet someone on December 16 at Sparks Steak House in Manhattan. After a meeting with his lawyer, Castellano drove to Sparks where he was gunned down by Gotti's killers. Watching the killing with Gotti from a nearby car was Gambino lieutenant Salvatore "Sammy the Bull" Gravano, who ironically would later rat on Gotti and scores of other mobsters.

The Columbine High School Massacre

6201 South Pierce Street
Littleton, Colorado
303-982-4400

On April 20, 1999, two high school students named Eric Harris and Dylan Klebold casually walked into Columbine High School and began firing from a multi-gun arsenal, and lobbing homemade bombs throughout the school. In all, they killed 12 students and 1 teacher and injured 23 before committing suicide.

Investigators concluded that the brutal, indiscriminate carnage inflicted by Harris and Klebold was intended to wipe out most of their high school. Were it not for the heroic efforts of many of the faculty, students, and law enforcement officials, it is believed the casualties would have been much higher. A permanent memorial is located at Robert F. Clement Park, which is adjacent to the school. In the aftermath of the massacre, police across the country altered training procedures based on the event as to better prepare for another worst-case scenario.

Cosby, Ennis

405 Freeway (north)
Skirball Center off ramp (near Mulholland Drive)
Bel Air, California

Ennis Cosby, son of entertainer Bill Cosby, was heading north in his car at about 1:45 A.M. on January 16, 1997. After getting a flat tire, he pulled the car off onto the exit leading to Mulholland Drive (in the Sepulveda Pass). As he changed the tire on the west shoulder of the road, a man emerged from the shadows and shot him to death. Eighteen-year-old Mikail "Michael" Markhasev, from nearby Orange County, was arrested for the crime, tried, found guilty and sentenced to life in prison. (Ironically, this was almost the exact same location where Frank Sinatra, Jr. was released by kidnappers in 1963 after he had supposedly been abducted.)

Dahmer, Jeffrey

Oxford Apartments
924 North 25th Street, Apartment 213
Milwaukee, Wisconsin

Certainly one of the most infamous, ghoulish serial murderers of all-time is Jeffrey Lionel Dahmer. On July 22, 1991, two Milwaukee police officers noticed a distraught, handcuffed man running down the street. Terrified, he said his name was Tracy Edwards and he was escaping from the apartment of Jeffrey L. Dahmer, a person who, for the last five hours, had terrorized and threatened to kill Edwards and eat his heart out.

Though the shy, unassuming Dahmer had been arrested before for disorderly conduct and molesting children, nothing could prepare the cops for what they found in his apartment. After being led there by Edwards, they discovered human remains, including skulls in the freezer and parts of bodies, along with photographs of dead men who had either been mutilated or completely dismembered.

In February of 1992, Dahmer was sentenced to 15 life terms in prison for his crimes. He himself was murdered in prison by a fellow inmate on November 28, 1994.

Denny, Reginald

Intersection of Florence and Normandy Avenues
South Central Los Angeles, California

When the "not guilty" verdicts were read in the Rodney King trial on April 29, 1992, few had any idea what was about to break loose. Least of all Reginald Denny, a mild-mannered white truck driver who was at the wrong place at the wrong time – ground zero for the 1992 L.A. riots. This is where Denny was yanked from his truck and beaten nearly to death as a TV camera from a helicopter captured the entire incident. Denny managed to survive, and later even forgave the thugs who brutally pounded him.

Dillinger, John

Biograph Theater
2433 North Lincoln Avenue
Chicago, Illinois

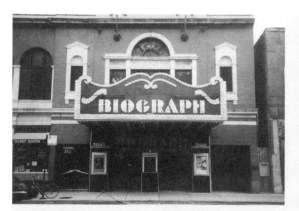

On the evening of July 22, 1934, John Dillinger stepped out of this downtown Chicago theater where he and two girlfriends had watched a film called *Manhattan Melodrama* starring Clark Gable. As soon as they reached the sidewalk, Melvin Purvis of the FBI stepped forward and identified himself. He ordered Dillinger to surrender, but no dice. Dillinger turned to run, but several shots rang out and Dillinger went down, his left eye shredded by one of the bullets fired by the other agents. "Public Enemy Number One," the most prolific bank robber in modern American history, was dead.

Einhorn, Ira

3411 Race Street, 2nd floor
Philadelphia, Pennsylvania

In the 1960s, Einhorn was a hip guru and outspoken activist (he even ran for mayor once). But in 1977, he was charged with the murder of Helen "Holly" Maddux, his live-in lover. He denied the charges, even after detectives found the young woman's decomposed body in a trunk in his closet at this address.

Einhorn fled to France and was tried and found guilty in absentia—but it was not until recently that French officials finally allowed Einhorn to be brought back to America for a trial in person, where he was eventually convicted of the crime.

Evers, Medgar

2332 Margaret West Alexander Drive
Jackson, Mississippi
601-981-2965

Medgar Evers is known for his endless contributions to the black civil rights movement. When he was in his late twenties, he was accepted into the NAACP and became a full time chapter organizer. In his early thirties, Medgar was named state field secretary for the NAACP. On the night of June 12, 1963 while getting out of his car in front of this house, Medgar was shot in the back by Byron de la Beckwith. He died 50 minutes later at a local hospital.

Evers' murder prompted President John F. Kennedy to push for a civil rights bill that would ban segregation. This, in turn, spurred Martin Luther King, Jr. and 250,000 people to march to Washington, D.C., where King gave his famous "I Have a Dream" speech. Although Evers died at the young age of 37, he was one of the most renowned civil rights activists in U.S. history. Evers' house, now a museum, was used in the movie *Ghosts of Mississippi*, and many of the current furnishings were put in place during the filming.

Fisher, Amy

One Adam Road West
Biltmore Shores, Long Island, New York

The is the house where 16-year old Amy Fisher (dubbed the "Long Island Lolita" by New York media), knocked on the door and shot Mary Jo Buttafuoco in the face when she answered it. Incredibly, Mary Jo survived the May 19, 1992 attack. Fisher had allegedly been having an affair with Mary Jo's garage mechanic husband, the infamous Joey Buttafuoco. Fisher served seven years and has since made amends with Mary Jo.

Fleiss, Heidi

1270 Tower Grove Road, Beverly Hills, California

This is the house in which Heidi Fleiss ran a multi-million dollar brothel which was frequented by the rich and famous. Heidi's story was told in the film *Madam of Beverly Hills*. Eventually, she spent two years in a California jail for tax evasion, money laundering, and pandering.

Ford, President Gerald

Pathway that runs diagonally from 12th Street and L Street to the State Capitol Building (the event happened about 10 yards from the sidewalk, near a magnolia tree) Sacramento, California

Gerald Ford may have been setting the country back on course after the Watergate scandal, but that didn't stop two different women from taking shots at him. On September 5, 1975, Charles Manson follower Lynette "Squeaky" Fromme waited for President Ford here, outside a Sacramento, California hotel. As he reached to shake her hand, she pulled out a Colt .45. Fromme pulled the trigger, but the loaded gun didn't fire. (Seems she had neglected to put a round in one of the chambers.) Secret Servicemen took her down before she could attempt to fire another shot, and today, Fromme is serving a life sentence in prison.

Ford, President Gerald

Westin St. Francis Hotel
335 Powell Street, Union Square, San Francisco, California
800-228-3000

On September 22, barely two weeks after Squeaky Fromme's attempt on President Ford's life, 45-year-old Sara Jane Moore yanked a pistol from her purse and fired on Ford from a distance of about 30 feet as he made his way toward the St. Francis hotel's Post Street exit after having lunch at the hotel (Moore was across the street from the exit, nearby where the Disney store is located today). The disturbed, ex-

housewife, and newly-christened radical, missed, in part due to a bystander who jostled her arm. President Ford was unharmed, and Moore was sentenced to life in prison.

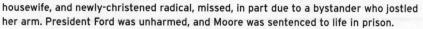

Gacy, John Wayne

8213 West Summerdale Avenue
Des Plaines, Illinois

This is the infamous house where, in late 1978, investigators questioning John Wayne Gacy, Jr. about the disappearance of Robert Piest discovered the crawl space that would eventually prove to be where the serial killer had buried some 29 bodies. The news stunned locals. After all, Gacy had been a well-liked and respected member of the community. He was politically active, appeared to be a loving husband and father, and donated time and effort to charity. Gacy was also well known for dressing up as "Pogo the Clown" to entertain local children. Gacy was put to death for the grisly murders on May 9, 1994.

Gallo, Joey

Umberto's Clam House
129 Mulberry Street, corner of Hester
New York, New York

This was the site of Little Italy's most famous mob hit. At 5:00 A.M. on April 7, 1972, three gunmen smashed through the restaurant's side door, shooting Joey Gallo, a maverick mob leader. Gallo, hit three times, staggered outside and collapsed in the middle of Hester Street. As the famous local saying goes, "He ordered clams, but he got slugs."

Garfield, President James

Union Station (Present-day site of The National Gallery of Art)
Located on the National Mall between Third and Ninth Streets at
Constitution Avenue, NW
Washington, D.C.
202-737-4215

Less than four months after his inauguration, President Garfield arrived at the Union Station in Washington, D.C. on July 2, 1881 to catch a train for a summer's retreat on the New Jersey seashore. As Garfield made his way through the station, Charles Guiteau, angry because he did not get a government job that he thought he deserved, rushed Garfield and fired two shots into him. One grazed Garfield's arm; the other lodged in his abdomen. Exclaiming, "My God, what is this?" the president collapsed to the floor remaining fully conscious, but in a great deal of pain. The wound eventually spread into peritonitis, and President Garfield died September 19, 1881.

Garrett, Pat and Billy the Kid

Fort Sumner Monument
Fort Sumner, New Mexico
505-355-2573
3 miles east of Fort Sumner on Highway 60/84, and 3 1/2 miles south of Highway
60 on Billy the Kid Road

On the night of July 14, 1881, outlaw William Bonney, (Billy the Kid), was hiding out in Fort Sumner, New Mexico. That night, after getting hungry, he wandered off to the house of his friend Pete Maxwell to see about getting some food. Billy supposedly got suspicious when he eyed some strangers at the corner of the house so he ducked into the nearest room. Billy was right to be nervous. The two strangers were deputies, out to arrest Billy for the murder of a former sheriff, William Brady. And his luck got worse after that. The room he ducked into was Pete Maxwell's, who was getting grilled by legendary Lincoln County sheriff Pat Garrett about the Kid's whereabouts.

"¿Quien es? ¿Quien es?" or "Who's there? Who's there?" were the last words Billy the Kid uttered. Garrett, recognizing the criminal's voice, shot Billy in the chest and killed him. The next day, Billy was buried a short distance from the old fort, and his gravesite has become a fairly popular tourist stop, even though it's located in the middle of almost nowhere. The original structure of the Maxwell house here at the Fort Sumner monument is completely gone, replaced today by a visitor's center.

Gotti, John

247 Mulberry Street (just below Prince Street)
New York, New York

Until recently, this was the site of the Ravenite Social Club, a longtime Mafia hangout. Most notoriously, John Gotti, "the Dapper Don," was arrested here on December 12, 1990, and charged with racketeering and murder. Even though the Ravenite's facade had been bricked up to evade FBI surveillance, the Feds managed to bug the building and record enough evidence to prosecute Gotti. Over time, many of the incriminating audio and videotapes were made public. The ground floor's brick facade was recently replaced with a shiny glass storefront, and a boutique has opened.

Hearst, Patty

Hearst, Patty

2603 Benvenue Avenue, #4 (at Parker Street)
Berkeley, California

This is where 19-year old heiress (and granddaughter of publishing baron William Randolph Hearst) Patty Hearst was abducted in February 1974 by a band of counter-culture revolutionaries called "The Symbionese Liberation Army." The gang beat up Hearst's boyfriend, Steven Weed, as they dragged her away. Soon, the world would learn that Hearst had joined forces with the group, which would result in one of the most captivating, bizarre stories of the century.

S.L.A. Bank Robbery

Hibernia Bank
Sunset District Office
1450 Noriega Street
San Francisco, California

Remember the crude video images of a machine gun-toting Patty Hearst moving through a bank? This is where it happened at 9:40 A.M. on April 15, 1974. In under four minutes, Hearst and her radical accomplices robbed the bank of over $10,000, wounded two bystanders, and fled in a getaway car. Just days earlier, Hearst had announced her allegiance to the Symbionese Liberation Army, and that she would fight under the name "Tania." Once the Hibernia Bank, today it's a Hollywood Video store.

Hearst, Patty

Mel's Sporting Goods

11425 S. Crenshaw Boulevard
Inglewood, California

Patty Hearst was also captured here on videotape brandishing a rifle as her S.L.A. comrades robbed the place. Though the store is gone, supposedly a bullet hole is still visible in a light pole outside the store.

S.L.A. Death Site

1466 E. 54th Street (near Compton Avenue)
Los Angeles, California

This is where six S.L.A. members (without Patty Hearst) were killed on May 17, 1974, in a fire resulting from a police siege which burned their South Los Angeles hideout (a one-story, stucco house) to the ground. Today, burn marks from the fire are still visible on the trees in front of where the house once stood.

Patty Hearst Capture Site

625 Morse Street (between Guttenberg and Lowell)
San Francisco, California

Hearst's saga came to an end here, a year and a half after being kidnapped. During trial, she claimed to have been brainwashed by her abductors, and though she was found guilty by a jury, she later had her sentence commuted by President Jimmy Carter.

Hickock, "Wild Bill"

Old Style Saloon No. 10
657 Main Street
Deadwood, South Dakota
800-952-9398

It's one of the great legends of the Wild West – the shooting of "Wild Bill." After his law-enforcement career ended, James Butler "Wild Bill" Hickock toured with Buffalo Bill Cody's Wild West Show, then retired here in Deadwood for a lonely life of drinking and gambling. That life ended August 2, 1876, when he was shot in the back of the head by a disgruntled laborer, Jack McCall, who had lost a few dollars to Hickock in a poker game. Some also theorized that McCall believed Hickock had killed his brother back in Kansas and was retaliating for the murder.

At the time, Hickock held aces and eights (two pairs). Ever since, that's been known as the "dead man's hand." Today, you can see re-enactments staged at this popular tourist attraction, and even see the Hickock "death chair."

WILD BILL'S DEATH CHAIR
HISTORIC DEADWOOD, 1876

Hoffa, Jimmy

Machus Red Fox Restaurant
6676 Telegraph Road
Bloomfield Hills, Michigan

Paroled from federal prison 3 1/2 years earlier, former Teamsters President Jimmy Hoffa had announced his plans in 1975 to again seek the union leadership. On July 30, Hoffa left home for an afternoon meeting. He told people the participants would include Anthony Giacalone, reputed by federal authorities to be a captain of organized crime in Detroit.

Hoffa was seen waiting outside in the parking lot of the Machus Red Fox restaurant in Bloomfield Township, and it is known that he made at least two calls from a pay phone outside the hardware store behind the restaurant. But 27 years after James Riddle Hoffa set off for lunch, his remains have not been found and no one has been arrested for his murder. (Though many wild rumors persist as to where his remains might be found.) In September 2001, some reports claimed that DNA tests by the FBI had tied Hoffa to a car driven by his associate Charles O'Brien the day Hoffa disappeared – suggesting that charges might someday be brought in the case.

James, Jesse (and the "James Gang")

Between Adair and Anita, along county road G30
(1 1/2 miles west of Adair)
Adair, Iowa

On July 21, 1873, Jesse James and his notorious gang committed what is considered to be the first train robbery in the west. Word had come down to the outlaws that the Rock Island and Pacific train was loaded up with a huge shipment of gold. The gang, thinking this might be the haul of their lives, anticipated a find of more than $100,000 worth of gold. Much to their surprise, the robbery yielded "only" about $2,000 in notes. It seems their timing had been just a bit off. The real haul of valuable gold sped by some 12 hours later.

Today, a locomotive wheel bears a plaque with the inscription: "Site of the first train robbery in the west, committed by the notorious Jesse James and his gang of outlaws July 21, 1873." It was erected by the Rock Island Railroad in 1954.

Kaczynski, Ted

Stemple Road
Lincoln, Montana
Lincoln Chamber of Commerce: 406-362-4949

Directions to Stemple Road: Take the Forest Service Road to Stemple Pass, about 3 miles outside Lincoln. Stemple Road is located on Highway 200 in Lincoln. (There is one blinking light in the center of the town-that's the intersection of Stemple Road.)

The Unabomber, Ted Kaczynski, lived just off this mountain pass road until his arrest in April 1996, when FBI agents stormed his small wilderness cabin in Montana. The strange, elusive terrorist was blamed for 16 mail bombs that killed 3 people and injured 23 during an 18-year period. While the actual cabin is kept under wraps at a California Air Force base, you can still see where the cabin used to sit. The former Harvard math teacher turned mad bomber now resides at the "SuperMax" penitentiary in Colorado.

Kennedy, President John F.

Oswald, Lee Harvey

214 W. Neeley Street
Oak Cliff, Dallas, Texas

This is the house where the well-known "backyard photos" of Oswald holding his rifle were taken. This two-story wood frame structure is crumbling, but the back staircase railing, prominent in the background of all of the Oswald photos, is still intact and easily recognizable (though the original staircase is long gone).

Sixth Floor Museum (Book Depository Building)

411 Elm Street, Dallas, Texas
888-485-4854

It was from here, at the sixth floor window of the Texas School Book Depository (now called the Dallas County Administration Building), that Lee Harvey Oswald (allegedly)

took aim and killed President John F. Kennedy on November 22, 1963. Also called the "Sniper's Nest," the window is visible from the street – it's the last window on the far right on the building's sixth floor side facing Dealey Plaza. Inside the fascinating museum that now exists on the sixth floor, boxes of books have been stacked around the window to simulate what it would have looked like in November 1963.

Zapruder, Abraham

The pergola on the north side of Elm, in Dealey Plaza, Dallas, Texas

The pergola gave a good view of the presidential motorcade, and spectator Abraham Zapruder stood on one of its low columns to take the famous home movie of the motorcade.

Kennedy, President John F.

Parkland Hospital Emergency Room

5201 Harry Hines Boulevard
Dallas, Texas
214-590-8000

Although newer buildings have gone up around the Emergency Room, its entrance looks exactly as it did in 1963 when Kennedy was taken after being shot.

Boarding House

1026 N. Beckley Avenue, Dallas, Texas

After Kennedy was assassinated, the School Book Depository was sealed off. Since Oswald had already been interrogated, he returned home to this boarding house, went inside, got a pistol, and hid it inside his jacket. He then hopped a 1:00 P.M. bus about 50 yards west of the house, and rode it approximately one mile south to Jefferson Street.

Officer D.J. Tippit

Tenth Street and Patton Avenue, Dallas, Texas

The houses once standing on the corner have been demolished, but this is where Oswald allegedly shot Officer D.J. Tippit after being stopped. It is believed Tippit stopped Oswald after getting a description of J.F.K.'s assassin.

The Hardy Shoe Store

213 West Jefferson Avenue, Dallas, Texas

After the shooting at Tenth and Patton, Oswald supposedly ducked into this shoe store. He was spotted by shoe salesman Johnny Brewer, who then followed Oswald to the Texas Theater and alerted the ticket taker to call the police. (The shoe store is now a bridal shop.)

Kennedy, President John F.

The Texas Theater

231 West Jefferson Avenue, Dallas, Texas

The police rushed into this theater, took the stage and asked Johnny Brewer to identify the man he'd just followed from the shoe store. Oswald was fingered, and though he put up a struggle, he was then taken into custody. Built by billionaire Howard Hughes, the Texas Theater opened in 1931 and began showing the city's first talking pictures. After being closed for seven years, it reopened in 2002.

City Hall

2001 Commerce Street, Dallas, Texas

This is where Jack Ruby shot Oswald as he was being taken away to jail. The basement entrance to the ramp where cop cars were waiting to deliver Oswald to the county jail can still be accessed from inside the building. Take the stairs at the left of the lobby to the basement and go down the hall to the glass doors, the only addition since the murder.

Love Field

8008 Cedar Springs Road, Dallas, Texas
214-670-6073

Lyndon Johnson was sworn in on Air Force One at Love Field, and a plaque commemorating the ceremony was placed on a granite pillar at the front entrance to the airport, just inside the double doors from the parking lot.

Kennedy, Robert F.

Ambassador Hotel
3400 Wilshire Boulevard
Los Angeles, California

On June 5, 1968 at 12.15 A.M., Senator Robert F. Kennedy was making his way from the ballroom at the Ambassador Hotel to give a press conference after winning the California Primary. The prearranged route went through a food service pantry. While walking through this area, a Palestinian Arab, Sirhan Sirhan, stepped forward and fired a .22 revolver at the senator. Although Sirhan was quickly subdued, Kennedy and five others were shot, although only Kennedy was fatally wounded.

Sirhan was arrested at the scene, charged and convicted of first degree murder. He was to have been executed, but the U.S. Supreme Court voided the constitutionality of the death sentence before the sentence could be carried out. Sirhan has been incarcerated at Corcoran State Prison, California, ever since.

The Ambassador Hotel itself still stands, but it has been closed since 1988 and there are no immediate plans to re-open it. The ballroom looks much the same as it did the night Kennedy was here, and there is an "X" carved into an old tile in the pantry floor where Kennedy lay slumped after being shot.

A few other historic moments at this hotel...

• Shirley Temple and Bill "Bojangles" Robinson used to rehearse their dance numbers in one of the ballrooms.

• The Oscar statuette was introduced inside the Coconut Grove, during the 1930 Academy Awards.

• Buster Crabbe used the hotel's Olympic-sized Lido Pool to practice for the Olympics.

• F. Scott and Zelda Fitzgerald snuck out of the Ambassador in the middle of the night after setting fire to their bungalow.

• Physicist Albert Einstein called the front desk once to complain about a honeymoon argument between boxer Jack Dempsey and his wife.

• Russian Premier Nikita Krushev threw a famous fit after hearing that, for security reasons, he could not go to Disneyland. (To appease the Communist leader, Walt Disney sent Mickey Mouse over to cheer him up.)

• In the 1940s, Marilyn Monroe got her start here with the Emmalean Snively's Blue Book Models.

• Richard Nixon composed and delivered his famous "Checkers" speech from inside the hotel.

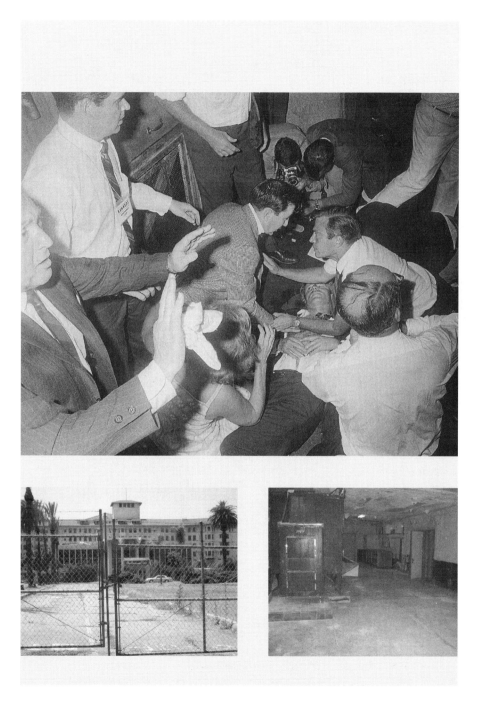

King, Jr., Martin Luther

The National Civil Rights Museum (formerly the Lorraine Motel)
450 Mulberry Street, Memphis, Tennessee
901-521-9699

Dr. Martin Luther King, Jr., leader of the American civil rights movement, was assassinated on April 4, 1968 in Memphis, Tennessee while lending support to a sanitation workers' strike. He was shot by James Earl Ray at approximately 7:05 P.M. Ray's bullet struck King as he was standing on his balcony at the Lorraine Motel; King died approximately one hour later.

Although no television cameras were in the vicinity at the time of the assassination, television coverage of the event quickly followed. From 1968–1982, business at the Lorraine Motel languished, and in 1982 the property was foreclosed. In 1991, the National Civil Rights Museum opened at the site.

King, Rodney

11777 Foothill Boulevard, Lakeview Terrace, California

In 1993, after a high speed chase, an allegedly drunken motorist named Rodney King was beaten by police officers for resisting arrest. The incident was captured on videotape by a nearby resident and beamed worldwide within days. When the officers charged in the crime were acquitted, it set off the infamous 1992 L.A. riots. The actual beating site is a large, dirt lot in this remote part of the San Fernando Valley, directly across from the Mountainback Apartments at 11777 Foothill Boulevard.

Levy, Chandra

1260 21st Street, NW, Washington, D.C.

Chandra Levy, an intern in the nation's Capitol, disappeared on May 1, 2001. On May 22nd, 2002, the remains of the attractive young woman were discovered in a heavily wooded section of nearby Rock Creek Park. California congressman Gary Condit, who allegedly had been having an affair with Levy, was thought by many to be a suspect in her disappearance. While he was never implicated in the crime, he was voted out of office due to the negative swirl surrounding his involvement with Levy.

Lincoln, Abraham

Ford Theater

511 10th Street, NW
Washington, D.C.
202-347-4833

John Wilkes Booth, a popular actor, ended his full-time stage career in May of 1864. The Maryland native wanted to spend most of his time on his primary interest – supporting the Confederate States of America. Within months, Booth was working actively with Confederate partisans.

A plan to capture President Lincoln and exchange him for Confederate prisoners of war brought Booth into contact with Dr. Samuel Mudd, John Surratt, Mary Surratt (John's mother), Lewis Thorton Powell, David Herold, George Atzerodt, and others. This plan failed when, on the day chosen for the capture, President Lincoln changed his plans and did not travel on the road where conspirators were waiting. This March 17, 1865 kidnapping failure was quickly followed by two major Confederate defeats. Richmond, the capital of the Confederacy, was abandoned to Union troops, and on Palm Sunday, April 9th, Robert E. Lee surrendered his army to General Grant. Soon after these defeats, Booth decided to assassinate President Lincoln while Powell was to kill Secretary of State Seward, and Atzerodt was to kill Vice President Andrew Johnson.

On April 14, 1865 (at about 10:15 P.M.), Booth opened the door to the State Box at the Ford Theater where the President and his party were seated. He shot Lincoln once in the back of the head, stabbed Henry Rathbone in a struggle, and then jumped to the stage, 11 feet below. Breaking his leg in the fall, he made his way across the stage, left through the back door, and escaped on his horse.

Lincoln, Abraham

The Petersen House

516 10th Street NW
Directly across the street from the Ford Theater,
part of the Ford's Theatre National Historic Site

After the shooting, Lincoln was taken across the street to the Petersen House. During the night and early morning, a parade of government officials and physicians was allowed to come inside and pay respects to the unconscious President. Despite the best efforts of the physicians involved, the external and internal hemorrhaging continued throughout the night and on the next day, April 15, 1865, at 7:22 A.M., a doctor leaned over the president and felt his final breath. Lincoln was just 56 years old.

Garrett Farm

Bowling Green, Virginia
(The highway marker is on Route 301, near Route 17, adjacent to the properties of the A. P. Hill Army Base)

After John Wilkes Booth shot President Abraham Lincoln on April 14, 1865, at Ford's Theatre in Washington, D.C., he began a grueling trek (made harder by his broken leg) through southern Maryland, across the Potomac River, and into Virginia where he eventually met his death.

Most historians agree that Lincoln's assassin was killed in Garrett's barn on April 26, 1865. However, due to the mystery surrounding the autopsy and subsequent burial of Booth, some surmised that Booth didn't really die that night. But today, it seems almost certain that the actor-assassin did in fact die here that night, shot inside the barn while it burned, then pulled out until he died three hours later.

The marker text reads: "John Wilkes Booth . . . The Garrett place is where John Wilkes Booth was allegedly cornered and killed by Union troops on April 26, 1865. Although several groups believe Booth escaped from the Garrett farm, no proof has been uncovered to confirm nor totally rule out the beliefs. The house stood a short distance from this spot."

Lindbergh, Charles, Jr.

Lindbergh Home (now the Albert Ellis Residential Group Center)
188 Lindbergh Road, Hopewell, New Jersey
609-466-0740

The kidnapping and murder of Charles Lindbergh, Jr., son of aviation pioneer and American hero, Charles Lindbergh (five years after his famous, solo cross-Atlantic flight) remains one of the most notable crimes in this country's history—the true crime of the century.

On the night of March 31, 1932, Charles, Jr.'s nursemaid, Betty Gow, went to check on the electric heater in the baby's room. To her shock, she found the child's crib empty. Turning on the light in his son's room, Lindbergh discovered a small note which was left on the window sill. "Anne," he said, turning to his wife, "they have stolen our baby."

Despite other notes left by the kidnapper in the next few months, everything wound up at a dead end. Two months later, the baby's body was found in a shallow grave in the woods about four miles from the Lindbergh home. A trucker who had stopped to relieve himself stumbled upon the decomposed body along with a handmade ladder, chisel, and some ransom notes.

In 1934, German Immigrant Bruno Richard Hauptmann was arrested for the crime (based initially on some of the ransom money that was found in his possession). A year later he was tried, convicted, and executed at the New Jersey State Prison. Today, the house (which is virtually unchanged from the night of the crime) is used by the Albert Elias Residential Community Home, a residential facility designed to serve younger male juvenile offenders. The youths there are also responsible for the historic maintenance of the house that the Lindbergh family deeded to the State of New Jersey.

List, John

431 Hillside Avenue, Westfield, New Jersey

In 1971, bookish, conservative, 35-year old John List inexplicably slaughtered his mother, wife, and three children in the ballroom of the family mansion. He left behind a note in which he justified the homicides by explaining that, due to his inability to make enough money (he thought he was in danger of losing his job), he didn't feel his family would be happy with the turn their lives would soon be taking. So he "put them out of their misery" and then disappeared. It was one of the most ghoulish massacres in American history.

Eighteen years later, the case was still cold. But in 1989, the popular television series *America's Most Wanted* commissioned an age-enhanced bust of List to aid viewers in identifying the confessed murderer. The creation was so accurate that 350 viewers called with tips, one of which led to List's arrest. List remains in prison today, serving five consecutive life sentences.

Luby's Massacre

1705 East Central Texas Expressway, Killeen, Texas
254-628-8500

It took less than 15 minutes, but it became the biggest mass murder by gunfire in United States history. At lunchtime on October 16, 1991, George Hennard, Jr. drove his pickup truck through the Luby's Cafeteria's front window and then began firing off his two guns. He prowled the crowded restaurant, deliberately hunting women (primarily) and shooting most in the head at point blank range.

By the time Texas police arrived, he'd killed 22 people (one died later and 27 others were hurt). Though he was shot four times by the police, he took his own life with a bullet to the head – the last one he had in his magazine.

MacDonald, Jeffrey

544 Castle Drive, Fort Bragg, North Carolina

On the cold, rainy night of February 17, 1970 at Fort Bragg, North Carolina, military policemen responded to a telephone call from Green Beret group surgeon Jeffrey R. MacDonald. Shockingly, the MPs arrived at the apartment to discover the freshly killed bodies of MacDonald's wife, Colette, 26, and their daughters, Kimberly, 5, and Kristen, 2.

MacDonald, who had sustained minor injuries, told the cops that a drug-crazed bunch of hippies committed the murders while chanting, "Acid is groovy. Kill the pigs." Prosecutors were suspicious at once, given that MacDonald's injuries were so slight. He was ultimately convicted of the murders in a civilian criminal court and remains in prison, despite numerous appeals that continue to this day.

Malcolm X

Harlem's Audubon Ballroom
3940 Broadway Avenue, New York, New York

On February 21, 1965, Malcolm X was shot to death as he delivered a speech in Manhattan's Audobon Ballroom. The following March, three men – Talmadge Hayer, Norman Butler, and Thomas Johnson – were convicted of murdering the 39-year-old black leader. Though prosecutors suggested at trial that the slaying was plotted as "an object lesson for Malcolm's followers," no direct evidence linked the Nation of Islam – from which Malcolm had publicly broken – to the killing, though that speculation still thrives.

Manson, Charles and the Manson Family

The Spahn Ranch

23000 Santa Susana Pass Road San Fernando Valley, California (Located along the south side of Santa Susanna Pass Road near the entrance to the Iverson Movie Ranch. The movie/tourist sets burned down in the wild-fires of 1970. Since that time, the property has been regraded and subdivided into at least three separate parcels.)

A ranch outside Los Angeles owned by George Spahn, an 81-year-old, blind man who had operated it as a nostalgic Western Movie Ranch, became the home for Charles Manson and his followers. Spahn soon became dependent on the girls in Charlie's family to help him with his daily activities, not knowing they were also acting as "ears" for Manson at the same time.

While here, the paranoid Manson developed a theory based on visions and the Beatles' *White Album*. He interpreted the song "Helter Skelter" as an omen telling of an impend-ing race war in which blacks would rise up and kill off all white people, with the excep-tion of him and his "family." Today, nothing original is left on this private property where the Manson Family once lived.

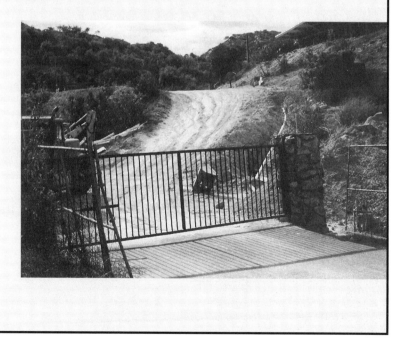

Manson, Charles and the Manson Family

Tate, Sharon

10048 Cielo Drive (Originally 10050 Cielo Drive), Beverly Hills, California

The beautiful, willowy actress's husband Roman Polanski was not home on August 9, 1969 when Charles Manson's fanatical family members snuck up on Tate (who was eight months pregnant) and her houseguests (including coffee heiress Abigail Folger). The gang brutally butchered everyone in the house; Tate plead in vain for them to spare the life of her unborn child.

A "revenge" crime for Manson's warped view that he'd been deprived of a recording career by the house's former owner (record producer Terry Melcher), this horrendous act changed the city overnight, making celebrities much more paranoid about their own security. The owners of the house tore the original down and built another in its place – and it is impossible to see the house from the gate (the address was changed to discourage trespassers).

LaBianca, Leno and Rosemary

3311 Waverly Drive (at St. George Street) (Originally 3301 Waverly) Los Angeles, California

This was the site of the second Manson Family strike in the summer of 1969. Allegedly, the Manson Family knew someone who used to live near this house, the home where grocery store owner Leno La Bianca lived with his wife, Rosemary (the Family did not know the La Biancas). Written in the victim's blood around the house were "Death to Pigs" and of course, the famously misspelled "Healter Skelter." Though the address has been altered, the house where the murders took place remains virtually unchanged.

Corcoran Correctional Facility

4001 King Avenue, Corcoran, California

This is the central California maximum security prison where Charles Manson is serving his life sentences.

McDonald's Massacre

(now the Southwestern College Education Center)
460 West San Ysidro Boulevard (about a mile north of the Mexican border)
San Ysidro, California

On July 18, 1984, James Huberty declared to his wife that he was going to "hunt humans." Soon, he would slaughter 21 innocent people in one of the worst mass shootings in U.S. history. After a standoff with cops, Hubert was shot and killed by a single bullet. McDonald's tore the restaurant down and donated the land. A local college was built in its place, and today a monument with 21 columns (one for each victim) can be found there.

McKinley, President William

Northwest side of Delaware Park
Buffalo, New York

On September 6, 1901, Leon Czolgosz shot President William McKinley as he greeted citizens in the Temple of Music, a pavilion of the Buffalo, New York, Pan-American Exposition. Eight days later, on September 14th, McKinley was dead, and America's most popular president since Lincoln was mourned throughout the world. A bronze tablet marks the spot where the shooting took place.

McMartin Preschool Trial

McMartin Preschool (now Strand Cleaners)
927 Manhattan Beach Boulevard, Manhattan Beach, California

It was the longest and costliest trial in American history – the McMartin Preschool case. And in the end, Peggy McMartin Buckey and her son Ray were acquitted in the sensational Manhattan Beach case. Peggy McMartin Buckey, Ray Buckey, and Virginia McMartin were among 6 people indicted in 1984 on 115 counts of child molestation.

Ultimately, after ballooning to 208 counts involving 41 children, the case was whittled down to 65 counts of molestation and conspiracy against Buckey and her son. The case cost taxpayers more than $13 million. The preliminary hearing alone took 18 months. The entire case took 7 years to wind through the courts, and involved 6 judges, 17 attorneys and hundreds of witnesses, including 9 of the 11 children alleged to have been molested.

After the trial ended, Ray Buckey was retried on eight counts on which the first jury had deadlocked, but a mistrial was declared when the second jury also deadlocked. A number of jurors in both trials said they believed that children had been molested, but that the prosecution had failed to prove that the Buckeys were the ones who had molested them.

The Menendez Brothers

722 North Elm Drive, Beverly Hills, California

This is the site of the infamous Menendez murders, committed in August of 1989 by brothers Lyle and Erik Menendez. As their parents, Kitty and Jose Menendez, were watching TV and eating ice cream, the pair blew them apart with multiple shotgun blasts. The juries in the first trials of their cases were deadlocked, but a new jury found them both guilty of first degree murder. The murders were the subject of two 1994 made-for-TV movies: *Menendez: A Killing in Beverly Hills* and *Honor Thy Father and Mother: The True Story of the Menendez Murders.*

Midnight in the Garden of Good and Evil House

429 Bull Street, Savannah, Georgia
888-728-9255

A murder at this ornate mansion, known as "the Mercer house," inspired the best-selling John Berendt book and subsequent Clint Eastwood-directed movie, *Midnight in the Garden of Good and Evil*. In 1981, Danny Hansford was found shot to death here at the exquisite home of his employer and lover, Jim Williams. Though Williams was tried for the murder four times, the flamboyant antiques dealer was never convicted.

Mob Summit

625 McFall Road, Apalachin, New York

The "Apalachin Conference" of 1957 is one of the landmarks of organized crime history. Just 20 days after syndicate boss Albert Anastasia was killed, more than 50 of the top syndicate leaders in the country got together at the country home of Joseph M. Barbara here in upstate Apalachin, New York. When police had learned that Barbara was making hotel reservations for a large number of people in the Apalachin area, they decided to notify two federal agents from the Alcohol and Tobacco Tax Unit and get a closer look.

Four officers drove onto the grounds on November 14, 1957, and as soon as the gangsters spotted the car, they assumed they were in for a mass arrest and fled the house. Some made it to their cars to escape, but others (some of whom were more than 60 years old and dressed in tailored suits), fled through the countryside on foot. Police set up roadblocks and, soon, many were under arrest.

The Nanny Murder Trial

33 Bemuth Road, Newton Highlands, Massachusetts

On February 4, 1997, local police received a phone call from Louise Woodward, reporting that Matthew Eappen was having difficulty breathing. Woodward had been hired by Sunil and Deborah Eappen to baby-sit their sons just four months earlier. When paramedics arrived at the Eappen household, they found that the baby had a two-and-a-half-inch skull fracture. Matthew's eyes were also bulging, a tell-tale sign of "shaken baby syndrome." After spending four days on life support, Matthew died on February 9th.

According to prosecutors, Woodward admitted to shaking Matthew, dropping him on the floor, and throwing him on a bed. They alleged that the motive was Woodward's frustration with Matthew's uncontrollable crying, and that the violent shaking was her way of trying to silence the 8 1/2 month old baby. Her trial, which created an international stir and became known worldwide as the "Nanny Murder Trial," resulted in the jury's guilty verdict being overturned by Judge Hiller Zobel.

O.K. Corral

Freemont Street and Allen Street
Tombstone, Arizona
520-457-3456

The O.K. Corral at the corner of Freemont and Allen Streets in Tombstone was the site of the most famous Western gun battle ever. It happened on Wednesday, October 26, 1881, and the setting was a vacant lot in the vicinity of the stables and sheds of the O. K. Corral (not in the Corral itself, as owner Bob Love points out).

The showdown played out with Morgan, Virgil, Wyatt Earp, and Doc Holliday on one side, and Ike and Billy Clanton, Tom and Frank McLaury, Billy Claiborne, and Wes Fuller on the other. It lasted just 30 seconds, and at the end, Frank McLaury was killed by Wyatt Earp, Tom McLaury was killed by Doc Holliday, and Billy Clanton died from various chest wounds. Today, it remains a popular tourist attraction where (of course), the gunfight is reenacted over and over and over again. Beyond just the O.K. Corral, the entire complex here gives one a true sense of what the old west was like in both a fun and interesting way.

Ramsey, Jon Benet

755 15th Street
Boulder, Colorado

On Christmas Day, 1996, in the upscale Chautauqua section of Boulder, six-year-old beauty queen Jon Benet Ramsey was discovered missing. Soon, after a search of the house, the little girl was found in the basement, murdered. To date, nobody has been arrested for what was one of the most intensely covered crimes in U.S. history.

Reagan, President Ronald

Washington Hilton Hotel
2015 Massachusetts Avenue, NW, Washington, D.C.
866-597-9330

On March 30, 1981, President Reagan was shot outside the Washington Hilton Hotel. Reagan was rushed to George Washington Hospital, a bullet within an inch of his heart. The president showed grace and a quick wit in the face of death, even telling a joke or two within hours of the shooting (when wife Nancy asked what had happened, he simply said, "Honey, I forgot to duck").

Reagan was shot in the chest, but surgeons removed the bullet and he made a full recovery. Three other people, including Reagan's press secretary, James S. Brady, were also shot. John W. Hinckley, Jr., of Evergreen, Colorado, was charged with the shooting. In 1982, a jury declared that Hinckley was insane at the time of the attempted assassination and found him not guilty of the attempted murder charge. A federal judge later ordered that Hinckley be placed in a mental hospital, where he remains today. (Hinckley was obsessed with actress Jodi Foster and claimed that he committed the act to gain attention from her.)

Rosenberg, Julius and Ethel

10 Monroe Street
Knickerbocker Village
New York, New York

On February 2, 1950, Klaus Fuchs, a physicist who had worked on the development of the atomic bomb, was arrested for conspiring with the Soviet Union. More spy-ring investigations followed, as did more arrests. The arrest of Julius and Ethel Rosenberg garnered an incredible amount of attention and controversy. The pair were both active in radical politics, and Julius had once lost his job in the Army as a civilian engineer due to allegations of communist activities.

The Rosenbergs were charged with selling atomic weapons secrets to the Soviet Union, and debate raged over the guilt and/or innocence of the New York couple. Ultimately however, despite their own denials and seemingly slim evidence, they were found guilty. On June 19, 1953, the Rosenbergs were executed by electric chair at Sing Sing Prison in Ossining, New York. This address was the home of the Rosenbergs.

Salem Witch Trials

Salem Witch Museum
Washington Square, Salem, Massachusetts
978-744-1692

In the early spring of 1692, Salem townspeople became terrified as hysterical young girls screamed out names in fits
of hysteria. By summer, hundreds had been accused and
imprisoned of witchcraft, defenseless against accusations in
a society driven by superstition and fear. Some believe the
fits were a result of smallpox, and coupled with the paranoia
of possible Indian attacks, things spun wildly out of control.

The court, formed to try the victims, acted quickly. Bridget
Bishop was tried on June 2nd and hanged on June 10th,
thereby setting the precedent for a summer of executions.
The Salem Witch Museum, located near the exact sites of
these events, brings you back to 1692. Visitors are given a
dramatic history lesson using stage sets with life-size figures, and much more.

St. Valentine's Day Massacre

2122 North Clark Street, Chicago, Illinois

On February 14th, 1929, in the S-M-C Cartage Company warehouse, seven pals of gangster "Bugs" Moran waited to meet with their boss. But Bugs was running late, and
arrived just in time to see a cop car pull up and five men get out. Moran took cover and
watched as the five men (presumably cops) entered the warehouse. Gun fire rang out
from the building. The five cops ran out, dove into the car and sped off into the
snowy Chicago night.

Witnesses soon discovered that the seven
gangsters had been lined up against the
rear wall of the warehouse and riddled with
machine gun fire. Moran, who by now knew
he was the target of the hit, was heard to
say, "Only Capone kills guys like that!"
Bingo. Capone had set the whole thing up,
with his men arriving in a stolen police car
and wearing fake uniforms.

It was the most notorious gangland shoot-
ing in United States history. The warehouse was demolished in 1967, and today the site
is a fenced-off courtyard with five trees, adjacent to a nursing home. The tree in the
middle is approximately where the wall that the seven men were lined up against stood.

Shepard, Matthew

Snowy Mountain View Road
Approximately one mile northeast of Laramie, Wyoming

Matthew Shepard, a 21-year old homosexual man, was lured from a college campus bar shortly after midnight on October 7, 1999 by Aaron McKinney and Russell Henderson, who tempted Shepard by falsely saying that they were also gay. He was driven to a remote area near the Sherman Hills neighborhood east of Laramie, then tied to a split-rail fence and sadistically beaten while he begged for his life. He was then left for dead in the cold until a cyclist found him at 6:22 P.M., some 18 hours after the attack. Unconscious and suffering from hypothermia, Shepard died shortly after.

Russell Henderson pleaded guilty to felony murder with robbery and kidnapping and was given two life sentences without the chance for parole. Aaron McKinney was found guilty and sentenced to two life terms. He was spared from facing the death penalty because Matthew Shepard's mother, feeling that it would represent revenge and not justice, asked that it not be imposed.

Sheppard, Marilyn

28944 Lake Road, Bay Village, Ohio

On July 4, 1954, a pregnant Marilyn Sheppard was murdered and beaten to death in her own suburban bedroom. Soon after, her successful physician husband Sam Sheppard was arrested and charged with the slaying. He maintained his innocence, claiming he'd tried to fight off a "bushy-haired stranger," was knocked completely unconscious, and awoke to find his wife dead. However, Sheppard was convicted and spent 10 years behind bars. In 1966, he was re-tried and his conviction was overturned, thanks to a young, upstart lawyer named F. Lee Bailey. The Sheppard murder case is believed to have been the inspiration for the successful 1960's TV series, *The Fugitive*, starring David Janssen. The Sheppard house where the murder took place has since been razed and a new one has been built in its place.

Siegel, Bugsy

810 Linden Drive, Beverly Hills, California

This is the home where mob hit-men blew away mobster Bugsy Siegel in 1947 (they drove by and shot him through the front windows while he was sitting in the living room). Siegel had just built the first major hotel in Las Vegas, the Flamingo. His life story was told in the 1991 movie *Bugsy*, starring Warren Beatty.

Simpson, O. J.

Simpson Home

360 North Rockingham Avenue, located north of Sunset Boulevard, at the southeast corner of Rockingham and Ashford
Brentwood, California

This was the site of the $5 million Tudor mansion of O.J. Simpson, where he and Nicole were married, where he was arrested for her murder on June 17, 1994 (following the Bronco freeway chase), and where he lived after being found "not guilty" in the trial. The scene of much of his trial's focus, Simpson's house became a huge tourist attraction in the months following the tragic events. He was  forced to sell the home after losing a civil lawsuit. In July of 1998, the new owner of the estate bulldozed the home and all of the other buildings on the property.

The Murder Scene

Nichole Simpson's Condominium
875 South Bundy Drive (now changed to 879 South Bundy)
Brentwood, California

 At around midnight on June 12, 1994, Nicole Simpson was found murdered outside of this condominium, lying in a pool of blood on the sidewalk (her throat had been slashed). Her acquaintance, Ronald Goldman, had also been savagely stabbed to death. In the years since the murders, the new owners remodeled the outside of the home to discourage rubbernecking. However, it's an easy address to find, the actual site of the murders is still partially visible, and it remains a popular destination.

Mezzaluna Restaurant (now Peete's Coffee)

11750 San Vicente Boulevard (at Gorham Avenue)
Brentwood, California

After a school recital, Nicole Simpson and her family went to dinner at the nearby Mezzaluna trattoria at around 6:30 P.M., where Ronald Goldman worked as a waiter. Goldman later offered to return a pair of lost  prescription glasses to Nicole's house – where they both were murdered. The restaurant closed in mid-1997 and is now a coffeehouse.

Simpson, O. J.

Ronald Goldman's Apartment

11663 Gorham Avenue, Brentwood, California

This is the apartment building where victim Ronald Goldman lived. A waiter at Mezzaluna restaurant, Goldman stopped here to change his clothes on that fateful night, on his way from the restaurant to Nicole Simpson's condo.

O'Hare Plaza Hotel

6600 N. Mannheim Road, Rosemont, Illinois
847-827-5131

This was the Chicago-area hotel where O.J. was staying when he was "notified" of his ex-wife's murder. He had taken the red-eye here the previous evening from Los Angeles, and it was in his room at this hotel that he allegedly cut his hand on a glass upon hearing the news (his alibi for the severe cut on his knuckle).

Paul Revere Middle School

1450 Allenford Avenue, Brentwood, California

At 5:00 P.M. on June 12, 1994, just a few hours before the murders, O.J. Simpson and his wife Nicole attended their daughter's dance recital at this school. (The video of Simpson directly outside the school after the recital was played many times during the trial.)

McDonald's

20712 Santa Monica Boulevard, Santa Monica, California
310-829-3223

This is where O.J. drove with Kato to grab a few burgers just an hour or so before the murders took place. O.J. stopped by Kato's room to borrow some cash, mentioned he was going out to grab a bite, and then Kato asked if he could tag along. This trip resulted in some important observations for the trial, such as what Simpson was wearing that night, and where his Bronco was originally parked at the house. It also pinned the time of Simpson's last known whereabouts to about 9:40 – 9:45 P.M. (which is when they returned to the house). (Note: The Burger King where it was wildly rumored that these two stopped to make a drug score is a few blocks east on Santa Monica Boulevard, just east of Bundy Drive on the north side of the street.)

Smart, Pamela

4E Misty Morning Drive, Derry, New Hampshire

This is the home where 24-year old Gregory Smart was killed on May 1, 1990. His wife, high school teacher Pamela Smart, was eventually arrested and convicted for plotting the murder, which was acted out by several of Smart's students. One of the students, 15-year old William Flynn (the shooter), had been having an affair with the teacher, and later confessed that she had coerced him into committing the crime.

Smart was tripped up by her teaching aid, Cecilia Pierce, who divulged to police that she'd heard Smart plotting the murder with Flynn. Smart then even reportedly attempted to have Pierce killed from prison. Flynn is currently serving a 28-year-to-life sentence; Smart is a serving a lifetime sentence without parole. The incident was made into a 1995 movie *To Die For*, starring Nicole Kidman.

Smith, Susan

John D. Long Lake, Union, South Carolina

A permanent memorial marks the spot where two little boys, three-year old Michael and fourteen-month-old Alexander Smith were brutally drowned by their mother on October 25, 1994 so that she could eventually run off with her boyfriend. Despite the fraud that she perpetrated in the days after the crime (claiming a black man had hijacked her car), she eventually confessed after the police proved to her that her story was plausible. Incredibly, she was spared the death penalty, and today serves a life sentence without the possibility of parole.

Speck, Richard

Jeffrey Manor
2319 East 100th Street, Chicago Illinois

On the night of July 13, 1966, 25-year old career lowlife Richard Speck opened the screen door to a townhouse where a group of nurses lived. He then began tying the nurses up with bedsheet strips that he had torn with his knife. Frightened by Speck's knife and gun, the women put up little resistance.

Though there were only a few nurses home when Speck first arrived, more nurses continued to come home. Horrifically, Speck took each nurse, one by one, into various rooms of the townhouse and killed them (most by strangulation, some by stabbing). Speck was captured after a massive manhunt and was tried and convicted in 1967 and sentenced to die. However, the U.S. Supreme Court abolished the death penalty in 1972, and so Speck was re-sentenced to eight life terms. He died in prison in November of 1991, just short of his 50th birthday.

Spungen, Nancy

Hotel Chelsea
222 West 23rd Street, Room 100, New York, New York
212-243-3700

With Nancy Spungen as his manager, ex-Sex Pistol Sid Vicious played a few gigs at Max's in Kansas City and CBGB'S in New York, but the drugs were taking their toll. Sid and Nancy took a room at the Chelsea Hotel in New York. It was in the bathroom here that Nancy was killed on October 12, 1978; she was found with stab wounds in her abdomen.

Sid Vicious was charged with her death, but three people were seen leaving the room in the early hours of October 12th and $14,000 was missing. Sid was imprisoned at Riker's Island, but was bailed out for $50,000 (paid for by Malcolm McLaren, manager of the Sex Pistols). He was released on February 1, 1979, and died at his new girlfriend's apartment during a party celebrating his release. His mom had given him $100 to score some heroin to celebrate and it killed him.

The Hotel Chelsea, of course, is famous for many other things, as well. A true Bohemian landmark, it's been called home by writers, musicians and other artists for decades, including Janis Joplin, Thomas Wolfe, Bob Dylan, Edie Sedgewick, Jimi Hendrix, Arthur Miller, Mark Twain, Dylan Thomas, and many others.

Stuart, Charles

Tobin Bridge, northbound side, Boston, Massachusetts

It was the most ghoulish crime scene imaginable. On October 23, 1989, Charles and Carol Stuart left childbirth class at the hospital. Moments later, Charles Stuart called police on his cell phone to report he and his wife had just been shot. Carol Stuart died that night; their "unborn" son, 17 days later. Charles Stuart told police a black man had shot them.

The police promptly began a manhunt in the largely black neighborhood of Roxbury. As it turns out though, Charles Stuart was having an affair and had money problems. No black man had come near them – Charles Stuart shot his wife, then himself. On January 3, 1990, with police increasingly suspicious of him, Stuart checked into the Sheraton-Tara Hotel in Braintree. The next day, he drove back to the Tobin bridge, stopped his car mid-span, and committed suicide by jumping off the bridge.

Wallace, George

Laurel Shopping Center
Baltimore-Washington Boulevard (US-1), Laurel, Maryland
301-490-3315

In 1972, George Wallace entered the Democratic presidential primaries, but his campaign ended abruptly on May 15, 1972, when an assassination attempt by Arthur H. Bremer critically wounded him and left him paralyzed below the waist in the parking lot of this suburban mall. However, he was overwhelmingly reelected governor in 1974, and made another unsuccessful bid for the Democratic nomination in 1976.

In 1982, Wallace renounced his segregationist views and was again elected governor, but this time with support from black voters. He retired at the end of that term and died in Montgomery on September 13, 1998. Today, Arthur Herman Bremer is incarcerated at the Maryland Correctional Institution, where he is due to be released in 2025.

"Watergate" Hotel

The Premiere Hotel, Room 723
2601 Virginia Avenue NW, Washington, D.C.
800-965-6869

On June 17, 1972, a member of the Watergate burglary party stayed in room 723 to spy on the break-in proceedings happening across the street at the Democratic National Headquarters, then housed in the Watergate Office Building. (That address is 2600 Virginia Avenue, NW.) Then, he got to see his five other partners get busted as they fiddled with the taping equipment they'd planted back in May. Today, room 723 is loaded with memorabilia from the event – just ask for "The Watergate Room."

White, Stanford

Madison Square Garden II
East side of Madison Avenue, the entire block from 26th to 27th Streets
New York, New York

On June 25, 1906, New York City's leading architect and playboy, Stanford White, was shot to death while attending a musical at the rooftop theater of the former Madison Square Garden. Harry K. Thaw, an eccentric heir to a Pittsburgh railroad fortune, pulled the trigger that ended Stanford White's life. The two men had been battling over Thaw's beautiful wife, the beguiling model and showgirl, Evelyn Nesbit.

It was dubbed the "Murder of the Century" by the press, and it is believed that coverage of the trial superceded any other modern event up until that point. White had actually designed Madison Square Garden II, and was killed in the rooftop apartment he kept in the opulent building. After one deadlocked jury, Thaw eventually served some time in an insane asylum, but was eventually released. He died in 1947 from a heart attack.

Whitman, Charles

University of Texas
Austin, Texas

On the morning of August 1, 1966, Charles Joseph Whitman, student, honorably discharged marine, sharp-shooter, and ex-Eagle Scout killed his mother in her apartment and his wife at their residence. He then went out and bought a variety of ammunition and a shotgun; at about 11:30 A.M., he ascended 231 feet to the observation deck of the Tower of the University of Texas in Austin, taking with him a footlocker, six guns, knives, food, and water.

He clubbed the receptionist (who later died) on the 28th floor, then killed 2 persons and wounded 2 others who were coming up the stairs. At 11:48 A.M., he started shooting people on the ground. During the next 96 minutes he opened fire on people crossing the campus and walking on nearby streets, shooting 45 individuals and killing a total of 14.

While police returned his fire, other law enforcement worked their way into the tower. At 1:24 P.M., police officers Rammer Martinez and Houston McCoy shot and killed Whitman. Though the autopsy on Whitman revealed a brain tumor, doctors have never been able to agree on whether or not it played a part in Whitman's gruesome actions.

Williams, Wayne

James Jackson Bridge
James Jackson Parkway and South Cobb Drive
Atlanta, Georgia

An investigation was opened in July 1979 in regards to a string of 24 black children and teens who had been murdered. Almost two years later, police made their arrest in the case. On May 22, 1981, while staking out this bridge, police heard a splash in the Chattahoochee River just before dawn. Wayne Williams, a 23-year-old local musician, was found driving over the bridge with a nylon rope, gloves, and a bloodstain in his car. He was questioned and then released. But when the body of Nathaniel Cater was pulled from the Chattahoochee near the same bridge two days later, Williams was put under surveillance and eventually arrested for Cater's slaying on June 21. (Forensic evidence had linked Williams with him.) Williams was eventually convicted of murdering two of the victims and is now serving concurrent life sentences for the crimes.

Wonderland Murders

8764 Wonderland Avenue, Los Angeles, California

On the balmy summer night of July 1, 1981, four people were bludgeoned to death in a split-level home on Wonderland Avenue, a cramped street in the steep, wooded section of Hollywood called Laurel Canyon.

It has been widely speculated that the murders were a hit ordered up by underworld figure, Eddie Nash. Nash had been robbed recently and allegedly had a hunch that the heist had been orchestrated by an adult film star, John Holmes, who had fallen on hard times and was struggling to support a $1,500 a day cocaine habit. To punish Holmes, police and prosecutors theorized that Nash forced him to lead Nash's thugs to the house on Wonderland Avenue where Holme's accomplices were staying. Holmes was then allegedly made to watch as each of the victims were brutally murdered.

However, even though the Wonderland investigation ran 10 years and included three trials, prosecutors were never able to land one conviction. (While Nash evaded those charges, he was indicted in May 2000 on racketeering charges, including the bribery of a juror in his 1990 trial.) Among the detectives on the case was Tom Lange, who later became one of the lead investigators in the O.J. Simpson murder case.

The Zodiac Killer

Intersection of Cherry and Washington Streets, northeast corner, just in front of 3898 Washington, San Francisco, California

From 1966 into the 1970s, the self-proclaimed "Zodiac Killer" was to claim responsibility for the deaths of 37 people throughout the Bay Area. He cryptically gave information about these killings through letters and cards he mailed to various newspapers and authorities.

And it was in this exclusive neighborhood on October 11, 1969, that the much-feared "Zodiac" killer came his closest to being caught. After two children witnessed a dead cab driver's wallet being stolen from him, they called the police. The police dispatcher had mistakenly broadcast that a black man had been spotted committing the crime, so when cops stopped a white man just a block from the crime, they believed it when he said he'd just seen a black guy running the other way. When the cops recovered a correct description of the suspect, they then realized that they had let him escape.

Chillingly, several days later the Zodiac Killer sent a letter to the cops detailing their mistake, complete with a swatch of the murder victim's bloody shirt. Though there have been highly suspicious suspects in the case, an arrest has never been made, and the Zodiac killer file remains open.

Celebrity Deaths and Infamous Celebrity Events

Ace, Johnny

City Auditorium (now Jones Hall)
615 Louisiana Street, Houston, Texas

Johnny Ace was a promising black R&B singer in the early 1950s. During his short career, Ace recorded several hit "heart ballads" including "Pledging My Love," "Cross My Heart," "The Clock," "Saving My Love For You" and "Please Forgive Me." He accidentally shot and killed himself while playing Russian roulette backstage on Christmas day, 1954. His last words, to Willie Mae "Big Mama" Thornton, were "I'll show you that it won't shoot."

Ace's recordings continued to gain popularity after his death, and he was immortalized (as was John Lennon) in the song "The Late Great Johnny Ace" by Paul Simon. Demolished in the summer of 1963, City Auditorium is now the site of another popular theater, Jones Hall.

Allman, Duane

Bartlett Street and Hillcrest Avenue
Macon, Georgia

It was almost dusk on October 29, 1971 when guitarist Duane Allman, trying to avoid a flatbed truck, crashed his motorcycle and died at this intersection. Just about a year later, Allman Brothers Band bassist Berry Oakley died in a similar accident just two blocks south of Allman's crash site.

Arbuckle, Roscoe "Fatty"

St. Francis Hotel (12th floor suite, rooms 1219, 1220, and 1221)
335 Powell Street, San Francisco, California
800-228-3000

On Labor Day, September 5, 1921, silent film star Roscoe "Fatty" Arbuckle's hotel party was crashed by starlet Virginia Rappe. She became violently ill from internal injuries related to bladder dysfunction and Arbuckle assumed she had had too much to drink.

When Rappe died four days later, word was spread that Arbuckle had raped and crushed the woman. The story stuck. Twelve weeks later, Arbuckle was tried by San Francisco District Attorney Matthew Brady. Fueled by inflammatory press coverage, Arbuckle was convicted in the eyes of the public. However, the case was so weak that the charge was reduced from murder to manslaughter. Two more trials followed until Arbuckle was at last acquitted, but regardless, the star's career was ruined.

Belushi, John

Chateau Marmont Hotel, Bungalow #3
8221 Sunset Blvd., Hollywood, California
800-242-8328

Built in 1929, this hotel has been host to many major stars of Hollywood and visiting celebrities from all over the world. And it was here that comic actor John Belushi died from a drug overdose. The last day of his life, Belushi had stopped at the Guitar Center to pick up a guitar that had been custom-made for Les Paul. After that, he started drinking at a club above the Roxy Theater called "On the Rox." Lastly, he visited the Rainbow Bar & Grill, where he had a bowl of Lentil soup. Then it was back to bungalow 2 at the Chateau Marmont.

Belushi was with Catherine Smith by now, and he had her inject him with a speedball – a combination of heroin and cocaine. Belushi overdosed, but Smith thought Belushi had just passed out, so she left for a while, only to return to find pandemonium had broken out after Bill Wallace – one of Belushi's friends – had discovered his body. They tried frantically to resuscitate him, but were unsuccessful. John Belushi was pronounced dead the morning of March 5, 1982.

Berg, Alan

1400 Block of Adams Street (in the middle of the block,
between Colfax Avenue and 14th Avenue on the east side;
garages are located at street level, the condos are located above)
Denver, Colorado

In 1984, Alan Berg, a Jewish talk-show host, was gunned down with 13 forty-five caliber bullets outside his home by members of The Order of the Silent Brotherhood, an Aryan Nations offshoot. In the weeks leading up to the shooting, Berg had been insulting the group on his talk show which was produced at KOA Radio. Today, David Lane, Bruce Pierce, and Richard Scutari, former members of The Order of the Silent Brotherhood, are all serving time for the murder of Alan Berg. This crime inspired *Talk Radio*, the play and movie by Eric Bogosian.

Berry, Halle

The intersection of Sunset Boulevard and Doheny Drive
West Hollywood, California

This is where, on February 23, 2000, actress Halle Berry allegedly ran a red light in her rented Chevy Blazer, collided with another car, and drove off. As opposed to being charged with a hit and run felony, she was only slapped with leaving the scene of an accident, in part because she suffered a 20-stitch gash on her forehead during the accident.

Eventually, Berry pleaded no contest to the misdemeanor charge, and was placed on three years' probation and ordered to pay $14,000 in fines, and to do 200 hours of community service. A civil suit is still pending. As a result of her mysterious behavior, the incident was bandied about in tabloids for many months after it occurred.

Bono, Sonny

Heavenly Ski Resort
Immediately west of the Nevada border,
south of Stateline and South Lake Tahoe
800-2HEAVEN

On January 5, 1998, the 62-year-old congressman and former pop star was killed after skiing into a 40-foot pine tree. Bono, an avid skier who was on vacation with his wife and two kids, skied off the main trail of the Upper Orion run into the tougher-to-navigate wooded area. In an eerie coincidence, Robert Kennedy's son, Michael, was killed in a similar accident in Aspen just several days before Bono's.

Bruce, Lenny

8825 Hollywood Boulevard,
Hollywood, California

It was in this Hollywood Hills home that renegade comedian Lenny Bruce killed himself from an overdose of heroin 1966. A brilliant satirist, Bruce called attention to himself due to his use of so-called "dirty words" in his nightclub act. The satire and darkness of Bruce's largely improvised shows redefined (and often overstepped) the taste standards of what was acceptable in the 1950s and 1960s. Portrayed in the 1974 film *Lenny* by Dustin Hoffman, Bruce was only 41 years old at the time of his death.

Bryant, Anita

Iowa Public Broadcasting Network (now the headquarters of Iowa Public Television)
2801 Bell Avenue, Des Moines, Iowa

On October 14, 1977, gay rights activist Tom Higgins, posing as a journalist, hit singer (and big time critic of the gay lifestyle) Anita Bryant in the face with a banana cream pie during a press conference at this television studio in Des Moines. The incident was a pivotal moment in the emerging gay rights movement, and Bryant's image was badly tarnished. She lost her lucrative endorsement deal with the Florida Citrus Growers, and soon disappeared from public view. Her divorce in 1980 marked the end of her career as a conservative Christian spokesperson. She later made a modest comeback as a singer and continues to perform today.

Carter, Rubin "Hurricane"

The Lafayette Bar and Grill
East 18th Street at Lafayette Street
Patterson, New Jersey

On June 17, 1966, at 2:30 in the morning, four people were shot in this bar. Two of the victims died instantly, another died a month later, and the fourth survived the gunshot to his eye. While making plans for a second fight for the middleweight championship, Rubin "Hurricane" Carter and a friend, John Artis, were charged with the triple murder.

Though Carter and Artis were both found guilty and sent to jail, there was always much speculation as to the men's guilt. While in prison, Carter developed a relationship with Lesra Martin, a teenager from Brooklyn. Through the help of Lesra's benefactors and a strong legal defense team, a New Jersey judge dismissed Carter's murder conviction, granting him freedom in 1986. Carter's life was documented both in the film *The Hurricane* (1999) starring Denzel Washington and in the dramatic song "Hurricane" by Bob Dylan (1976).

Cline, Patsy

Mount Carmel Road (2.2 miles west of Camden), Camden, Tennessee
877-584-8395

Thirty-year-old country singing star Patsy Cline had traveled to Kansas City to do a benefit concert for a popular disk jockey who had died there. Returning to Nashville in a private plane piloted by her manager, Randy Hughes, they encountered bad weather and crashed in a remote, wooded area near Camden, Tennessee on March 5, 1963. Both were killed in the crash, as were country performers Cowboy Copas and Hawkshaw Hawkins. The crash site (about a three mile hike off the main highway, 641 north) is marked with a commemorative plaque honoring the four victims.

Cobain, Kurt

171 Lake Washington Boulevard East, Seattle, Washington

On the morning of April 8, 1994, an electrician arrived at Kurt Cobain's house in Seattle and spotted what he thought was a mannequin lying on the floor of a small cottage/greenhouse above the garage. Upon closer examination, he realized that what he saw was the body of a young male with a shotgun on his chest. The police arrived and a body, dressed in jeans, a shirt, and Converse trainers, was removed for identification. Fingerprints confirmed that it was Kurt Cobain, Nirvana's much tormented frontman.

In 1996, Cobain's former wife Courtney Love announced that she was tearing down the garage/greenhouse where Kurt killed himself to discourage fans who come to visit.

Coleman, Gary

California Uniforms, Inc.
13248 Hawthorne Boulevard, Hawthorne, California
310-676-9180

In 1998, actor Gary Coleman (pint-sized "Arnold" on the TV sitcom *Different Strokes*) was involved in an altercation which led to his arrest on misdemeanor assault and battery charges. Coleman had just gotten a job as a security guard at Fox Hills Mall, and came to this shop for a uniform. A woman in the store asked for his autograph and he allegedly punched her. At trial, he testified that he had feared for his safety  after the woman (who was taller than he was) started insulting him. However, he ended up pleading "no contest" and was given a suspended sentence of 200 days, fined $200, and ordered to attend anger-management classes.

Combs, Ray

Glendale Adventist Hospital
1509 E. Wilson Terrace
Glendale, California

This is where game show host Ray Combs killed himself on the night of June 2, 1996. Combs had hosted the popular *Family Feud* for seven years (from 1988-1994), until he was replaced by the return of original host Richard Dawson. Earlier that very same day, Combs had attempted suicide at his home (at 1318 Sondra Drive, Glendale).

After he was taken to the hospital, he hanged himself with bedsheets even though he was on a 72-hour "suicide watch." Combs had become distraught after his comedy club in Cincinnati failed, thus causing financial problems. His marriage was also reportedly in trouble, and he had been experiencing chronic pain from a severe 1994 auto accident that had left him temporarily paralyzed.

Cooke, Sam

Hacienda Motel (now Polaris Motel)
9137 South Figueroa Street
Los Angeles, California

Popular soul singer Sam Cooke ("You Send Me," "Wonderful World," "Another Saturday Night") was shot to death at the site of the former Hacienda Motel in December of 1964 by a motel manager armed with .22 pistol. Cooke had taken a young woman to the seedy motel, and after the shooting she claimed that he had tried to rape her. However, evidence suggests that she may have been a prostitute who may have tried to rob Cooke (leading to Cooke's panic and subsequent chase). When Cooke broke down the door of the man-

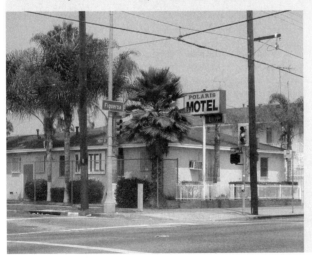

ager's office, where he mistakenly believed the woman had gone, the shocked manager shot and killed him.

Crane, Bob

Winfield Apartments (now the Winfield Place Condominiums), # 132A
7430 East Chaparral Road (1/4 mile east of Scottsdale Road), Scottsdale, Arizona

On the afternoon of June 29, 1978, actress Victoria Berryl knocked on the door to this apartment. She expected her knock to be answered by former TV star Bob Crane. There was no answer. She pushed the open the unlocked door and went inside. There she found his half-naked body lying in bed. His face was so badly beaten that he was unrecognizable from the left side. An electric cord was wrapped around his neck. Crane's pal and partner in sordid behavior, John Carpenter, was eventually charged but found not guilty of the crime in 1994.

Crawford, Joan

426 North Bristol, Brentwood, California

This is the famous house – at the time considered to be the most beautiful house in the tony neighborhood of Brentwood – where actress Joan Crawford lived with her adopted

daughter Christina (and son Christopher). Christina alleged in her book, *Mommy Dearest*, that Joan physically and emotionally abused her in this house. The best-selling book was made into a popular film of the same name, starring Faye Dunaway as Crawford.

Croce, Jim

Natchitoches Regional Airport
450 Wallenberg Drive, Natchitoches, Louisiana (off Interstate 49)

Known for hits such as "Bad, Bad Leroy Brown," and "Time in a Bottle," singer/songwriter Jim Croce had just finished a show at Prather Coliseum, the basketball arena at Northwestern State University, on the evening September 20, 1973. Croce's small private plane crashed immediately after takeoff from runway 17, hitting the trees just east of the runway and killing Croce and five members of his entourage.

Originally, Croce was to have spent the night in Natchitoches and fly to Dallas the next day, but there was a last minute change of plans and Croce ended up leaving immediately after the show. Today, a plaque commemorating Croce's last concert can be found in the Student Union at Northwestern State University.

Dean, James

James Dean's Home

14611 Sutton Street
Sherman Oaks, California

This was the last place that James Dean lived, and where he left from the morning of September 30, 1955. The house has since undergone much remodeling.

Competition Motors (Now called Vine Auto Body Shop)

1219 Vine Street
Hollywood, California

At about 8:00 A.M. the morning of the accident, James Dean came here to get some final tunings made to his new race car. He watched over the mechanics until about 10:00 A.M., at which point he left for the Farmer's Market to have breakfast before hitting the road to Salinas. Today, the side of the building is adorned with images and text relating to Dean's last day – a vivid landmark for anyone interested in this event.

CIRCA 1952
Johnny VanNewman — CALL ME (650)
3446032
LESLIE STEELE

IN 1955   JAMES DEAN
BOUGHT & WORKED ON HIS PORSCHE
SPORTSCARS IN THIS BUILDING.
THIS MURAL IS FOR JIMMY
AND HIS LOVE OF MACHINES.

Dean, James

Farmer's Market

6333 West 3rd Street (at Fairfax Avenue)
Los Angeles, California
323-933-9211

James Dean had his last breakfast—a donut at the Old Ranch Market within Farmer's Market (L.A.'s oldest outdoor market) — before hitting the road toward Salinas, where he would be killed several hours later.

Blackwell's Corner

Highways 46 and 33
Lost Hills, California
805-797-2145

This was the last stop made by James Dean and his crew at about 5:00 P.M. on the day he was killed. A gas station/grocery store, Dean parked here for about 15 minutes to grab an apple and a Coke before driving into the Polonio Pass. Though it's been rebuilt, Blackwell's Corner still enjoys its reputation as "James Dean's Last Stop," and the nice folks working inside seem more than happy to provide details of the event.

Dean, James

Crash Site

Intersection of Highways 46 and 41, about 26 miles east of Paso Robles
Cholame, California

Cholame may just be a speck on the map between Bakersfield and Paso Robles, California, but it is an important speck. After all, it's where the 24-year old actor was killed on September 30, 1955. To be more precise, it's at the remote junction of Highways 41 and 46 that Dean's Porsche Spyder 550 was struck by a black and white 1954 Ford Tudor, driven by a 22 year-old man named Donald Turnupseed.

The roads have been significantly revamped since the accident, but you can still get a sense of what happened if you visit the area. Dean, who was traveling to Salinas for an October 1st rally, was headed west on 46 (then called "466"). The approach to the intersection is a fairly steep hill, and accounts vary as to how fast Dean was going. Turnupseed was approaching the intersection from the opposite direction, which is flat. At the "Y" intersection of the two roads, Turnupseed veered left onto Highway 41, and never saw Dean coming toward him.

Police surmised that the combination of the color of Dean's car and the twilight dusk camouflaged the Porsche. Turnupseed's Ford slammed into Dean's Porsche, almost head-on. Dean's crumpled car was thrown into ditch against a nearby fence, which is where Dean died. Dean's passenger Rolf Wutherich ended up with a smashed jaw, broken leg, and multiple contusions. Turnupseed walked away from the accident with a gashed forehead and a few bruises. No charges were filed against the young man.

The Jack Ranch Café

About 100 yards east of the intersection of Highways 46 and 41
Cholame, California
805-238-5652

This unpretentious roadside diner serves as an unofficial museum to the crash that killed James Dean. Inside you'll find articles, books, and souvenirs related to the event. Outside is a memorial to the crash. Erected in 1977 by a Japanese businessman and huge Dean fan, the metal statue supposedly reflects the exact site where the crash occurred, some 900 yards away.

Dean, James

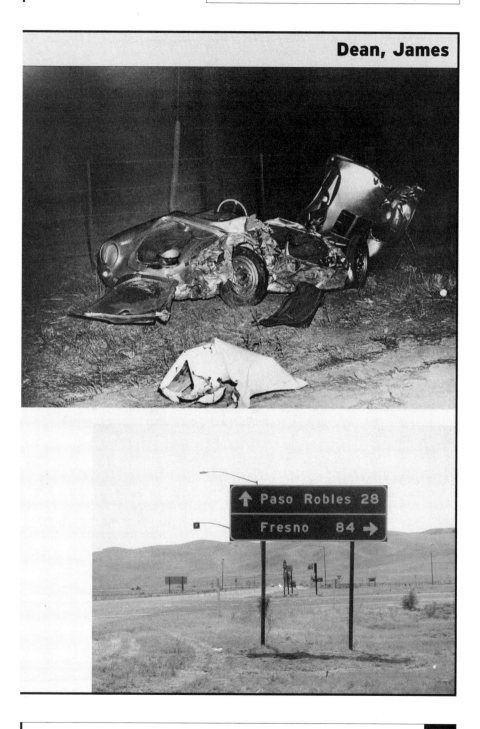

DeLorean, John

Sheraton Hotel at LAX Airport, Room 501
9750 Airport Boulevard
Los Angeles, California

On October 19, 1979, carmaker John DeLorean was arrested by FBI agents for possession of a suitcase full of cocaine, which he had hoped to sell to raise money for his struggling company. DeLorean had been filmed and recorded at meetings in Washington, D.C.'s L'Enfant Plaza Hotel as well as L.A.'s Bel Air Sands, but it was the tape from the meeting in the Sheraton Plaza that made the event famous (the camera had been placed in a gutted-out television).

DeLorean was taken into custody, but ironically, he had just missed a call from a banker who wanted to offer a legitimate $200 million loan that would have saved his company. DeLorean was acquitted in 1984.

Denver, John

Located east of Point Pinos at the northern tip of Monterey Peninsula, between Asilomar Avenue and Acropolis Street, off Ocean View Boulevard in the Pacific Ocean
Monterey, California

The folk rock troubadour had moved to the Carmel area not long before October 12, 1997, the day he crashed his small, "experimental" craft into the sea. Planning a trip

down south, he was actually giving the secondhand plane a test run when the accident occurred. The experts suspect that Denver accidentally adjusted a rudder which caused a nosedive that he was too low to correct. Many of Denver's fans gather nearby to honor the anniversary each year, and also to help clean up the beach in honor of the ecology-minded troubadour.

Dogg, Snoop Doggy

Woodbine Park (on Motor Avenue at National Boulevard)
Palms district, West Los Angeles, California

In 1993, Rap singer Snoop Doggy Dogg was arrested for murder. Allegedly, on August 25, 1993, he drove a black Jeep Cherokee during a drive-by shooting at this park. Philip Woldemariam, an alleged gang member, was shot and killed. Dogg claimed self-defense, and was eventually acquitted of the murder charges. The jury deadlocked on lesser charges, which were later dropped.

Downey, Jr., Robert

29169 Heathercliff Road, Malibu, California

The 31-year-old actor was busted in Malibu on July 16, 1997 for wandering into his neighbor's house and passing out on their bed. The neighbor, Lisa Curtis, returned home, found a strange man asleep in her house, and called the police, who arrested him for trespassing and being under the influence of drugs.

Dunne, Dominique

8723 Rangely Avenue, West Hollywood, California

This was the home of 22-year-old actress Dominique Dunne, who played the older sister, "Dana," in the *Poltergeist* movies. Dunne had recently ended her relationship with her boyfriend, John Sweeney – a chef at the popular restaurant Ma Maison – causing him to become abusive. On October 30, 1982, Sweeney arrived at her home and strangled Dunne in the driveway. She died several days later at Cedars-Sinai Hospital.

Her father, author Dominick Dunne, later became an outspoken commentator during the O.J. Simpson trial. Incidentally, Sweeney only spent 2 1/2 years in jail (3 years and 8 months including the time he spent in detention pending trial), most of it at the medium-security state prison in Susanville, California. Today, after changing his name, it is believed he is a chef in the Seattle area.

Francis, Connie

Howard Johnson's Westbury Plaza
475 Yonge Street (one block north of College), Westbury, New York

This is where, in 1974, the popular, dark-haired, bubbly singer Connie Francis ("Who's Sorry Now?," "Where the Boys Are," etc.) was raped at knife point after performing a concert at the nearby Westbury Music Fair. Eventually, Francis won a $3 million judgement when she sued the motel for lack of security. The episode left her emotionally scarred and put her career on long-term hiatus.

Fuller, Bobby

1776 North Sycamore Avenue
Hollywood, California

This was the apartment of Bobby Fuller, the singer who (as lead singer of The Bobby Fuller Four) recorded the hit song "I Fought the Law (and the Law Won)." On July 18, 1966, just five months after that song hit the Top Ten, Fuller died from carbon monoxide poisoning in his car while parked just outside of this building. Police labeled the 22-year-old's death a suicide.

Gabor, Zsa Zsa

8551 Olympic Boulevard (at Le Doux Road, in a parking spot on northwest corner, just west of La Cienega Boulevard)
Los Angeles, California

In June 1989, Gabor was pulled over for speeding by a Beverly Hills cop. However, she sped away and was pulled over again at this site, three blocks from the initial incident. When the cop began writing her a ticket, she slapped him, and eventually did jail time for the assault. (Not to mention also generating hundreds of both sarcastic headlines and late-night television jokes.)

Garcia, Jerry

Serenity Knolls
145 Tamal Road, Forest Knolls, California
415-488-0400

On Monday, August 7, 1995, Jerry Garcia, lead guitarist and vocalist with the Grateful Dead, drove up this road in West Marin and checked himself into this substance treatment center after telling friends and bandmates that he was going to Hawaii. A week earlier, he had checked out of the Betty Ford Treatment Center after staying two weeks of a proposed month-long stay.

When a counselor at the facility made a routine bed check at 4:23 A.M. on Wednesday, August 9th, they discovered he had died in his sleep. Paramedics were called but were unable to revive him. Jerome John "Jerry" Garcia was pronounced dead, just eight days after his 53rd birthday.

Gaye, Marvin

2101 South Gramercy Place
Los Angeles, California

This is the family home where legendary Motown singer Marvin Gaye was shot to death by his minister father, Marvin Gaye, Sr., during an argument at their home in April 1984. The father pleaded guilty to voluntary manslaughter, but received only five years' probation.

Gaye's career had recently turned around but the resurgence brought with it an increased reliance on cocaine. He returned to the U.S. and moved in with his parents in an attempt to regain control of his life. But the return only exacerbated his troubles; he and his father quarreled bitterly and constantly, and Gaye threatened suicide on a number of occasions. Finally, on the afternoon of April 1, 1984 – one day before his 45th birthday – Gaye was shot after a final argument and died on the lawn in front of the house after staggering outside.

Grant, Hugh

Pick up site: Northeast corner of Sunset Boulevard and Courtney Avenue
Arrest site: Three blocks away at the intersection of Curson and
Hawthorn Avenues, Hollywood, California

On June 27, 1995, English actor Hugh Grant picked up hooker Divine Brown here on Sunset Boulevard. Busted in the act just a few blocks away, Grant ultimately received probation and paid a small fine. Rather than harm his career, if anything, the incident seemed to bolster it.

Hartman, Phil

5065 Encino Avenue (at the NW corner of Embassy)
Encino, California

This is the house where, on May 28, 1998, the comic-actor was executed in his sleep by his wife, Brynn. She committed suicide soon after as police approached the house and the couple's children were taken outside. Hartman, a star on *Saturday Night Live*, had recently landed a featured role on the TV sitcom *NewsRadio*. He was just 49 years old.

Hathaway, Donny

Essex Hotel
160 Central Park South, New York, New York
212-247-0300

In 1979, soul singer Donny Hathaway tragically fell 15 stories to his death at this posh hotel. Hathaway was probably best know for his duets with Roberta Flack, including "Where Is the Love?" and "The Closer I Get To You." (He also sang the theme to TV's *Maude*.) He reportedly suffered from bouts of depression, and was hospitalized on more than one occasion.

On January 13, 1979, Hathaway and his manager returned to his hotel room after having dinner with Flack. Later that night, Hathaway's body was discovered below his 15th-floor window. The hotel room door was locked from the inside, and there was no sign of foul play. The window's safety glass had been removed and laid on the bed. It appeared that Hathaway had jumped to his death.

Hemingway, Margaux

139 Fraser Street
Santa Monica, California

This is the apartment where the actress and model killed herself on July 2, 1996. Ironically, this was also the anniversary of the suicide of her famous grandfather, Ernest Hemingway. After neighbors reported that she hadn't been seen in over a week, police were notified. Margaux was found inside her apartment, dead after taking an overdose of pills.

Herman, Pee Wee

South Trail Theater
6727 S. Tamiami Trail, Sarasota, Florida
941-924-6969

While visiting his parents in Sarasota, Florida, Pee Wee Herman (Paul Reubens) decided to go catch a movie. And it was on that date, July 26, 1991, that Herman was arrested by police for exposing himself in an X-rated movie theater. Pee-Wee dolls were recalled from toy stores and CBS dropped plans to broadcast the remaining five *Pee Wee's Playhouse* episodes.

Soon after, Herman, the butt of ten thousand wisecracks – got a rousing ovation that September when he walked onstage at the *MTV Video Music Awards* and casually inquired, "Heard any good jokes lately?" Today, the adult theater has been replaced by a restaurant.

Holden, William

535 Ocean Avenue
Santa Monica, California

William Holden (star of *Sunset Boulevard* and *Network*) was found dead in his apartment on the fifth floor of the Shorecliff Towers in Santa Monica in 1981. After allegedly drinking a great deal, Holden fell over, struck his head on an end table, and bled to death. The Oscar-winning actor (*Stalag 17*) lives on today with the William Holden Wildlife Foundation, created in his honor to maintain his commitment to helping preserve wildlife.

Holly, Buddy

Surf Ballroom

**460 North Shore Drive
Clear Lake, Iowa
641-357-6151**

Still going strong today, this is the club where "The Winter Dance Party Tour" played the night Buddy Holly, Ritchie Valens, and Big Bopper were killed. Interestingly, the payphone in the lobby is the same one both Buddy Holly and Ritchie Valens used to make their very last phone calls. Holly called his wife; Ritchie called his brother.

Crash Site

Off State Road 20, north of Clear Lake, Iowa

Directions: Take Interstate 35 (the main road) to Clear Lake. From I-35, take Highway 18 west into town. Turn onto a road marked S28 going north from 18 (there's a gas station on the northeast corner of the intersection). Drive 5 1/2 miles on S28 and turn right onto 310th Street. Turn immediately onto Gull Avenue, a gravel road. Drive north on Gull one half mile and stop at 315th Street. Park. Walk to the west past the sign marking 315th Street into the cornfield. Walk west on the north side of the wire fence for half a mile. Four oak trees (one for each victim) mark the exact site of the crash (where a memorial sits).

"The Winter Dance Party Tour" was planned to cover 24 cities in a short 3 week time frame, and Buddy Holly would be the biggest headliner. Waylon Jennings, a friend from Lubbock, Texas, and Tommy Allsup would go as backup musicians. Ritchie Valens, probably the hottest of the artists at the time, The Big Bopper, and Dion and the Belmonts rounded out the list of performers. It was the dead of winter and the tour bus had heating problems when they arrived at the Surf Ballroom in Clear Lake, Iowa on February 3, 1959. They were cold and tired. So harsh was the situation, that Buddy had decided to charter a plane for himself and his guys.

Dwyer Flying Service was called and charged $36 per person for a single engine Beechcraft Bonanza. At the last minute, Waylon Jennings gave his seat up to the Big Bopper, who was ill and had a hard time fitting comfortably into the bus. When Buddy learned Jennings wasn't going to fly, he said, "Well, I hope your old bus freezes up." Jennings said, "Well, I hope your plane crashes." Allsup flipped Valens for the remaining seat and Valens won.

The plane took off just after 1:00 A.M. from Clear Lake and never got far from the airport before it crashed, killing all on board. At the next tour stop in Moorhead, Minnesota, the rest of the performers looked for local talent to fill in, deciding the show must go on. They found a 15-year-old singer named Bobby Vee, which was the start of his career.

Holly, Buddy

Jones, Anissa

2312 Littler Lane
Oceanside, California

On August 28, 1976, Anissa Jones, "Buffy" from the 1966–1971 TV series *Family Affair*, died at this house from a drug overdose. Autopsy reports indicated Anissa died from "self-administered overdose of barbiturate, phencyclidine, cocaine and methaqualone poisoning." The death was ruled an accident. After *Family Affair* ended, Jones appeared in occasional guest shots, but eventually drugs took over her life. At 18 years old, she received a $75,000 trust fund and used it to buy a car, get an apartment, and purchase incredible amounts of drugs. She died five and a half months later.

Joplin, Janis

Landmark Hotel (now the Highland Gardens Hotel), Room 105
7047 Franklin Avenue
Hollywood, California

This is where Janis Joplin accidentally overdosed on October 4, 1970. She died in her room at the Landmark Hotel in Los Angeles, having scored a particularly pure batch of heroin. Her sad, lonely death followed that of Jimi Hendrix, who'd died just two weeks earlier. (Jim Morrison would die within a year.) Janis was cremated and her ashes were scattered along the Marin County coastline of California. The album she was recording

at the time, *Pearl*, was released after her death. Although Janis Joplin's career lasted only a few years, she has been hailed as the greatest white female blues singer who ever lived.

Kerrigan, Nancy

Cobo Arena
600 Civic Center Dr., Detroit, Michigan
313-983-6616

Minutes after practicing in Detroit's Cobo Arena for the 1994 National Figure Skating Championships and a berth on the U.S. Olympic team going to Lillehammer, skater Nancy Kerrigan was whacked across the right knee with a pipe-like piece of metal. "Why? Why? Why?," she sobbed.

Why? Because Jeff Gillooly, husband of Kerrigan's competitor Tonya Harding, had hired an attacker to put her out of competition. Though Harding won that championship, she bombed in the Olympics and was then implicated in the crime with her husband and his accomplices. Gillooly went to jail, but Harding did not serve any time. They are no longer married.

Kidder, Margot

412 Ross Street
Glendale, California

This is where actress Margot Kidder was found cowering in the bushes in the backyard of a stranger's home. After being missing for days, she had buzzed off her hair, was missing teeth, and was ranting incoherently. Apparently, Kidder had suffered a mental breakdown following a number of unfortunate incidents in her life, including a painful 1990 car accident, bankruptcy and an alcohol problem. Police were called and she was taken in handcuffs to Olive View Medical Center in Sylmar.

Kovacs, Ernie

Intersection of Beverly Glen and Santa Monica Boulevards
Westwood, California

On the night of Saturday, January 13, 1962, legendary TV comedian Ernie Kovacs was driving home from a Christening party for the son of Milton Berle. Driving home on his usual route, south on Beverly Glen, Kovacs supposedly reached for one of his trademark, foot-long Havana cigar specials. Attempting to light it, legend has it he lost control of his car and smashed broadside into a utility pole, which is no longer there.

Lennon, John

The Dakota Apartments
One West 72nd Street
New York, New York

John Lennon was killed by Mark David Chapman on December 8, 1980, as he returned to his New York apartment from a recording session. At almost 11:00 P.M. that night, Lennon's limo pulled up outside the Dakota and doorman Jose Perdomo left his post to open the car doors for Lennon and his wife, Yoko Ono. Yoko got out first, followed closely by her husband. As Yoko passed him, Chapman said "Hello." As Lennon passed, the Chapman pulled a snub-nosed .38 revolver from his pocket, dropped into combat stance, and said, "Mr. Lennon?" As Lennon turned, Chapman fired five shots, four of which hit Lennon.

Mortally wounded, Lennon staggered up the steps into the Dakota's front lobby and collapsed; he died later that evening at Roosevelt Hospital, after losing 80% of his blood. After shooting Lennon, Chapman took *The Catcher in the Rye* out of his pocket and tried to read it as he paced the sidewalk and waited for the police to come get him.

Though Chapman's lawyer initially entered a plea of insanity, Chapman later changed the plea to guilty. He was sentenced to 20 years to life in prison, a sentence which he is serving in New York's Attica prison. Chapman was denied parole at his first parole hearing in October of 2000.

Linkletter, Diane

Shoreham Towers
8787 Shoreham Drive
West Hollywood, California

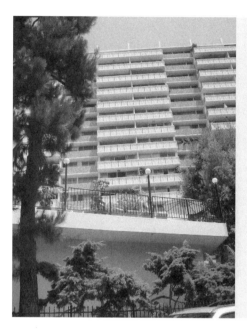

On October 5, 1969, television star Art Linkletter's daughter, Diane, jumped to her death from her sixth floor apartment while high on LSD. Linkletter, a known drug user, had phoned her brother Robert, threatening suicide. He calmed her, promised to get there as soon as possible, but after hanging up the phone, she screamed and jumped from her kitchen window, killing herself.

Lombard, Carol

Mount Potosi (near the Red Rock Ranch State Park)
Approximately 30 miles southwest of Las Vegas,
on the eastern slope of Death Valley
702-363-1922

On January 16, 1942, actress Carole Lombard, her mother, her press agent, and 19 other people were killed when their DC-3 airplane crashed near Las Vegas, Nevada. They were returning from a war-bond promotion tour, and her death was the first war-related female casualty that the U.S. suffered during World War II.

Supposedly, the plane veered off-course because the captain was in the back chatting with Lombard, leaving the less experienced first officer flying solo. The plane clipped a rocky ledge on Mt. Potosi, flipped and exploded. At the foot of the mountain, Lombard's husband, Clark Gable, waited with the rescue squad of ambulances and motor cars that had marshaled in the faint hope that some of those on the plane had survived. Tragically, all aboard had been killed. The Red Rock Ranch, where her plane crashed, was owned by Chet Lauck and Norris Goff, who played "Lum and Abner" on radio. It is now a state park.

Lynyrd Skynyrd

Off Highway 568, near Gillsburg, Mississippi.

Near dusk on October 20, 1977, while flying from Greenville to Baton Rouge, the plane carrying southern rock legends Lynyrd Skynyrd crashed, killing singer/songwriter Ronnie Van Zant, guitarist Steve Gaines, backup singer Cassie Gaines (Steve's sister) and road manager Dean Kilpatrick. Pilot Walter Wiley McCreary and co-pilot William John Gray, both of Dallas, also died.

The aircraft had become low on fuel and both engines quit before the twin engine Convair 240 (built in 1947) could reach McComb Airport, so a forced landing was made in a wooded area. The swamp where the plane crashed is eight miles from McComb Airport. In all, 20 other members of the band and road crew were injured, many critically. The actual crash site is a good distance from the nearest road, so a track had to be cut from the thick forest. Today, the track has grown over, so the site is nearly impossible to reach.

Madonna

6432 Mulholland Highway (at Canyon Lake Drive, just below the Hollywood sign) Hollywood Hills, California

This is Madonna's former estate, the "Castillo del Lago," where on May 29, 1995, a stalker scaled the wall and was shot three times in a struggle with one of the Material Girls' armed guards. The stalker was later convicted and sentenced to a lengthy prison term. Earlier, another stalker had been arrested at the same Madonna estate and sentenced to a year in jail. Both men claimed to be Madonna's husband. Back in the 1930s, long before Madonna lived here, this gaudy terra cotta and yellow-striped palace was a casino run by mobster Bugsy Siegel.

Mansfield, Jayne

Slidell, Louisiana
Directions: Drive from Biloxi toward New Orleans along old Highway 90. The site is just before the Rigolets Bridge, near a restaurant called the White Kitchen.

Like all the bleach-blonde sex goddesses, Jayne Mansfield's career was waning in the wake of Marilyn Monroe's death when she met her own untimely end at the age of 33. In Slidell, Louisiana, at about 2:00 A.M. the morning of June 29, 1967, a 1966 Buick Electra carrying Mansfield and six other passengers — including Mansfield's three children and dog — plowed into the back of a tractor-trailer, obscured by haze released by a mosquito fogger. While the children survived, Mansfield, her lawyer and boyfriend Sam Brody, driver Ronnie Harrison, and the dog did not.

Michael, George

Will Rogers Memorial Park
9650 Sunset Boulevard (just across from the Beverly Hills Hotel)
Beverly Hills, California

On April 8, 1998, pop star George Michael decided to enter the men's room at this well-mannered park and engage in what police described as a "lewd act." (The park was under fairly regular surveillance after cops realized that it had become a "hot zone.") Michael was alone in the restroom at the time—which is located near the northwest corner of the park. Michael was arrested, found guilty of the charge, and eventually sentenced to perform community service.

Mineo, Sal

8563 Holloway Drive (just off the Sunset Strip)
West Hollywood, California

This is the two-story apartment complex where actor Sal Mineo (*Rebel Without a Cause*) was stabbed to death by a robber in the carport behind his apartment building, in February of 1976. The 30-year old actor had been in the stages of trying to shed his

teen-idol image, and so he'd recently turned to directing. On this night, returning from rehearsal of the play *P.S. Your Cat Is Dead*, a neighbor heard him screaming out for help, but he got there too late—Mineo was already dead. Nothing was stolen, and a white male with long hair had been seen running from the scene.

Mineo's killer, Lionel Ray Williams, was eventually caught and convicted and sentenced to life in prison in 1979, for what was believed to have been a random act of murder. (Williams was found-out when, while a prison inmate in Michigan, he began bragging to fellow inmates that he had killed a star.)

Mix, Tom

Florence, Arizona

Directions: From Phoenix, take U.S. 60 east to Florence Junction. Follow Arizona 79, the Pinal Pioneer Parkway, south. You'll pass through Florence then continue south about 20 miles toward Oracle Junction. The Tom Mix Memorial is near mile 116, the marker at Tom Mix Wash.

A black iron silhouette of a riderless bronco stands at the spot in the road where Tom drove to his death on October 12, 1940. Tom Mix died after ignoring warnings about a gully bridge that was out due to road work. The gully into which his 1937 Cadillac plunged has been renamed Tom Mix Wash.

Mix was the highest paid actor in the 1920s and easily the most famous cowboy actor of his era. By the mid-1930s though, he had made his last picture, and by 1940 Mix's popularity had waned.

He had come to Phoenix for a promotional visit at a downtown moviehouse. After making his appearance at the RKO Theatre, he made the rounds of a few downtown bars. By nightfall he was drunk, and decided to drive toward Tucson on the Florence Highway in his new Cadillac roadster. Mix took one of the curves at 80 miles per hour, his Caddie left the road and plowed into a clump of mesquite; he died instantly. His body was taken to Los Angeles for a burial service at which thousands of fans turned out.

Murphy, Audie

Blackburg, Virginia (near Roanoke)

Directions: To reach the site from the town of Blackburg, take Main Street to Mount Tabor Road (also known as Route 624). Go 12 miles just past Route 650 and turn left onto a gravel road (FSP 188.1). Continue on 1.8 miles and then turn right at the top of Brush Mountain. Continue 1.6 miles to the parking lot gate.

On May 28, 1971, Audie Murphy died in an airplane crash here on the slopes of Brush Mountain. Murphy was the most decorated U.S. soldier in World War II; a true American hero. He joined the infantry at age 18 and soon entered World War II. In January 1945, his heroic actions helped put an end to the Nazi advance into France, and he received the Congressional Medal of Honor, our nation's highest military award. During World War II, he also earned 24 medals from the United States, 3 from France and 1 from Belgium.

After the war, Murphy stayed in the public eye, writing his memoirs *To Hell and Back*, and starring in over 40 films. The Veterans of Foreign Wars erected a monument to Audie Murphy's memory here on the crash site as a tribute to the much decorated patriot. The trail behind the monument leads to a scenic overlook with breathtaking views of Sinking Creek Valley.

Neil, Vince

The Esplanade at Sapphire Street
Redondo Beach, California

Mötley Crüe frontman Vince Neil had been living it up at his Redondo beach home for three days, when he decided to make a run to a local liquor store for more booze. Nicholas "Razzle" Dingley (a member of the Finnish punk band Hanoi Rocks), went along for the ride. Coming home from the booze run, Neil, driving with a personal blood alcohol level almost twice the legal limit, swerved sharply to avoid a parked fire truck. His red 1972 Ford Pantera then smashed into a white Volkswagen, killing "Razzle" Dingley. Neil escaped with minor injuries, but the man in the Volkswagen was left with brain damage and paralysis. Though Neil was arrested for vehicular manslaughter, amazingly, he got off with just a 30-day jail sentence.

Nelson, Rick

Near FM Road 990, outside DeKalb, Texas

Directions: Take Highway 82 east of out DeKalb and cross the train tracks to FM Road 1840. FM Road 990 will come up in about half a mile and you make a right onto it. From there, the crash site is about 400 yards west of 990 a half mile from the intersection of 1840 and 990.

Rick Nelson was the all-American kid on *The Adventures of Ozzy & Harriet* and had several major hits in the late 1950s and early 1960s, such as "Hello Mary Lou," "It's Late," "Poor Little Fool," and "Travelin' Man." In 1972, he hit the top 20 with "Garden Party."

While on tour on December 31, 1985, Rick Nelson's plane went down due to a fire started in a faulty heating unit. The rumors of a fire caused by freebasing coke were entirely incorrect, yet still persist. The fire began in the rear of the plane, and the fumes quickly spread throughout the plane causing the crash. Rick Nelson was only 45 years old. The pilot and co-pilot survived, but Nelson, his fiancée, and five other people perished when the DC-3 hit the ground.

Ngor, Haing S.

945 North Beaudry Avenue (between Chinatown and Dodger Stadium)
Los Angeles, California

Cambodian actor Haing S. Ngor was shot to death here in the driveway of his home on February 25, 1996. He is probably best known for having won the Oscar for Best Supporting Actor in graphic, real-life drama, *The Killing Fields*. Investigators believed that Ngor was killed by gang members after refusing to relinquish a gold locket containing a picture of his late wife — who, in 1975, sadly, had been allowed to die in childbirth by the Khmer Rouge soldiers.

Nicholson, Jack

The corner of Riverside Drive and Moorpark Street (near the Lakeside Golf Course)
Studio City, California

On February 8, 1994, Jack Nicholson allegedly hopped from his car here and attacked motorist Robert Blank's Mercedes-Benz with a golf club. It seems Blank had cut him off in traffic. He smashed the windshield and dented the roof with his golf club, and then drove away. Though Nicholson was charged with misdemeanor assault and vandalism, Blank also sued him, eventually settling out of court.

Notorious B.I.G.

6060 Wilshire Boulevard
Los Angeles, California

It was here outside the Petersen Automotive Museum, the site of a *Soul Train* awards party on March 9, 1997, where rapper (real name Christopher Wallace, also known as Big E. Smalls) was gunned down and killed by a drive-by shooter shortly after midnight while sitting inside his Chevrolet Suburban. It has been reported recently that Smalls may have supplied the gun which killed rival rapper Tupac Shakur in Las Vegas the year before he himself was murdered (as well as possibly putting a one million bounty on Shakur's head). However, the Smalls family disputes the charges leveled by *Los Angeles Times* Pulitzer Prize-winning journalist, Chuck Phillips.

Parker, Charlie

Stanhope Hotel
995 Fifth Avenue
New York, New York
212-774-1234

On the night March 12, 1955, while visiting his friend, the "jazz baroness" Nica de Koenigswarter, legendary sax player Charlie Parker died here at this luxury hotel of pneumonia. Though he was only 34 years old, the coroner estimated Parker's age to be 64 due to the wear and tear on his drug-and-alcohol ravaged body. Parker was a revolutionary giant among jazz musicians of the time, but it would take the general population years to discover his musical genius.

Parsons, Gram

Joshua Tree Inn

**61259 29 Palms Highway
Joshua Tree, California
760-366-1188**

Room 8 is the destination for many music aficionados from the world over. While registered in this room on September 18, 1973, musician Gram Parsons (a veteran of the Byrds and the Flying Burrito Brothers), died at the age of 26 after too much tequila and morphine. Parsons had just finished his "Fallen Angels" tour featuring his duet partner, Emmylou Harris.

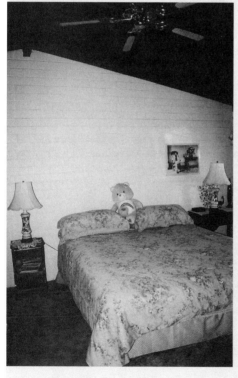

On the peach-colored wall of the room hangs the same mirror and picture that hung here back in 1973. Also, a journal is kept on a bedside table for the scores of fans who come to pay homage. Yvo Kwee, the owner, says that the mirror sometimes rattles inexplicably around 4:00 A.M. and the backdoor sometimes opens itself.

Parsons, Gram

Joshua Tree National Park

74485 National Park Drive
Twentynine Palms, California
760-366-5500

A few miles from the Inn is one of the most bizarre landmarks in rock and roll. It seems that after Parsons died his road manager and pal Phil Kaufman and an accomplice hijacked Parsons' body from Los Angeles International Airport where it was on its way to New Orleans. The two drove back out to Joshua Tree National Park, up to a landmark called Cap Rock (where, it has been reported, Parsons used to get high with his musical soul-mate Keith Richards and look for UFOs) and lit Parsons' body on fire, as per an earlier agreement he had made with Parsons.

Kaufman and his accomplice were eventually charged with misdemeanor theft for stealing the coffin and fined just over $1,000. Though he never achieved great commercial

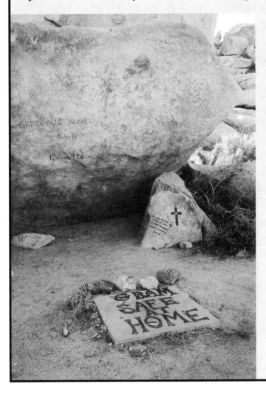

success, Gram Parsons still has a small but intense following. Some of these fans laid a plaque at Cap Rock, featuring the words "Safe at Home" (the name of one of Parsons' songs). The site continues to draw people from all over the world. The road leading to the West entrance of Joshua Tree State Park is located just down the street from the Joshua Street Inn. The number at the park is 760-367-5500, and Cap Rock is located about 10 miles in from the park's West entrance.

Phoenix, River

The Viper Room
8852 Sunset Boulevard
West Hollywood, California

This is the Johnny-Depp-owned club where 23-year-old actor River Phoenix (*Stand By Me*) died of an overdose of heroin and cocaine. He collapsed on the sidewalk outside of this club, on Halloween night of 1993. He was pronounced dead at Cedars-Sinai hospital, located nearby at 8700 Beverly Boulevard.

Polanski, Roman

12850 Mulholland Drive
Hollywood Hills, California

It was here in actor Jack Nicholson's house, where director Roman Polanski (*Chinatown* and *Rosemary's Baby*) allegedly had sex with a 13-year-old girl. The scandalous event resulted in Polanski's 1977 trial, conviction, and self-exile in Europe.

Presley, Elvis

Graceland
3734 Elvis Presley Boulevard
Memphis, Tennessee
1-800-238-2000

Where the King lived . . . and died. Even though you're not allowed to see the bathroom where it all ended, you can tour the mansion (which even houses the famous pink Cadillac.) Located on 14-acres, it features a pool room, "jungle room," trophy building, and much more. Don't forget to pay respects in the Meditation Garden. (In 1976, it was reported that Bruce Springsteen was escorted away by Graceland security guards after trying to climb over the main gates and meet Elvis, who was still alive at the time.)

Prinze, Freddie

Beverly Hills Plaza Hotel
10300 Wilshire Boulevard, Los Angeles, California
310-275-5575

The son of a Puerto Rican mother and a Hungarian father, Freddie Prinze was a 20-year-old stand-up comedian when he landed a starring role on the sitcom, *Chico and the Man*. It debuted in 1974 and was a huge rat-
ings success. By 1977, Prinze was one of the biggest stars on TV. At the height of his popularity, despondent over person-al problems and apparently under the influence of drugs, he shot himself in the head and died several hours later at the nearby U.C.L.A. Medical Center.

This is the location where he killed himself, though hotel employees are tight-lipped about the room in which it happened. However, on his death certificate, "#216" is noted as the address of the incident.

Pryor, Richard

17267 Parthenia Street (west of Hayvenhurst), Northridge, California

This is the house where, back in the 1980s, comedian Richard Pryor accidentally set himself on fire while free-basing cocaine, then ran through the streets looking for help. "One thing I learned," said Pryor, "was that you can run really fast when you're on fire!" Pryor used the inci-dent as a springboard to review his life in the 1986 movie, *Jo Jo Dancer, Your Life is Calling*.

Pusser, Buford

North side of Highway 64 near Lawton, Tennessee (about halfway between the towns of Adamsville and Selmer), Adamsville, Tennessee
731-632-1401 (City of Adamsville information)

Revered in his home state as a mythical figure, Buford Pusser was the target of assas-sination attempts, one of which killed his wife and left him physically scarred, his jaw shot off and replaced by wire and plastic. Pusser left the Sheriff's department in 1970 and three movies would be made about his life: *Walking Tall*, *Walking Tall II*, and *Walking Tall: The Final Chapter*. On the night of August 21, 1974, the 36-year-old Pusser was killed in a one vehicle car crash on Highway 64 between Selmer and Adamsville, Tennessee. There's an interesting museum dedicated to Buford Pusser at 342 Pusser Street, Adamsville, Tennessee (731-632-4080).

Rather, Dan

1075 Park Avenue, New York, New York

One night in 1986, CBS anchorman Dan Rather was walking on Park Avenue when he was supposedly accosted by two men. According to his report, the men repeatedly asked him, "Kenneth, what's the frequency?" Rather, not knowing what to say, was beaten up for his lack of response. He managed to escape their grasp and headed into the lobby of this building as the men ran away.

When the story broke the next day, it seemed so strange and incomplete, that some began to question the legitimacy of it. But the incident became memorable to the point that the band REM even released a hit song called "What's the Frequency Kenneth?" – forever memorializing the event. Some years after it happened, an incarcerated man supposedly confessed to the attack, claiming insanity at the time.

Redding, Otis

Lake Monona (The memorial is located in the William T. Evjue Rooftop Garden, part of the Monona Terrace), Madison, Wisconsin

This was where the plane carrying soul singer Otis Redding and his backup band the Bar-Kays crashed on the afternoon of December 10, 1967. They were traveling from Cleveland to do two shows in Madison that evening when the plane went down on approach to Madison Airport. No cause was ever uncovered, though witnesses heard the engine sputtering.

A memorial to Redding was erected on the western shore of Lake Monona that consists of three benches and a plaque in Law Park on John Nolan Drive. If you sit on the middle bench and face east, you're facing the part of the lake where the plane went down.

Reeves, George

1579 Benedict Canyon Drive, Beverly Hills, California

This is where actor George Reeves, TV's *Superman*, was found dead of a gunshot wound on June 16, 1959. The incident was immediately controversial in that his relatives believed he was murdered, thereby disputing the official ruling of suicide. Interestingly (and somewhat morbidly), he was buried in the same suit that he wore on the show while playing "Clark Kent."

Rhoads, Randy

Flying Baron Estates
Leesburg, Florida

On March 18, 1982, the Ozzy Osbourne band played what would be their last show with Randy Rhoads at the Civic Coliseum in Knoxville, Tennessee. On the way to Orlando they were to pass by the Flying Baron Estates, home of the tour bus driver Andrew C. Aycock. They stopped there to get some spare parts for the bus and the next morning Aycock took out a red and white 1955 Beechcraft Bonanza F-35 that was parked at the estate and started giving rides. With Randy Roads and a woman named Rachel Youngblood on board, the plane "buzzed" the band's tour bus several times. Then, the plane's left wing struck the left side of the band's tour bus and hit a nearby pine tree, killing all on board.

Rogers, Will

13 miles south of Barrow, Alaska

Humorist and American icon Will Rogers was killed with his good friend, flying ace Wiley Post, on August 15, 1935. Post's Lockheed Orion-Explorer crashed at Point Barrow, Alaska in fog due to engine failure, and both men were killed on impact. A Will Rogers and Wiley Post Monument was placed across from the Wiley Post-Will Rogers Memorial Airport. However, the exact crash site is marked 13 miles down the coast at a spot that is only reachable by boat or by taking a four-wheeler across the tundra. Each year around the anniversary of the crash, Barrow holds a 13 mile run in honor of the two men.

Sabich, Spider

Starwood section of Aspen, Colorado

Vladimir "Spider" Sabich was a world-class skier who lived life as an adventure. His two-year romance with Claudine Longet, singer-actress and ex-wife of singer Andy Williams, ended tragically when he was shot to death on March 21, 1976 in their Aspen home. Felled with a single bullet from a .22 caliber pistol, he bled to death on the way to a hospital. Longet was charged with felony reckless manslaughter but convicted of a lesser charge: criminally negligent homicide, a misdemeanor.

Longet said Sabich was showing her how to use the gun when it went off. Ballistics experts testified the gun's safety catch didn't work. She was sentenced to 30 days "at a time of her own choosing." She served the time in the Pitkin County Jail following a vacation in Mexico and later married one of her defense attorneys.

Savitch, Jessica

Odette's
South River Road, New Hope, Pennsylvania
215-862-2432

On the evening of Sunday, October 23, 1983, NBC newswoman Jessica Savitch had dinner with Martin Fischbein, Vice President of the *New York Post*. They drove from her apartment in New York City to New Hope, a quaint village near Philadelphia. They dined at a restaurant called Chez Odette, now known simply as Odette's.

About 7:15 P.M. they left the parking lot, with Fischbein behind the wheel and Jessica in the back seat with her dog, Chewy. Fischbein missed the "No Vehicles" signs in the pouring rain and drove out the wrong exit and up the towpath of the old Delaware Canal. Veering too far to the left, the car fell over the edge and into the water and landed upside-down, trapping the occupants. The Bucks County coroner came to the conclusion that while both had drowned, Fischbein was apparently knocked unconscious in the crash. Jessica had not been; in fact, she struggled to escape. Drugs or alcohol played no role in the crash. It was simply an ill-timed accident.

Schaeffer, Rebecca

120 North Sweetzer Avenue
Los Angeles, California

On the morning of July 18, 1989, this up-and-coming actress who starred in the sitcom *My Sister Sam* was shot and killed by Robert Bardo, a deranged fan who had become obsessed with her. This is the tragic event that made the term "stalker" a part of our everyday vernacular. Bardo, who was captured soon after and prosecuted by a pre-O.J. Simpson trial Marcia Clark, is now serving a life sentence without parole.

Rebecca Schaeffer's murder helped prompt then-California Governor George Deukmejian to sign a law prohibiting the DMV from releasing addresses (it also pushed the Los Angeles Police Department to create the first Threat Management Team). The law was the first of its kind and later helped to convict Jonathan Norman, who was sentenced to 25 years in prison for attempting to carry out threats against director Steven Spielberg.

Selena

Days Inn
901 Navigation Boulevard
Corpus Christi, Texas
866-231-9330

On March 31, 1995, the popular Tejano singing star singer Selena (Selena Quintanilla-Perez) was shot and killed by Yolanda Saldivar, 34, the former president of the Selena fan club. After holding police at bay for nine hours, she finally gave up and admitted that she had shot her onetime friend. Selena was just 23 years old.

According to testimony from the trial, Selena was meeting with Saldivar to discuss allegations that Saldivar had embezzled money from her when the shooting occurred. The defense argued that Saldivar had accidentally fired the shot that killed Selena, while the prosecution maintained that the shooting was deliberate. Saldivar was eventually found guilty and sentenced to life in prison. If you're interested in searching for room 158, where the murder occurred, forget it – the hotel renumbered the entire floor.

Shannon, Del

15519 Saddleback Road
Canyon Country, California

This the home where singer Del Shannon committed suicide. Shannon's first big hit was "Runaway" in 1964. It charted at number one for four straight weeks. He had other hits such as "Keep Searchin' (We'll Follow the Sun)" and "Hats Off to Larry," but nothing matched the success of "Runaway." On February 8, 1990, Shannon shot himself in the head with a .22 caliber rifle. He had apparently been suffering from depression.

Shawn, Dick

Mandeville Auditorium
UC San Diego
9500 Gilman Drive
La Jolla, California
858-534-3900

On April 17, 1987, comic actor Dick Shawn died suddenly from a heart attack while performing in his one-man show, *The Second Funniest Man in the World* at this Southern California college theater. Everyone laughed for the first few minutes because they thought it was part of the act. When he still didn't get up, someone finally decided to see if he was okay. Unfortunately, he wasn't.

Shakur, Tupak

On Flamingo Road, just east of Las Vegas Boulevard, near the intersection of Koval Lane, Las Vegas, Nevada

Though the popular gangsta rap star Tupac Shakur had made headlines over a series of run-ins with the law, none got more attention than the gangland-style hit that ended up taking his life on September 13, 1996. After leaving the Tyson/Seldon fight at the MGM Grand Hotel in Las Vegas (he was videotaped getting into an altercation on the way out), the BMW Shakur was riding in with record executive Suge Knight was stopped on Flamingo Road near the Strip. Based on eyewitness accounts, two men jumped out of a Cadillac and blasted 13 rounds into the BMW, hitting Shakur four times (Knight suffered a minor head wound). Shakur died several days later as a result of the wounds suffered in the ambush.

Sinatra, Frank

Golden Nugget Casino (now Bally's Atlantic City)
Park Place and Boardwalk, Atlantic City, New Jersey

After a 1983 show at the Golden Nugget, Sinatra and Dean Martin went to play blackjack in its casino. They demanded that the dealer deal from the hand, not the plastic "shoe" required in Atlantic City, and use only a single deck. New Jersey casinos generally mingle four to eight decks. When the dealer hesitated, the singers became abusive. Four employees—a dealer, floorperson, pit boss, and shift manager – complied.

In August 1984, the Casino Control Commission fined Golden Nugget $25,000 and suspended the employees for up to two weeks for breaking the rules. At that meeting, Commissioner Joel Jacobsen called Sinatra "an obnoxious bully" with a "bloated ego." Sinatra scrapped an engagement later that month at the Golden Nugget, and his lawyer issued a statement saying, "He will not perform in a state where appointed officials feel the compulsion to use him as a punching bag." But the incident blew over and he returned the next year, performing at a number of casinos – including Bally's and the Sands – where he played his last Atlantic City engagement on November 20, 1994.

Snyder, Jimmy "The Greek"

Duke Zeibert's restaurant (now Morton's)
3251 Prospect Street Northwest, Washington, D.C.

"The black is the better athlete, and he practices to be the better athlete, and he's bred to be the better athlete because this goes way back to the slave period. The slave owner would breed this big black with this big black woman so he could have a big black kid. That's where it all started." Those were some of the words uttered by sportscaster Jimmy "The Greek" Snyder on January 16, 1988 to a reporter at a popular D.C. eatery. These remarks got Snyder fired after 12 years as a CBS football analyst, and although Snyder later apologized, his career as a broadcaster was over.

Stratton, Dorothy

10881 Clarkson Road
West Los Angeles, California

This was the end of the line for Playmate and actress Dorothy Stratton. "Discovered" in Canada by her hustler boyfriend Paul Snider, Stratton was "Playmate of the Month" in August 1979, and soon after the pair married. But the obsessed, megalomaniac Snider soon made her life tortuous. She eventually left him for film director Peter Bogdonavich, which drove Snider nuts. (He had hired a private detective to follow her around and report on her activities.)

One evening, Snider convinced her to come to their apartment, where he tied her up and put a shotgun to her head, pulling the trigger. He then turned the gun on himself. In the 1983 film *Star 80* about her life, the murder scene was filmed in the actual apartment where she died.

Switzer, Carl

10400 Columbus Avenue
Mission Hills, California

He was cute, freckle-faced "Alfalfa" on *The Little Rascals* (And *Our Gang* comedies) in the 1930s and early '40s. But like many child actors, after Carl Switzer outgrew his cuteness the roles stopped coming (though he did have a small part in *It's A Wonderful Life*). As he got older, he took jobs primarily as a hunting and fishing guide, but his life ended at this house on January 21, 1959 at the age of just 31.

Switzer was shot and killed by Moses Stiltz here at the home of Rita Corrigan (wife of stuntman "Crash" Corrigan). The two were arguing over money when Stiltz shot Switzer in a back bedroom. The shooting was ruled as a justifiable homicide and Stiltz never served any time for the shooting.

Taylor, William Desmond

404-B South Alvarado (the northeast corner of Alvarado and Maryland)
Los Angeles, California

This is the former site of the Alvarado Court Apartments, near MacArthur Park, where, on February 1, 1922, renowned film director William Desmond Taylor was shot to death in his bungalow. The biggest scandal to hit young Hollywood, it was a true murder mystery that was the talk of the town for years. Many show business figures headed the list of suspects, including silent film actress Mabel Normand. However, to this day the case remains unsolved.

Thunders, Johnny

St. Peter's Guest House, Room 37
1005 St. Peter Street, New Orleans, Louisiana
504-524-9232

Though over the years there were always many rumors that he had died, this was actually the last stand for the heroin-addled guitar slinger, Johnny Thunders. He died here on April 23, 1991. The former New York Doll had thought about moving to New Orleans, finding some new musicians, and maybe starting a new band, but he never got the chance to complete his plan. Thunders checked into room 37 of the St. Peter Guest House in the late hours of the 23rd of April, and the following morning he was dead. Apparently, he had scored heroin upon arriving and dealt himself a lethal shot and died overnight.

Todd, Thelma

17531 Posetano Road, Pacific Palisades, California

The sexy young actress Thelma Todd had made a name for herself by vamping it up in comedies with the Marx Brothers (*Horse Feathers, Monkey Business*), Laurel & Hardy, and Buster Keaton. She also ran a popular beachside restaurant, "Thelma Todd's Sidewalk Cafe," located in this building just north of Sunset Boulevard.

Her death remains mysterious. In 1935 at the age of 30, Todd's lifeless body was found in her car – parked in the garage just above her café – and police ruled it an accidental suicide. But many, due to the large amount of blood that was found, suspected something more sinister; perhaps an organized crime hit. Nobody was ever arrested for the crime, and Todd's life story was told in the 1991 TV movie *White Hot: The Mysterious Murder of Thelma Todd,* with Loni Anderson playing the lead.

Turner, Lana

730 North Bedford Drive, Beverly Hills, California

It was one of the biggest scandals in Tinseltown history. On Good Friday of 1958, actress Lana Turner's 14-year-old daughter (Cheryl Crane) stabbed her mother's lover, mobster Johnny Stompanato, to death. Crane testified that the couple had been fighting when the burly Stompanato allegedly threatened to kill her mother. That's when Crane grabbed a 10-inch kitchen knife and buried it in Stompanato's stomach, killing him. Based on a defense of justifiable homicide, Crane was later acquitted of the crime.

Vaughn, Stevie Ray

Alpine Valley Resort
East Troy, Wisconsin (85 miles northwest of Chicago)
1-800-227-9395

Guitar hero Stevie Ray Vaughan was killed in a post-gig helicopter crash in East Troy, Wisconsin, on August 27, 1990. He was 35. Vaughn and three members of Eric Clapton's entourage perished when their helicopter crashed into a ski slope about a mile from the Alpine Valley Music theater, where they'd just finished playing a concert.

Versace, Gianni

1116 Ocean Drive, South Beach, Miami, Florida

Cunanan, Andrew

5701 Collins Avenue, Miami Beach, Florida

At 8:45 A.M., on July 15th, 1997, world famous designer Gianni Versace was returning home from a short walk to the nearby News Café, where he purchased magazines. He was wearing shorts with $1,200 in the pocket, sandals, and a dark colored shirt. He walked up the steps to the front gate, put the key in and was about to turn it, when Andrew Cunanan approached him. Versace was shot twice – once, point blank in the center of his face, the other in his neck. He fell to the steps, and landed on his right side.

On July 25, 1997, two weeks after gunning down Versace, murderer Andrew Cunanan killed himself on a houseboat about 40 blocks away from where he had shot the designer. Cunanan, who had left a trail of dead across a number of states, shot himself in the mouth with the same pistol he had used on all of his other victims. For two months before killing Versace, he'd holed up at the somewhat seedy Normandy Plaza Hotel (rooms 205 and 322) located at 6979 Collins Avenue in Miami Beach.

Villechaize, Hervé

11537 West Killion Street
North Hollywood, California

This is the home of, the 3-foot, 11-inch actor who played "Tattoo," Mr. Rourke's assistant on the original TV series *Fantasy Island*. Increasingly despondent over the poor state of his health, Villechaize shot himself to death on the backyard patio of this home in North Hollywood, on September 4, 1993. He had suffered medical problems from his under-sized lungs and nearly died of pneumonia the year before.

Von Bulow, Claus

Clarendon Court
Bellevue Avenue at Rovensky Avenue, across from Rovensky Park
Newport, Rhode Island

In 1979, Claus Von Bulow was convicted of trying to murder his wealthy wife Sunny at this opulent Newport mansion by injecting her with insulin (allegedly, so he could make off with her money.) In 1982, however, he was acquitted after a successful appeal. Today, Sunny is still alive, but comatose at New York City's Columbia-Presbyterian Hospital.

Warhol, Andy

The Factory (former site)
33 Union Square West, New York, New York

Valerie Solanas walked into the Factory, Andy Warhol's studio, on June 3, 1968, pulled out a gun that was given to her by a guy she met in a copy shop, and fired on America's most famous artist. Warhol would eventually recover from the injuries. Solanas, a radical feminist and sometime acquaintance of Warhol, was sentenced to three years in jail for assault; she later spent time in various mental hospitals.

Wilson, Dennis

Basin C at dock 1100
Marquesas Way, Marina del Rey, California

This is where Beach Boys' drummer Dennis Wilson died at the age 39 in a drowning accident off of a friend's boat. With his brothers and Mike Love, Dennis helped the Beach Boys turn out such hits as "California Girls," "Fun, Fun, Fun" and "Wouldn't It Be Nice." Apparently, on December 28, 1983, Wilson had too much to drink, decided to go swimming, and subsequently drowned.

Wood, Natalie

Two Harbors, Catalina Island (26 miles off the coast of California)

Around Thanksgiving 1981, Natalie Wood, her husband Robert Wagner, and a friend— actor Christopher Walken – sailed their yacht to Catalina's main harbor, Avalon. They spent the night there and then set off for the more remote seaport area known as Two Harbors, on the island's north side. The group had a few drinks at a little place called Doug's Harbor Reef Saloon, and then headed back to their boat. Based on the skipper's account, tensions later arose with Wagner after Wood flirted with Walken. Wood went to her cabin alone, and then about an hour later was discovered missing. Searchers soon found her dead in the water, about a mile east of Two Harbors, off Blue Cavern Point.

Let's Go to the Movies

The African Queen

Holiday Inn Key Largo and Marina
99701 Overseas Highway
Key Largo, Florida
305-451-2121

Though the boat in the 1951 classic John Huston film starring Humphrey Bogart and Katherine Hepburn appeared to be blown apart in Kabalego Falls, Uganda (where the film was shot), it actually still exists here in Florida. Since the early 1980s, it has lived on as a tourist treat at this hotel.

The Alamo

FM 674 (7 miles north of Bracketville), Bracketville, Texas
830-563-2580

Made for almost eight million dollars in 1960, John's Wayne's epic *The Alamo* was, at the time, the costliest movie ever made. It became too expensive to shoot at its original Mexico location, so John Wayne leased 400 acres on a ranch at this site, located about 100 miles west of San Antonio. The full-size movie set was built here and remains open today as not just a tourist attraction, but also a location for many other movies.

American Beauty

Spacey/Burham home: 11388 Homesdale Street, Brentwood, California

Colonel's home: 330 South Windsor Boulevard, Hancock Park (Los Angeles), California

These two homes were used in the filming of the 1999 Oscar-winner, *American Beauty*. Interestingly, both the exteriors of Spacey/Burnham home and the Colonel's home next door were movie sets. But for the interiors, the producers used these two actual homes. Incidentally, the fast-food drive-through where Lester catches his wife cheating with "The King" is actually a Carl's Jr. restaurant located at 20105 Saticoy Street, Canoga Park, California.

American Graffiti

Petaluma, California, Petaluma Visitors Program
1-877-273-8258

The movie was inspired by the small town of Modesto, where filmmaker George Lucas grew up. But this is where it was primarily shot. You can take a walking tour of the town's many movie sites, with a guide from the tourist information office at 799 Baywood Street. A few points along the way:

The main drag used in the movie is Petaluma Boulevard North, between D Street and Washington Street.

Richard Dreyfuss gets drafted into the Pharaohs gang in front of the Old Opera House, 149 Kentucky Street.

The used car lot where Dreyfuss is made to chain the axle of the police car is still a vacant lot. It's located along the McNear Building, 15-23 Petaluma Boulevard North.

The Amityville Horror

112 Ocean Avenue, Amityville, New York

This much is true: On November 13, 1974, Ronald DeFeo murdered his mother, father, two brothers, and two sisters with a high-powered rifle in this, their Long Island home. He is currently serving a 150-year sentence for the murders. But what happened after the crimes is what makes this house so famous.

In 1976, George and Kathleen Lutz, the new owners of the house, had begun spreading (and selling) a story around the country stating that ghosts and evil spirits had scared them out of the house they had recently purchased. And although the family's versions of this story changed many times, the book called *The Amityville Horror —A True Story* became a #1 bestseller, and the movie *The Amityville Horror* was a box office smash.

Today, it is widely accepted that the entire thing was a cash-generating hoax. The Lutz's (with the help of author Jay Anson) evidently fabricated the basis of their story, but even so, the actual house remains a popular landmark.

Animal House

Because of Universal Picture's tight budget for 1978's *Animal House*, director John Landis had to find a real college campus for the filming. Fortunately for the filmmaker, the University of Oregon agreed to lend their campus to the production, and the rest is frat-house history.

The entire movie ended up being filmed in Oregon, and many of the movie's most famous locations remain today, with the unfortunate exception of the actual "Animal House." The building used for shooting the Delta House's exterior scenes was located at 751 East 11th Street, across from the small Northwest Christian College. Back then, it was a halfway house for criminals. In 1986, the building was torn down (Delta House Bricks were sold as souvenirs for $5 each). It is now an empty lot.

But you can still find the following locations:

The Sigma Nu fraternity, at 763 E. 11th Avenue, was used for the Delta House interiors and for the Tri Pi sorority exteriors, where Belushi peeped in the sorority windows.

The Kappa Sigma fraternity, at 1090 Alder Street, is where the Toga Party was shot.

The Phi Kappa Psi house, at 729 E. 11th Avenue, was both the interior and exterior of the uptight Omega House.

The dining area in the Erb Memorial Union (EMU), was where the infamous Belushi "zit" scene and ensuing food fight were staged.

The school office building where the horse drops dead is Johnson Hall, the university's administration building. All of the scenes in Dean Wormer's office were actually filmed in the offices of the university president.

Remember when Pinto and Clorette made out in the middle of the football field? That was shot in Autzen Stadium.

Located about 15 miles southeast of Eugene, the Dexter Lake Club is the roadside club where the boys go out and "surprise" Otis Day and the Knights. It is located at 39128 Dexter Road in Dexter, Oregon. As of the writing the building is not occupied and is listed for sale.

Annie Hall

Cajun Bistro
8301 Sunset Boulevard
West Hollywood, California

This 1977 film is considered by many to be Woody Allen's best (it won the Oscar that year for Best Picture), and although it was filmed primarily in New York, one of the most popular scenes was filmed at an existing landmark in West Hollywood, California. It's the scene near the film's end at the health food restaurant where Woody's character Alvy Singer (with Diane Keaton) orders alfalfa sprouts and mashed yeast before being arrested in the parking lot for bad driving. Back then it was The Source, a popular health food restaurant. Today, it's The Cajun Bistro.

The Bagdad Café

46548 National Trails Highway
Newberry Springs, California
760-257-3101

Located off old Route 66 east of Barstow on Highway 40, this is the oddly charming roadside café from the 1988 film starring Marianne Sagebrecht and Jack Palance. Originally called "The Sidewinder Café," today it's been re-named in honor of the movie that made it famous.

The Birds

**Bodega Bay, CA
The Potter Schoolhouse
17110 Bodega Lane, Bodega, California**

The center of the attacks in Hitchcock's 1963 classic was this small town located 50 miles north of San Francisco. Several miles inland is the town of Bodega, and the Schoolhouse where Suzanne Pleshette teaches (and the birds gather outside) still stands (though it's a private home).

The Blair Witch Project

**Seneca Creek State Park
25 miles west of Burkittsville, Maryland**

**Patapsco Valley State Park
8020 Baltimore National Pike, Ellicott City, Maryland
410-461-5005**

Seneca Creek State Park was actually the "Black Hills Forest" featured in this surprise low-budget smash from 1999. The rest of the film was made throughout Burkittsville, Maryland and the 200-year old Griggs House that was featured in the movie still stands in Patapsco State Park, western Baltimore County.

The Blob

Colonial Theater
227 Bridge Street
Phoenixville, Pennsylvania
610-917-1228

Downingtown Diner (now The Chef's Diner)
81 West Lancaster Avenue
Downingtown, Pennsylvania
610-873-6700

The 1958 sci-fi thriller about the odd mass of gelatin from outer space (starring a young Steve McQueen) was shot in Valley Forge (15 miles west of Philadelphia) and nearby Phoenixville and Downingtown, Pennsylvania. While most of the scenes were shot on interior stages, several actual town locations were used, including the Colonial Theater and the Downington Diner, which was the location of the film's climax.

Breakfast at Tiffany's

727 Fifth Avenue (at 57th Street)
New York, New York

This is where Holly Golightly (Audrey Hepburn) spent her mornings eating breakfast to the strains of "Moon River." It is not uncommon to find people posing for photos outside of the store, in the exact spot near the window into which Hepburn used to gaze. Perhaps the most popular jewelry store in the world, it remains virtually unchanged from the day they shot the scene in 1961.

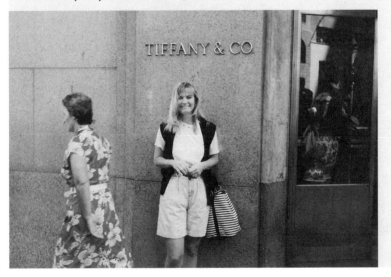

The Breakfast Club

9511 Harrison Street, Des Plaines, Illinois

This 1980's teen angst classic was actually filmed at Illinois State Police Station (formerly, Maine North High School), located in Des Plaines, Illinois. The library where the majority of the film is set was built from scratch in the building's former gymnasium. The high school had been closed for two years before the filming of the movie, and was used by the park district before the Illinois State Police bought it and turned it into a Police Station.

The Bridges of Madison County

Winterset, Iowa

Madison County is a real place in Iowa (it's where John Wayne was born), and it's where the famous bridges are located. Specifically, they're in a place called Winterset (the place Meryl Streep visits to buy her new Frock), which is about 30 miles southwest of Des Moines on I-169.

Of the original 19 bridges that were built and named after the closest resident, only 6 remain. In the movie, you can the Roseman Bridge which was built in 1883 and the longest of the bridges, the Holliwell Bridge.

The farmhouse where Streep lived (at onetime an abandoned ruin) is still maintained as a tourist attraction and it's open from May to October. For brochures, maps of the county with bridge locations, other historical information, and movie sites, contact the Madison County Chamber of Commerce toll-free at (800) 298-6119.

Bullit

San Francisco, California

Steve McQueen ("Frank Bullit") drove the Mustang Shelby himself during the highwire chase scene from this popular 1968 cop movie. (Two other stunt drivers drove the other car involved.)

Careening down real streets at upwards 100 miles per hour, it's unique in that it was filmed in real time – not slowed down or sped up for effect. It virtually set the standard for all future movie car chases, and is as riveting today as it was almost 35 years ago. (Cameras inside the cars recorded many of the jolts and bumps in the shock absorber-less cars.) You can't really follow the exact route because it's made up several area chases spliced together, but three specific highlight areas include:

1. Many of the shots take place on Fillmore Street between Broadway and Vallejo.

2. McQueen's car going airborne was shot at the intersection of Taylor and Vallejo.

3. Another exciting shot is of the two cars plunging down Chestnut Street.

Caddyshack

Rolling Hills Golf and Tennis Club
3501 West Rolling Hills Circle, South West 36th Street, Davie, Florida
407-834-6818

Located about 10 miles from Fort Lauderdale, this is the country club where most of the 1980 comedy took place. The poolside scenes however were shot at the Boca Raton Hotel and Country Club, 501 East Camino Real in Boca Raton, just north of Fort Lauderdale.

Carrie

Hermosa Beach Community Center
710 Pier Avenue (at Pacific Coast Highway), Hermosa Beach, California
310-318-0280

The 1976 thriller *Carrie* had its memorable prom scene shot in this gym. The Brian DePalma classic (co-starring John Travolta and Amy Irving) became famous primarily for the scene in which the aforementioned actors rigged a bucket of pig's blood to fall on the head of Sissy Spacek (whose portrayal of Carrie White got her nominated for the Best Actress Oscar that year). The gym is located in the back of the building and looks much the same today as it did in the movie.

Casablanca

Van Nuys Airport
6590 Hayvenhurst Avenue, Van Nuys, California
(Exact hanger location, 16217 Lindbergh Street)

It's one of the most famous scenes in movie history, and though there is some dispute among purists, this is generally believed to be the spot where it took place. The year was 1942 and the scene is Humphrey Bogart's poignant farewell to Ingrid Bergman at the end of *Casablanca*. Today it's called Van Nuys Airport, but back then it was Los Angeles Metropolitan Airport and it was used regularly for Hollywood productions.

While the bulk of *Casablanca* was filmed on a Warner Bros. backlot, a pair of key scenes were shot at this location. One was the arrival of Captain Strasser (played by Conrad Veidt),

the other, the tearful finale where Bogart tells Bergman one last time, "Here's looking at you, kid." Keep in mind, it's tricky to find. The hangar where the scene was filmed is no longer part of the airport complex and it's exact location is on the south side of Waterman Drive, west of Woodley Avenue, on a small street called Lindbergh.

Chaplin, Charlie

**Former Mack Sennet Studios
1712 Glendale Boulevard, Los Angeles, California**

Today it's a self-storage facility, but in 1912 the same building was a soundstage called "Keystone," named by Mack Sennet and the place where he created and filmed his famous "Keystone Kops" comedies. It's also where Charlie Chaplin supposedly first donned a hat, picked up a cane and created his "Little Tramp" character. Interestingly, some of the old wooden lighting grids are still visible against the ceiling inside the building.

Chaplin, Charlie

**1416 North La Brea Avenue, Hollywood, California
323-802-1500**

Hollywood consisted mainly of orange groves when film legend Chaplin built his own movie studio in 1917. For 20 years, Chaplin shot all of his classic silent films here including *The Gold Rush* (1925), *City Lights* (1931), *Modern Times* (1936), and *The Great*

Dictator (1939). He once left his footprints in some wet cement outside of the studio's Sound Stage 3, supposedly giving Sid Graumann the idea to immortalize actors by having them leave their handprints in the forecourt of his famed Chinese Theatre.

Chaplin left the studio in 1953, at which time CBS filmed several well-known TV series there, including *The Adventures of Superman*, *The Red Skelton Show*, and *Perry Mason*. Until 1999, it was the headquarters of A&M Records, and today it's the home of Jim Henson Productions. In honor of the studio's history, they've erected a statue of Kermit, dressed like Chaplin's "Little Tramp" character above the main studio gate. Though no tours are given, a plaque near the entrance notes that the studio has been designated as Historic Monument #58.

A Christmas Story

West 11th Street (across from Rowley's Inn)
Cleveland, Ohio

The quirky, charming 1983 holiday movie starring Peter Billingsley (in search of a Red Rider air powered BB gun) and Darren McGavin, though set in Indiana, was actually shot on this "Anywhere, U.S.A"-looking street in Cleveland.

Clerks

Quick Stop Groceries
58 Leonard Avenue, Leonardo, New Jersey

Director Kevin Smith actually worked in the convenience store where this 1994 indie hit was filmed. At number 60 Leonard Avenue (next door) is RST Video, the store next to the market in the movie. Impressively, *Clerks* was made for just $27,575, funded primarily by 10 credit cards that Smith had in his name, money that resulted from selling his comic book collection, a family donation, and paychecks from working at the Quick Stop and RST Video.

Close Encounters of the Third Kind

Devils Tower
Black Hills National Forest, Wyoming
Directions: Devils Tower is situated just 9 miles south of Hulett, Wyoming, 24 miles west of Aladdin, Wyoming, and 27 miles northwest of Sundance, Wyoming (307-467-5283)

Devil's Tower was declared the first U.S. National Monument in 1906. Part of an extinct volcano, it became a pop culture icon after aliens used it as the supposed landing site in the 1977 Steven Spielberg film. Three miles from the entrance, there's a visitor center that's open from April-October.

The base of the tower is at an elevation of 4,250 feet above sea level and the tower itself rises 865 feet above this point, towering above peaceful pines and a boulder field created over millennia by columns that have fallen and broken into pieces. Every year, more than 5,000 climbers from all over the world come to northeast Wyoming to scale this famous natural attraction.

Close Encounters of the Third Kind

**Hangars 5 and 6, Building 17, Brookley Industrial Complex
Old Bay Street, Mobile, Alabama**

No soundstage in Hollywood was large enough to house the spectacle, so Steven Spielberg used two former World War II blimp hangars to shoot the climax of his film, thus creating the largest indoor set in movie history. The hangers, located on a former Air Force base, are owned by Teledyne/Continental and, while no tours are offered, fans can see the buildings from behind a fence.

Culver Studios

**9336 Washington Boulevard
Culver City, California
310-202-1234**

Located in Culver City, the exterior of Culver Studios became famous in its own right after being featured in the opening credits of many of David O. Selznick International's productions, such as *Gone With the Wind*. The colonial mansion (easily visible from Washington Boulevard) is an exact copy of George Washington's Mount Vernon. The 1939 epic was shot on Stages 11 and 12 in 1939; the exteriors of Tara, Twelve Oaks, and the city of Atlanta were created on the back lot, and were then set on fire when it came time to film the burning of Atlanta sequence.

Deliverance

**Chattooga River (sections III and IV)
Rabun County
Northeastern corner of Georgia (on the border of North Carolina
and South Carolina)
Rabun County Chamber of Commerce (706-782-4812)**

It's hard to define exact sites in this 1972 backwater horror show that starred Jon Voight, Burt Reynolds, and Ned Beatty. The area is simply too broad. However, the river that the men canoe down is the Chattooga River which runs along the border of South Carolina. The waterfall is Tallulah Falls. This film was shot in sequence and the dialogue was looped – recorded without sync sound and dubbed in later by the actors. After the movie came out, tourists came to the area in droves, thus fueling a white water rafting craze.

Die Hard

FOX Plaza
2121 Avenue of the Stars, Century City, California

The 34-story "Nakatomi tower" that Bruce Willis saves from a bunch of terrorists in the 1988 thriller *Die Hard* is actually part of the Century City complex. Considered one of the greatest action movies of the late 1980s, *Die Hard* (directed by John McTiernan) created a new standard for action films. It spawned a series of sequels, and transformed Bruce Willis from merely the star of TV's *Moonlighting* to one of the most bankable action heroes in Hollywood history.

Diner

400 East Saratoga Street (Corner of Holliday), Baltimore, Maryland
410-962-5379

The diner was actually shipped in from Oakland, New Jersey when director Barry Levinson needed a meeting place for his 1982 film about college students in 1959. Though it's been relocated from where it was used in the film, it still remains in Baltimore (as the Hollywood Diner) and can be seen in two other Levinson productions, *Tin Men* and *Avalon*. It was also used in the Tom Hanks-Meg Ryan film *Sleepless in Seattle*, and television's *Homicide: Life on the Street*.

Double Indemnity

6301 Quebec Street, Hollywood, California

Generally considered to be one of the greatest films of all-time, *Double Indemnity* is certainly one of the greatest film noir achievements. Directed by Billy Wilder, this shady 1944 classic tells of an illicit affair between an insurance agent (Fred MacMurray) and

the wife of an oilman (Barbara Stanwyck). They hatch a plan to fraudulently sell her husband an accidental death insurance policy so that they can kill him and collect the insurance money, and the rest is movie-making history.

The house where Stanwyck lived (a centerpiece of the film) sits high up in the Hollywood Hills. It's tough to find, but well worth the effort in that it looks almost identical to how it appeared in 1944.

Duel

Route 14 near the Angeles National Forest, North of Los Angeles, California

This was Steven Spielberg's incredible debut. Made in an astonishing two weeks, this tense battle between an anonymous, taunting truck driver and a dweeby salesman (Dennis Weaver) remains a efficient thriller. Though most of the "duel" takes place on Route 14, the gas station/launderette is in a town called Acton just south of Route 14. The film's finale, where Weaver finally defeats the truck in a blaze of glory, is at Soledad Canyon, off Route 14 toward Raveena.

Easy Rider

Bryan's Gallery, 121 Kit Carson Road, Taos, New Mexico
800-833-7631

This is the jail cell where Dennis Hopper and Peter Fonda meet up with Jack Nicholson in the counter-culture 1969 road picture, *Easy Rider*. Though the exterior of the jail is in Las Vegas (at 157 Bridge Street), the interior still exists in Taos, New Mexico. Today, it's an art gallery located in the town square. A plaque describes the building's history.

E.T.

7121 Lonzo Street, Tujunga, California

This is the house used as Elliot's home in Steven Spielberg's classic 1982 film, *E.T.* Situated in the hills of the Tujunga Valley, northeast of the San Fernando Valley, it's located at the end of a cul de sac and can be easily recognized by the familiar mountain peak behind it.

The Exorcist

3600 Prospect Avenue
36th Street NW, Georgetown, Washington, D.C.

Though the window of Reagan's room was just a façade built for the movie, the rest of the house looks pretty much as it did in the 1973 horror film based on the book by William Peter Blithe. The interiors of the movie were shot in New York City at Ceco Studios, but you can see the set of stairs that Father Karras gets tossed down. They're on the side of the house leading from Prospect Avenue to M Street.

Fast Times at Ridgemont High

Canoga Park High School
6850 Topanga Canyon Boulevard (at Vanowen Street), Canoga Park, California

Van Nuys High School
6535 Cedros Avenue, Van Nuys, California

This 1982 comedy featured Sean Penn as the quintessential stoner/surfer Jeff Spicoli, and was written by Cameron Crowe (*Vanilla Sky*, *Almost Famous*, *Jerry Maguire*). The movie was actually shot at two high school campuses in the San Fernando Valley (Marilyn Monroe once attended Van Nuys High School). The mall featured in the film was known as the Sherman Oaks Galleria, located at 15303 Ventura Boulevard, Sherman Oaks, CA. It has since been turned into an office/shopping complex.

Field of Dreams

28963 Lansing Road, Dyersville, Iowa
888-875-8404

"If you build it, they will come," the voice in the movie promised. The off-screen narration may have been referring to baseball legends, but today it's tourists who flock to play on the very site where Kevin Costner's 1989 movie was filmed. You can run the bases, play catch, bat – even just sit in the bleachers and dream of simpler days. The house (part of the Lansing family farm) is also open to visitors. And of course, so is the cornfield. To the owner's credit, great efforts are taken to not over-commercialize the field and surrounding area. It is left pristine and simple, the way baseball diamonds are supposed to be.

Forrest Gump

Chippewa Square
Intersection of Bull and McDonough Streets
Savannah, Georgia

This lovely southern city has many squares, but this is the one made famous by the musing Tom Hanks character in the 1994, Robert Zemeckis-directed film that earned him his second Best Actor Oscar. (Zemeckis won for Best Director, and the film won for Best Picture.) The bench seen by filmgoers was placed there especially for the movie, and though it's since been removed, there's another one nearby where you can sit and talk to strangers.

The French Connection

Brooklyn, New York

Amazingly, one of the most famous chase scenes in movie history was shot at full speed and with real pedestrians and real traffic (in addition, there were five staged stunts as part of the chase). The incredible chases from the 1971 film were shot over the course of five weeks beneath the Bensonhurst Elevated Railway. The 26-block path of Brooklyn's Stillwell Line is as follows: It starts at the Bay 50th Street Station along Stillwell Avenue, into 86th Street and finally right into New Utrecht Street (ending at 62nd Street Station).

Friday the 13th

Camp No Be Bo Sco
11 Sand Pond Road (on Lake Cedar)
Just south of Blairstown on Route 818, northwest New Jersey

This was the site of the infamous Camp Crystal Lake, where Jason made his first appearance in the campy 1980 slasher film. As the plot went, the camp had been closed for over 20 years due to several gruesome murders. Enter seven young counselors who, despite warnings of a "death curse," plan on re-opening the camp. You know what happens next. Camp No Be Bo Sco is actually a Boy Scout camp from the 1920s.

From Here to Eternity

Kalaniannaole Highway
Halona Cove (by the Halona Blow Hole)
East of Diamond Head, Waikiki, Hawaii

Based on a novel by James Jones, this 1953 wartime classic has many memorable cinematic moments (like Frank Sinatra getting the daylights kicked out of him by an evil Ernest Borgnine in Sinatra's big comeback role as "Maggio"). However, the most memorable image from this (and almost any other movie) is the one of Burt Lancaster and Deborah Kerr embracing in a kiss in the midst of the surf. Fittingly, this is now called the "From Here to Eternity" beach.

Ghostbusters

14 North Moore Street
New York, New York

Though the interiors were shot on the West Coast, this was the actual headquarters of the slime fighters featured in the popular 1984 film, *Ghostbusters*. Sigourney Weaver's apartment building can be found at 55 Central Park West at 65th Street (overlooking the park). A few of the upper stories were added in via special effects.

Becoming one of the highest grossing films of all time, it was rumored that the film's well-known logo of the ghost in the red circle was based on the physical appearance of John Belushi.

The Godfather

New York City, New York

You could probably write an entire book based on *Godfather* shooting locations, but here are sites from some of the more well-known scenes in this 1972 film masterpiece.

1. The place where most of the film's interiors were shot was called Filmways Studios. Originally located at 246 East 127th Street in East Harlem, the studio has since closed and on the site is a supermarket.

2. The wedding scene at the Corleone compound is on Staten Island (a borough of New York) in the upscale area of Emerson Hill. The address is 120 Longfellow Road.

3. The Corleone family compound is right next door at 110 Longfellow.

4. Sonny beat the daylights out of his brother in law Carlo at 118th Street and Pleasant Avenue in East Harlem.

5. Later, Sonny gets obliterated in a flurry of gunfire at a tollbooth that was constructed at an old airfield (Floyd Bennet Field) southeast of Brooklyn at the end of Flatbush Avenue.

6. Moe Green is shot through the eye in the steamroom of the McBurney YMCA at 215 West 23rd Street.

7. Barzini is taken down on the front steps of the New York County Courthouse, 60 Centre Street in Lower Manhattan.

8. The Christening where Michael becomes a godfather took place inside Old St. Patrick's Church at 264 Mulberry Street in Little Italy (between East Prince and Houston Streets).

The Graduate

The Ambassador Hotel
3400 Wilshire Boulevard
Los Angeles, California

United Methodist Church of LaVerne
3205 D Street
LaVerne, California (just east of Los Angeles)

Though it's been closed for more than 10 years, this landmark hotel is steeped in history (see the Robert Kennedy entry in chapter three). Used for dozens of motion pictures, this once elegant hotel is the place where Benjamin (Dustin Hoffman) conducts his affair with Mrs. Robinson (Anne Bancroft). The church at the end of the movie where Benjamin disrupts Elaine's wedding – though supposedly in Santa Barbara – is actually the United Methodist Church of LaVerne.

The 1967 film directed by Mike Nichols became one of the most important films of the 1960s. Marrying a poignant Simon and Garfunkel soundtrack with the coming-of-age tale woes of Ben Braddock, a recent college grad coping with a darkly comic mix of alienation and moral conflict, *The Graduate* remains one of the most effective films of all time.

Grease

Venice High School
13000 Venice Boulevard
Venice, California

This was "Rydell High" from the 1978 blockbuster starring John Travolta and Olivia Newton John. It was used for exterior shots because it looked like a typical school from the '50s. The bleachers where Travolta and his crew sang "Summer Nights" are still standing behind the school, as are the lunch tables where Olivia Newton John and her girlfriends sang their parts in the song. The track where Travolta ran is just in front of the bleachers.

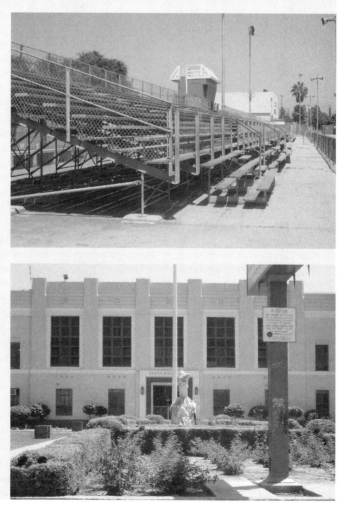

Halloween

1530 Orange Grove Avenue
Los Angeles, California

This is where Jamie Leigh Curtis made her movie debut in the creepy 1978 classic directed by John Carpenter. Set in the Midwestern town of Haddonfield, Illinois, the film was actually shot on this tree-lined, midwestern-looking street in Hollywood, just north of Sunset Boulevard. Most of the action in the movie took place in this house where Curtis was baby-sitting. The house where her best friend was murdered while baby-sitting is just down the street at 1537 Orange Grove Avenue.

The Hal Roach Studios

8822 Washington Boulevard (intersection of National Boulevard, near the train tracks)
Culver City, California

The Hal Roach Studios were, for over 30 years, famous as the place that produced everything from *Our Gang* and *The Little Rascals* to Laurel and Hardy classics. Roach sold the studio in 1955 to his son, Hal Roach, Jr., who eventually declared bankruptcy, and in 1963 the property was sold and the studio knocked down for good.

A historic plaque sits right near where Mr. Roach's office once resided. A trip back through the car dealership on the site reveals virtually nothing of what was once there, except for the abandoned train tracks near the entrance.

Heaven Can Wait

Filoli Mansion
Woodside, California
(off Highway 280 between San Francisco and San Jose)
650-364-8300

This was the mansion Warren Beatty lived in after assuming the body of a rich industrialist in his 1978 remake of *Here Comes Mr. Jordan*. The manor was also seen in the opening credits of TV's *Dynasty*. The house and gardens are open to the public from February to October.

High Noon

Main Street
Columbia, California (just off highway 49, north of Sonora)
Chamber of Commerce: 209-536-1672

Gary Cooper won a Best Actor Oscar and *High Noon* won three more Awards in what is considered to be the best Western ever produced. In the 1952 film, the townspeople of "Hadleyville," New Mexico completely turn their backs on the quiet sheriff as he faces the bad guys.

Several spots along Main Street were used, including the McConnell house (where Grace Kelly lived) and the exterior of the City Hotel and Saloon, a great place to visit for a taste of California history (209-532-1479). Many other films have been shot in this remarkably well-preserved gold rush town.

Several miles southeast of Columbia off Route 108 is Tuolumne City, where you'll find St Joseph's Catholic Church. This was the town church in Hadleyville where Gary Cooper went to plead for help from the town's residents. It is located on Gardner Avenue at Tuolumne Road.

Home Alone

671 Lincoln Avenue
Winnetka, Illinois

This was the MacAllister home where Macaulay Culkin outsmarted a pair of bumbling burglars in 1990's *Home Alone*. Not far from the home is the mall where he met Santa Claus–Winnetka Village Hall, 501 Green Bay Road.

Hoosiers

355 N. Washington Street
Knightstown, Indiana

The movie *Hoosiers* recounted the thrilling 1954 Boy's State Basketball Championship between powerhouse Muncie Central and tiny Milan High School. The smallest team in history to win the state title, Milan was victorious with a heart-stopping last second shot by Bobby Plump.

The Knightstown Hoosier Gym where the team (the fictitious Hickory High) played its home games in the movie is located in the quaint town of Knightsbridge. Today, after-school programs allow youths to play basketball in the gym, and church basketball leagues use it as well.

The bigger, more modern gym where Gene Hackman and the Hickory High players actually go to the state playoffs in the movie is the Hinckle Fieldhouse, located at Butler University, Indianapolis.

In Cold Blood

600 Oak Avenue
Holcomb, Kansas

The famous 1967 film based on the Truman Capote true-crime novel was actually shot in the infamous farmhouse where the gruesome 1959 murders were committed by Perry Smith and Dick Hickcock. (The trial in the movie was even shot in the actual courthouse were both men were tried—it's the Finney County Courthouse in Garden City, Kansas.)

On November 15, 1959, the murderers broke into the Clutter family home thinking they had a safe full of money. Upon learning that they did not have any such riches, they proceeded to kill (in cold blood) Herbert Clutter, his wife Helen, and their two teenage children, Nancy and Kenyon. The men were captured, convicted and hanged at the Kansas State Prison at Lansing on April 14, 1965.

Invasion of the Body Snatchers

Sierra Madre, California (just east of Pasadena)

The location of the 1956 sci-fi classic is virtually unchanged since the time the film was shot. Originally, director Don Siegel wanted to shoot where the movie's fictional town of "Santa Mira" was supposedly based – Mill Valley, just north of San Francisco.

However, they stayed in the L.A.-area in this little town near Pasadena. It's the meeting place where residents (turned aliens) met to distribute the "pods" from trucks. It's also where stars Kevin McCarthy and Dana Wynter attempt to escape the town, but blow their own cover by displaying emotion (they yell when a dog is almost struck by a truck).

It's a Mad, Mad, Mad, Mad World

Palos Verdes, California

The scrambling, star-filled, slapstick classic directed by Stanley Kramer in 1963 had dozens of Southern California locations, and almost as many stars – the film featured Sid Caesar, Spencer Tracy, Buddy Hackett, Ethel Merman, Phil Silvers, and Dick Shawn, among others. However, the movie's main destination, the "W" that everybody madly searched for, was formed by four palm trees located at one time in the park at Portuguese Point at the southwest tip of Palos Verdes Point, near Long Beach.

It's a Wonderful Life

Beverly Hills High School
241 South Moreno Drive
Beverly Hills, California

During the courtship scene between Jimmy Stewart and Donna Reed in this 1946 holiday classic, the two young stars are dancing in the Bedford Hills High School gymnasium. A button is pushed (by Carl "Alfalfa" Switzer from *The Little Rascals*) which results in the dance floor opening, thus causing everyone to fall into the swimming pool that is located under the gymnasium floor. The "Swim/Gym" is still functioning at Beverly Hills High. It's just south of the main school building, next to the school's sports field.

Jaws

Martha's Vineyard, Massachusetts

Steven Spielberg's 1975 classic was set on fictitious "Amity Island" but it was really Martha's Vineyard, the trendy retreat off the coast of Massachusetts. There are several easily identifiable locations that would be of interest to fans of the movie.

1. Joseph A. Sylvia State Beach is where swimmers go crazy after the attack on the young boy. Next to it is the American Legion Memorial Bridge where we see the shark swim safely back to sea.

2. At the intersection of Water and Main Streets in Edgartown is the town center where Chief Brody collects materials for the beach closure signs they suddenly need.

3. Quint's workshop was located in Menemsha, a fishing port at the southwest tip of the island. It's exact location was the inlet between the General Store and the Galley Restaurant. It's now an empty lot.

The Jazz Singer

KTLA Studios
5858 Sunset Boulevard (between Bronson and Van Ness)
Hollywood, California

This 1927 film location is notable because it was the first movie ever to be produced with sound. At the time, this wonderfully ornate building was the Warner Bros. lot (they moved to Burbank in 1929), and today it houses the studios of KTLA Channel 5.

Jurassic Park

Kauai and Oahu, Hawaii
Hawaii Movie Tours
800-628-8432

Most of Steven Spielberg's 1993 dinosaur smash was filmed on the Garden Isle of Kauai. Many of the places are hard to reach by car, but numerous helicopter tours can take you right down into the midst of them. Some of the more notable locations include:

Manawaiopuna Falls in Hanapepe Valley is where John Hammond's helicopter arrives.

The giant "Jurassic Park" gates stood by a water-filled canyon called Blue Hole near the center of the island. It's a long but beautiful five-hour hike to get there from Wailua, on the island's rugged eastern coast.

The electrical fence that the T-Rex broke through was built in Kauai's Olokele Valley.

On Oahu: The wonderful scene where the herd of Gallimimus charge past Sam Neill and the kids is actually on the island of Ohau at the Kualoa Ranch, Kamehameha Highway, Ka'a'awa Valley. The ranch can be toured and you can even pose for pictures under the fallen tree where Neil hides from the dinosaurs with the kids. (Remember when the T.

Rex appears and attacks the flock?) Located about 20 miles north of Honolulu, the number is 800-231-7321.

Note: The "Badlands" scene near the start of the movie was not actually in Utah, but at Red Rock Canyon in the Mojave Desert, 25 miles northeast of Mojave, California. It's a four-wheel drive trip to get there, and the park ranger can give you a map (661-942-0662).

King Kong

Shrine Auditorium
640 Jefferson Boulevard, Los Angeles, California
213-749-5123

When King Kong was brought on stage in a New York theater to be exhibited before hordes of flash-popping photographers and gawkers, it was actually shot here at this classic Los Angeles theater. Built originally in 1906 (and rebuilt in 1920 after a devastating fire), the Shrine has been used for everything from the Oscars to the Emmys to the Grammys. It is also where Michael Jackson's hair caught on fire during the filming of a Pepsi commercial in 1984.

The Lasky Barn/DeMille Studio Barn

2100 North Highland Boulevard, Hollywood, California
323-874-2276

This structure was rented by Cecil B. DeMille as the studio in which he made the first feature-length motion picture in Hollywood, "The Squaw Man" in 1913. It was originally located at the corner of Selma Avenue and Vine Street, and in 1927 was transferred to Paramount Studios.

The Museum is now located on Highland Avenue across from the Hollywood Bowl entrance. It was named a state historical monument in 1956. Though a small structure, the museum houses the largest public display of early Hollywood photographs and memorabilia and makes for a fascinating visit.

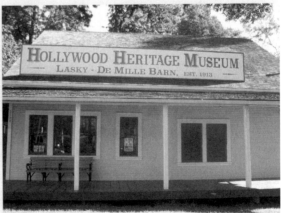

The Last Picture Show

Royal Picture House
115 East Main Street
Archer City, Texas
940-574-2489

Peter Bogdanovich's 1971 paean to small town life (based on a Larry McMurty novel) remains one of the most poignant films of its era. One of the centerpieces of the film was the Royal Picture House movie theater, which still stands and was recently renovated and reopened.

The Longest Yard

Georgia State Prison
200 Georgia Highway 147
Reidsville, Georgia
912-557-7301

Producers went to then-Governor Jimmy Carter about using the maximum security prison as the setting for the film. Carter agreed, and certain areas of the prison were sealed off to allow production. Burt Reynolds portrayed Paul Crewe, the arrogant, disgraced former NFL Quarterback (his career ended for point-shaving) who wound up in jail for car theft. While no real inmates were used in the movie, some professional football players were used, including Ray Nitschke, Joe Kapp, Sonny Sixkiller, and Pervis Atkins.

Melody Ranch

24715 Oak Creek Avenue
Newhall, California
661-255-4910

Originally Monogram Studios (opened in 1915), this ranch in the hills north of Los Angeles is where hundreds of classic westerns were filmed, including 35 John Wayne films (part of *High Noon* was also shot here). If you are a fan of singing cowboy Gene Autry, then the name "Melody Ranch" will raise fond memories of Gene and Smiley singing songs around the campfire. Gene's radio show was named *Melody Ranch*, and most of Gene Autry's western adventures were shot here.

The Music Box

927 Vendome Street
Los Angeles, California

Located in the Silverlake district just south of Sunset Boulevard, this is the legendary staircase where Laurel and Hardy struggled to haul a piano in their classic, Academy Award-winning 1932 comedy *The Music Box*. On one of the steps near the bottom, you'll spot a memorial plaque in the sidewalk bearing images of the boys. In the movie, there is a house they make it to at the top of the stairs – that was shot on a set. Here, you'll find a road, not a house, at the top.

My Dinner with Andre

Café des Artistes
Hotel des Artistes
1 West 67th Street, New York, New York
212-877-3500

Jefferson Hotel
Franklin and Adams Streets, Richmond, Virginia
804-788-8000

Louis Malle's talk-driven art film originally was to be shot in this popular New York City setting, but it would have cost too much money. So the Café des Artistes was re-created plate-for-plate inside the grand ballroom of the (then-closed) Jefferson Hotel in Richmond, Virginia. Today, the hotel (dating from 1898) has been re-opened, so you can visit the ballroom (though nothing remains of the movie set).

National Lampoon's Vacation

Six Flags Magic Mountain
26101 Magic Mountain Parkway
Valencia, California
661-255-4100

Remember the amusement park where Chevy Chase and his long-suffering family wind up after their eventful trip from the mid-west? The park that was closed, the one that John Candy was forced to open for the family, is actually Six Flags Magic Mountain in Valencia, California.

Nightmare on Elm Street

1428 Genesee Avenue
Hollywood, California

This is where Freddie Krueger terrorized Nancy Thompson in her dreams. The two-story home featured in this 1984 horror classic is located on a pleasant, tree-lined, residential street just two blocks east of Orange Grove Avenue–the street featured in the original *Halloween* movie. The neighborhood has a quaint, small-town feel, which is why it's used for so many motion picture productions.

Night of the Living Dead

Evans City Cemetery
Evans City, Pennsylvania
Directions: On Franklin Road, 1/4 mile up the hill from the intersection with
Route 68 (at the railroad crossing)

George Romero's creepy 1968 horror flick set the standard for other low budget horror movies, and the grim, grainy look of this film is still haunting today. Romero is from Pittsburgh originally, and so (like John Waters to follow) he kept his productions close to home. The cemetery from "Night" is in Evans City, just to the north of Pittsburgh, and the since-demolished farmhouse was located on banks of the Monongahela River.

North by Northwest

Wasco, California (about 25 miles northwest of Bakersfield on Highway 46)

One of Alfred Hitchcock's most famous scenes took place in this stylish 1959 thriller. Remember when Cary Grant is attacked by a crop dusting plane in the middle of a desolate Indiana farmland? The scene actually took place in Central California in a small town called Wasco ("The Rose Capital of the Nation"). As Robert Coe explains (he's the man who actually piloted the crop-duster which chased Cary Grant!), the exact field is about three miles north of town on Corchoran Road.

An Officer and a Gentleman

Tides Inn
1807 Water Street, Port Townsend, Washington
360-385-0595

This was the place where Richard Gere and Debra Winger spent their romantic night together, in Room 10 to be exact. Naturally, it's called the "Officer and a Gentleman" room. The Tides Inn is reachable from Seattle by ferry across the Puget Sound, and the area also features some other recognizable locations from the movie.

1. Fort Worden State Park, the "base" in the movie, is a restored former coastal artillery army base on Port Townsend's Olympic Peninsula. It is located at 200 Battery Way, Port Townsend, Washington (360-344-4433).

2. The balloon hanger, where Richard Gere and Lou Gossett, Jr. had their fight scene, is now a 1,200 seat performing arts pavilion.

3. The pool used for the diving/ rescue scenes is the swimming pool at Mountain View Middle School. It is located at 1919 Blaine Street, Port Townsend, Washington (360-379-4530).

One Flew Over the Cuckoo's Nest

Oregon State Mental Hospital
Between 24th and 25th Streets
Salem, Oregon (about 50 miles south of Portland)

The 1975 film starring Jack Nicholson and Louise Fletcher (who both won Oscars for their roles as R.P. McMurphy and Nurse Fletcher, respectively), was shot almost entirely on location at the Oregon State Mental Hospital in Salem. Dean Brooks, the hospital's actual superintendent, played the film's psychiatrist. Recently, it was named one of the twenty greatest films by the American Film Institute, and remains only one of three films to sweep the top five categories at the Oscars (the other two are *It Happened One Night* and *The Silence of the Lambs*.)

Pink Flamingoes

894 Tyson Street (at Reed)
Baltimore, Maryland

This 1972 John Waters' cult classic was shot (like most of Waters' productions) throughout his hometown of Baltimore. ("Trashtown, U.S.A." he's called it.) In *Pink Flamingoes*, the family's trailer was located on the grounds of an abandoned commune (it's since been carted away). But the scene that made this effort famous was the one in which Divine actually eats dog poop at the end of the movie. Still perhaps the most shocking act ever released in a commercial film, it happened right here on Tyson Street, just off Reed. At the time, the location was the home of Pat Moran, Waters's casting director. (The dog was hers, too.)

Planet of the Apes

Westward Beach
Westward Beach Road (between Zuma Beach and Point Dume)
Malibu, California

Many locations all over California and Arizona were used in this 1969 classic, but this is the one that people seem to remember best: The spot at the end of the 1969 film where Charlton Heston realizes that he's been on earth all along, where the crumbled remains of the Statue of Liberty sit near the surf. Of course, the statue was not really there – it was painted in as a special effect once the film was shot. However,  the cove is open to the public and is one of the area's prettiest stretches of beaches.

The Player

Rialto Theater
1023 South Fair Oaks Avenue
Pasadena, California

The is the theater to where the movie mogul (Tim Robbins) is lured in Robert Altman's 1992 satire of Hollywood. A writer is sending him death threats, and when he ultimately meets the writer at the Rialto, Robbins ends up killing him in a nearby parking lot.

Poltergeist

4267 Roxbury Street (north of Walnut, between Rachel Avenue and Tapo Street)
Simi Valley, California

This is the house where the Freeling's lived in the 1982 Steven Spielberg film, *Poltergeist*. (No, the house is not actually built upon an old burial ground.) The ordinary, suburban neighborhood served as the backdrop for the modern day ghost story about a tract home that suddenly becomes a gateway for enraged ghosts.

Pretty Woman

738 North Las Palmas Avenue
Hollywood, California

Considered to be the movie that made Julia Roberts a bonafide star, this "fairy tale" (directed by Garry Marshall) about the prince who rescues the streetwalker turned into one of the biggest blockbusters of all time. The building from the movie's final scene

where Richard Gere "rescues" Julia Roberts from the fire escape is a little hotel just north of Hollywood Boulevard. Other locations from the movie include:

1) Regent Beverly Wilshire Hotel, 9500 Wilshire Boulevard (310-275-5200)

2) Boulemiche Boutique, 9501 Santa Monica Boulevard (310-273-9653) – Where Roberts is snubbed by the staff.

Psycho

100 Universal City Plaza
Universal City, California
800-777-1000

Most of the 1960 Hitchcock sus-
pense classic, *Psycho*, was
filmed on the Universal lot. The
famous shower scene took place
on Stage 18-A, and the iconic
house still stands, changing
very little since the film was
made. Likewise, the car dealership where Janet Leigh swaps
cars was shot on location just
north of Universal Studios at
4270 Lankershim Boulevard
and – surprise – after all these
years it's still a car dealership.

Pulp Fiction

Hawthorne Grill
13763 Hawthorne Boulevard (at 137th Place, southwest corner)
Hawthorne, California

This is the coffee shop where John Travolta sat with Samuel L. Jackson discussing
heady matters when Amanda Plummer and Tim Roth pulled their guns. The place was
torn down in 1999 (after 40 years in business) and is currently a vacant lot. The spot
where Travolta and Jackson are eating Kahuna Burgers in their car before committing
their hit on the guys who crossed Marsellus is on Van Ness Avenue, immediately north
of Hollywood Boulevard, in Hollywood.

Pumping Iron

360 Hampton Drive
Venice, California
310-392-6004

Gold's Gym was the site of the landmark 1977 film, *Pumping Iron*, which introduced
Arnold Schwarzenegger to the movie-going public. It has also been the scene of various
body-building contests, including one notable Mr. America competition where Mae West
helped congratulate the winners.

Purple Rain

First Avenue
701 1st Avenue North
Minneapolis, Minnesota
612-338-8388

Originally called "The Depot," this club opened in 1970, and in 1982 it became First Avenue. A former Greyhound Bus station, this club was the central location in Prince's 1984 film, *Purple Rain*. It's still a thriving musical center, and in its history has hosted everyone from Frank Zappa to REM.

Raging Bull

Carmine Street Recreation Center
1 Clarkson Street (at Seventh Avenue South)
New York, NY
212-242-5228

This 1980 Martin Scorcese classic won the Oscar for Best Picture. The tough, gritty depiction of Jake LaMotta's life includes several recognizable places where movie fans can go and re-live some of the magic from this film, widely considered to be one of the best pictures ever made.

The public pool where Robert DeNiro first comes upon Cathy Moriarty is the Carmine Street Public Pools located in Greenwich Village. Long shots and crowd scenes at the boxing matches were filmed at the Olympic Auditorium (1801 South Grand Avenue, Los Angeles, California – also see *Rocky*) The actual fight sequences were shot on a studio stage.

Raiders of the Los Ark

Conservatory of Music
University of the Pacific
3601 Pacific Avenue
Stockton, California
209-946-2415

Of course, much of Spielberg's 1981 gem was shot all over the world – Kauai, France, England, Tunisia, etc. However, this is the location of the classroom where Harrison Ford teaches archaeology.

Rebel Without a Cause

Griffith Park Observatory
2800 East Observatory Road, Los Angeles, California

This Los Angeles Planetarium was the scene of the famous shootout at the end of this, arguably Dean's most famous cinematic moment. In fact, the movie scene became so famous that it firmly established the observatory as a well-known tourist landmark.

As of this writing, the park and observatory are undergoing renovations that will have it closed for at least two years. However, when you do get to visit, you'll see the bust of James Dean at the approximate site of where the scene was filmed. Interestingly, Dean's first professional acting job was a soda commercial filmed in Griffith Park near the observatory.

Return of the Jedi

The Moon of Endor
Jedediah Smith Redwood State Park
4241 Kings Valley Road, Crescent City, California

The towering redwood trees of Northern California (some up to 300 feet tall) served as the Moon of Endor in George Lucas's third *Star Wars* installment, *Return of the Jedi*. These were some of the first scenes from the series filmed in this country. Additionally, the Tatooine scenes (including the battle at Jabba's Sail Barge above the Sarlacc Pit) were shot near Yuma in the Arizona Desert in Buttercup Valley.

Richard Pryor Live on the Sunset Strip

Hollywood Palladium
6215 Sunset Boulevard, Hollywood, California
323-9627600

This popular, 1982 tour-de-force was filmed at the famous Hollywood Palladium. In the two-hour concert film, Pryor defined himself as one of the most powerful comic forces in history.

Opened in 1940 (with a show featuring Tommy Dorsey and Frank Sinatra), this venue has hosted the Grateful Dead, the Rolling Stones, the Who, the Clash, Talking Heads, James Brown, Led Zeppelin, Rod Stewart, the Police, and many others. (The Blues Brothers concert sequences were also filmed here.) Dignitaries such as England's Princess Margaret and Lord Snowden, Robert Kennedy, Ronald Reagan, Adalai Stevenson, Harry S. Truman, Dwight D. Eisenhower, John F. Kennedy, Lyndon B. Johnson and Richard Nixon have spoken here. Throughout the 1960s and '70s it was even home to the *Lawrence Welk Show*.

Rocky

The 1976 film *Rocky* featured several places in Los Angeles and Philadelphia that have become recognizable locations to millions of filmgoers.

Oscar De la Hoya Boxing Youth Center

1114 S. Lorena Street, East Los Angeles, California

This gym was seen in the film's opening amateur fight scene, and featured a religious mural overlooking the ring.

Shamrock Meats, Inc.

3461 East Vernon Avenue (at Alcoa Avenue), Vernon, California (southeast of downtown Los Angeles)

Of course, this is the place where Rocky trained for the title fight, punching the hanging sides of beef in the cold, refrigerated air. He was also interviewed here by a news reporter in the movie, in a comic scene that featured his brother-in-law, Paulie (who worked there), trying to poke his head into the shot.

Olympic Auditorium

1801 South Grand Avenue (at Olympic Boulevard), Los Angeles, California
Built originally for the 1932 Olympics, this is where the famous fight scenes with Apollo Creed were shot. (Some scenes from *Raging Bull* were also shot here.) Additional fight footage for the film was shot at the nearby Los Angeles Memorial Sports Arena.

Philadelphia Museum of Modern Art

26th Avenue (at Benjamin Franklin Avenue) Philadelphia, Pennsylvania

The famous 68-step staircase still attracts people who make the flight and then thrust their arms in victory a la Rocky when they reach the top.

Rosemary's Baby

Dakota Apartments
One West 72nd Street, New York, New York

Roman Polanski's macabre 1968 film took place primarily at this venerable Manhattan landmark apartment building. It's where Mia Farrow and John Cassavetes lived. Many famous people have lived here (it's adjacent to Central Park) and, of course, it's where John Lennon was murdered on December 8, 1980.

Safety Last

550 West 7th Street, Los Angeles, California

Everyone remembers the classic scene where Harold Lloyd hangs from a huge clock, dangling high above Los Angeles. That scene was from the 1923 silent classic called *Safety Last*, and it was filmed at the Brockman Building, located in downtown Los Angeles in the 500 block of 7th Street, between Grand Avenue and Olive Street (a block south of the Biltmore Hotel). While it looked like Lloyd was risking it all, he was actually never in any danger; the scene was shot on portion of the building that merely allowed a view of the city which gave the illusion of being up high.

Saturday Night Fever

Brooklyn, New York

Saturday Night Fever was one of those rare films that actually sparked a pop culture phenomenon: Disco. There are several key places you can visit that helped define some of the film's most dramatic, entertaining moments.

1. The movie's opening sequence with Travolta swinging the paint can was shot along 86th Street in Brooklyn.

2. The bridge where the gang likes to play daredevil stunts is the Verrazzano Narrows Bridge, where I-278 connects Brooklyn to Manhattan, south of Bay Ridge.

3. The Manero family lived in the house at 221 79th Street, Bay Ridge, Brooklyn.

4. The famous 2001 Odyssey Nightclub where Travolta tore up the pulsating dance floor while wearing the white suit is located in Brooklyn at 802 64th Street at 8th Avenue. It's now Spectrums, a gay dance club: 718-238-8213.

5. The famous dance studio where Travolta and Karen Lynn Gorney practice is the Phillips Dance Studio, 1301 West 7th Avenue, Brooklyn, New York (718-265-2081).

The Shining

Timberline Lodge
Route 26, Portland, Oregon (60 miles east)
503-272-3311

This lodge was used for the exterior shots of the Overlook Hotel in the creepy 1980 Kubrick-directed film of the Stephen King novel. However, the movie was shot almost entirely in studios in England. Jack Nicholson was at his eye-raising best here as Vermont schoolteacher, Jack Torrance.

Some Like It Hot

Hotel del Coronado
1500 Orange Avenue
San Diego, California
619-435-4131

This 700-room Victorian masterpiece is steeped in history. Built in 1888, it's where Frank L. Baum wrote *The Wizard of Oz* (it's believed that the hotel's ornate appearance actually inspired the description of Oz), and it was also featured as the Miami hotel where Jack Lemmon and Tony Curtis hid out in drag with Marilyn Monroe in the 1959 Billy Wilder comedy classic.

Sudden Impact

Burger Island
695 Third Street
San Francisco, California

It was in the fourth "Harry Callahan" film, *Sudden Impact* that Clint Eastwood's famed vigilante character created his catchphrase, "Go ahead – make my day." Clint confronts the bad guy holding the customers in a restaurant hostage, and when the criminal threatens to kill him, Clint utters his now famous line.

In the mid '90s, the original restaurant was moved across the street to 701 Third Street, where it operates today. The original structure has been torn down and a McDonald's restaurant is now sitting at the exact site where the scene was shot.

Sunset Boulevard

641 Irving Boulevard (just off Wilshire Boulevard)
Los Angeles, California

This is the site of the crumbling, gothic mansion where silent film star Norma Desmond (played by Gloria Swanson) lived in the 1950 classic, *Sunset Boulevard*. The gripping, caustic Billy Wilder film (which also starred William Holden as a struggling screenwriter who winds up dead in the swimming pool), bitterly documented what happened to some of the old guard of silent Hollywood when sound came into play.

While the mansion was torn down in 1957 to make way for an office building, the Alto Nido apartments where Holden lived in the film are essentially unchanged and can be found at 1817 North Ivar Street in Hollywood.

Taxi Driver

226 13th Street
New York, New York

This is the fleabag hotel where Robert DeNiro took Jodie Foster in the disturbing 1976 Martin Scorcese classic. It's also the site where the film's bloodbath finale was filmed. Other New York City locations include the outside of the St. Regis-Sheraton Hotel at 2 East 55th Street (where Cybil Sheppard picks up DeNiro), and Seventh Avenue at 38th Street, where the political rally was shot.

The Ten Commandments

Desert Excavation Site
Nipomo Sand Dunes, Guadalupe, California

Directions: From Fairview Avenue in Goleta, follow Highway 101 west for 66 miles (75 miles from downtown Santa Barbara) to the Main Street exit in Santa Maria. Turn left (west) and go 8.8 miles to the small town of Guadalupe. Continue several more miles to the entrance into Rancho Guadalupe Dunes County Park. Phone: 805-343-2455.

In 1923, filmmaker Cecil. B. DeMille built the largest set in movie history for his silent (and early Technicolor) epic, The Ten Commandments. After filming, the director ordered that the elaborate set be dismantled and secretly buried in the sand – which it was. For over 60 years it lay there, until 1983 when a group of dedicated film buffs decided to try and locate the remains (which by that time had truly become a lost city. They succeeded, and today the area is being uncovered as an authentic archeological dig site. Details can be found at www.lostcitydemille.com/.

This is Spinal Tap

Raymond Theater
129 North Raymond Avenue, Pasadena, California

This classic 1921 vaudeville theater (also used in Pulp Fiction) is where many of the concert scenes from this 1984 "Rockumentary" were shot by Rob Reiner. (From the Stonehenge production "extravaganza" to the stage pods, one of which trapped bassist Derek Smalls, played by Harry Shearer). From 1979 through 1991, The Raymond Theatre was known as the live music venue, Perkins Palace, and many memorable concerts were presented here, from Fleetwood Mac to Van Halen.

Top Gun

Kansas City Barbecue Restaurant
610 West Market Street
San Diego, California
619-231-9680

In the blockbuster 1986 film Top Gun, this popular eatery was the flyer's hangout where Anthony Edwards banged out "Great Balls of Fire." The movie, starring Tom Cruise, Val Kilmer, and Kelly McGillis, was a major hit due to the blend of the Giorgio Moroder score, the romance, and, of course, the wild F-15 dogfight sequences.

Towering Inferno

**Bank of America World Headquarters
555 California Street (at Kearney)
San Francisco, California**

A five-story set was built in Malibu to actually burn down in this 1974 disaster movie, but this location in San Francisco was used for the shots of the entrance to the building. Additionally, the lobby and the glass elevators that were used are located at the Hyatt Regency Hotel at 5 Embarcadero Center, also in San Francisco. The all-star cast featured Steve McQueen, Paul Newman, William Holden, Faye Dunaway, Fred Astaire, O.J. Simpson, Ava Gardner, Susan Blakely, and Jennifer Jones.

The Twilight Zone

**Indian Dunes Park (near Six Flags Magic Mountain Amusement Park)
Valencia, California**

Directions: Go north of Los Angeles on the 5 freeway, turn left on Highway 126 near Valencia. The site is on the left side, several miles down the road.

The park is no longer there, but this was the site where, at 2:20 A.M. on the morning of July 23, 1982, the final shot of Jon Landis's segment for the movie *The Twilight Zone* was being filmed. The segment, entitled "Time Out," featured veteran actor Vic Morrow and two child actors, Myca Dinh Le, and Renee Shin-Yi Chen, ages 7 and 6, respectively.

As Morrow waded through a knee-deep river with both kids in his arms (amidst a village under military siege), a helicopter was to come towards them. But something went terribly wrong and all three actors were killed by the out-of-control chopper (whose pilot may have been distracted by the many explosions going off). The park, a one-time popular dirt bike riding area, is gone now and the area is inaccessible private property.

Urban Cowboy

**Gilley's
4500 Spencer Highway
Pasadena, East Texas**

John Travolta rode the mechanical bull in 1980 at this site, where the famous country western club Gilley's used to sit. It burned down however, and to date, the lot remains empty.

Westerns

Lone Pine, California
Chamber of Commerce: 877-253-8981

For fans of old time western movies and TV shows, a trip to Lone Pine is like a trip to Mecca. This incredibly scenic Owens Valley location has been used for hundreds of locations for not just westerns, but comedies and science fiction movies, as well.

For years, directors, actors, actresses, and stunt doubles have made the trek to this amazingly scenic area, located about three hours northeast of Hollywood. John Wayne, Ronald Reagan and Mel Gibson, as well as animal stars like Trigger and Silver of western movie fame – even the elephant in *Gunga Din* – have all spent time here.

Each October, Lone Pine celebrates its own movie history by presenting the Lone Pine Film Festival, an event featuring films shot in the area. In 1990, Roy Rogers appeared at the first festival, and he dedicated a permanent marker in the Alabama Hills about four miles west of Lone Pine (at the corner of Whitney Portal and Movie roads).

When Harry Met Sally

Katz's Deli
205 East Houston Street (at Ludlow), East Village, New York, New York
212-254-2246

Shot in many locales throughout New York and Chicago in 1989, the scene that "made the most noise" was the one where Meg Ryan demonstrated (quite credibly) the ease with which an orgasm can be faked. At the very table where the scene was shot, a plaque reads, "You are sitting at the table where Harry met Sally."

White Heat

Mobil Oil Refinery
198th Street and Figueroa, Torrance, California

"Made it Ma – top of the world!" So screams James Cagney at the end of this classic 1949 gangster movie from atop the burning oil refinery. This demented, blaze of glory finale remains one of the most enduring images in motion picture history.

The Wild One

Johnny's Bar and Grill
526 San Benito Street (and up and down the street)
Hollister, California
831-637-3683

During the July 4th weekend of 1947, 4,000 motorcyclists (part of what was called "The Gypsy Tour") converged onto Hollister, a sleepy California town of about 4,500 people. Several small riots and fights broke out among some of the drunken bikers, which spilled out from this bar all along San Benito Street.

Several years later, the 1953 movie *The Wild One*, starring Marlon Brando and Lee Marvin, came out, and it is believed that it was loosely based on the 1947 events. Many feel that the film, a tale of two motorcycle gangs terrorizing small town America, greatly changed American culture with its shocking attack on small-town life and ideals. Thanks in some degree to myths surrounding the movie and the original event, bikers still flock to this small town every July 4th.

The Wizard of Oz

Sony Pictures Studios (formerly MGM)
10202 West Washington Boulevard, Culver City, California
323-520-8687

MGM's classic Culver Studio has since become Sony Pictures Studio where today, shows like *Jeopardy* and *Wheel of Fortune* are filmed. However, the soundstages still exist where many of the scenes from the *Wizard of the Oz* were filmed (and much of the history can be experienced during a two-hour walking tour).

The "yellow brick road" itself is long gone, but you can see where it once existed on Stage 27. The tornado scene was filmed on Stage 14, and the cornfield and apple orchard (where the evil apple trees came to life) were on Stages 15, 25, and 26. Munchkinland was filmed on Stage 27, and the poppy field was shot on stage 29.

R&B, Rock 'N' Roll, and All That Jazz

Alice's Restaurant

Housatonic Church–The Guthrie Center
4 Van Deusenville Road
Great Barrington, Massachusetts
413-528-1955

Alice's Restaurant isn't around anymore. But, as the song says, "Alice didn't live in a restaurant. She lived in the church nearby the restaurant . . . ." And the old Trinity Church, where Alice once lived and where the saga began, has become home to The Guthrie Center and The Guthrie Foundation. Arlo Guthrie, working to provide a place to bring together individuals for spiritual service, founded the Guthrie Center, an Interfaith Church, in 1991. So the Trinity Church where the song "The Alice's Restaurant Massacree" began and where the movie *Alice's Restaurant* was filmed, continues to service the local and international community.

Altamont Concert

Altamont Raceway
17001 Midway Road, Tracy, California
925-606-0274

It was billed as a West Coast Woodstock—a huge free concert in a windswept race-track headlined by the Rolling Stones. Instead, the gathering became one of the most violent days in the history of rock 'n' roll. For the final show of their 1969 American tour, the Rolling Stones "hosted" a one-day concert at the Altamont Speedway in Livermore, California. The show took place on December 6, 1969, was intended as a thank-you gesture to Stones fans. In addition to the Rolling Stones, the show's lineup included Santana, the Jefferson Airplane, the Flying Burrito Brothers, and Crosby, Stills, Nash and Young. The Grateful Dead never got to play, though they were scheduled to perform.

The haphazardly organized festival was "policed" by the Oakland chapter of the Hell's Angels motorcycle gang, a move that haunts the Stones to this day. The calamitous festival reached its climax during the Stones' set, when 18-year old Meredith Hunter rushed the stage with a gun and was stabbed to death before the band's eyes. The moment is the ugly centerpiece of the Maysles Brothers' classic 1970 documentary *Gimme Shelter*.

American Bandstand Studio

WFIL
4548 Market Street (46th and Market)
Philadelphia, Pennsylvania

The old WFIL Studio was the home of the original *Bandstand* and then *American Bandstand* from 1952–1963, arguably the show's most influential years. Built in 1947–48, it is notable as one of the first buildings in the United States designed specifically for television broadcasting, and was placed on the National Register of Historic Places on July 28, 1986. Today, it's an "incubator" building for small businesses.

America's Greatest Hits

Crossroads of the World
6671 Sunset Boulevard, Hollywood, California

Remember *America's Greatest Hits* from 1975? It featured "Horse With No Name," "Sister Golden Hair," and "Tin Man" to name a few. If so, then you'll probably recognize the Crossroads of the World center from the album cover illustration. Considered to be L.A.'s first modern shopping mall, Crossroads was built in 1936. The centerpiece building resembles a miniature ocean liner, an Art Deco facade complete with port-holes, railings, life preservers, and decks. An outdoor village of small, European-style bungalows surrounds the "ship," and rising above it all is a central 30-foot Streamline Modern tower, topped by an 8-foot, revolving globe of the Earth. Once a retail shopping center, today the Crossroads of the World is a quiet office complex.

Avalon Ballroom

Regency II Theater
1268 Sutter Street (at Van Ness), San Francisco, California
415-776-8054

In the 1960s, this is where Janis Joplin debuted with Big Brother and the Holding Company. A legendary concert venue through the 1960s, the Avalon's trademark was the swirly, psychedelic lights that were projected on the backdrop behind the stage. The area that served as the ballroom is on the second floor of this theater and access is not allowed to the public.

Beach Boys

Foster's Freeze
11969 Hawthorne Boulevard (just north of 120th Street), Hawthorne, California

The Beach Boys grew up in Hawthorne, California, and the "hamburger stand" mentioned in their hit song, "Fun, Fun, Fun," was actually this very Foster's Freeze (which they nicknamed "Frostie's"). It seems that Brian Wilson spotted a friend here driving by in her daddy's T-Bird. This Foster's Freeze is still open for business.

The Beatles

The Ed Sullivan Theater

1697 Broadway Avenue
New York, New York

This is where the Beatles made their United States television debut on February 9, 1964, during a musical segment of the *Ed Sullivan Show*. The CBS Television office had more than 50,000 requests for tickets to a studio that held 700. It is estimated that 73,700,000 viewers watched The Beatles' historic debut. Their thirteen and a half minute performance included the songs "All My Loving," "Till There Was You," "She Loves You," "I Saw Her Standing There," and "I Want to Hold Your Hand." Today, of course, this theater is famous as the place where David Letterman does his show.

The Beatles

Washington Coliseum

3rd and M Streets, NE, Washington, D.C.

On February 11, 1964, just two days after their debut on *Ed Sullivan*, the Beatles gave their first concert in the United States at the Washington Coliseum. Today, the building is used as a parking and storage facility for garbage trucks.

Deauville Hotel

6701 Collins Avenue, Miami Beach, Florida
305-865-8511

On February 16, 1964 , the Beatles made their second TV appearance on the *Ed Sullivan Show*. However, this time the performance was broadcast from the Napoleon Room of this popular resort hotel, not the Sullivan Theater in New York. The nightclub still exists and is located just off the hotel's main lobby. During their stay, the Beatles visited Muhammad Ali (then-Cassius Clay), who was there training for his upcoming championship fight with Sonny Liston.

Blue Jay Way

North of Sunset Strip, Hollywood, California

Directions: Turn north on Sunset Plaza Drive off Sunset Boulevard. Head north to Rising Glen when Sunset Plaza goes east. Go left on Thrasher, follow it around west, then turn north on Blue Jay Way.

On August 1, 1967, George Harrison was staying at a rented house on this street. He wrote the song "Blue Jay Way" while awaiting the arrival of former Beatles publicity man Derek Taylor, who had gotten lost in the fog. Shortly thereafter, the piece was recorded by the Beatles for the *Magical Mystery Tour* film and soundtrack record. You may have a hard time determining if you are actually on Blue Jay Way, because folks keep stealing the sign.

Candlestick Park

602 Jamestown Avenue
San Francisco, California
408-562-4949

On August 31, 1966, the Beatles gave their final American concert at Candlestick Park in San Francisco. The official song list that cold and windy night included: "Rock and Roll Music," "She's a Woman," "If I Needed Someone," "Day Tripper," "Baby's in Black," "I Feel Fine," "Yesterday," "I Wanna Be Your Man," "Nowhere Man," "Paperback Writer," and "Long Tall Sally."

Be-Bop

Minton's
Cecil Hotel
210 West 118th Street, Harlem, New York
212-864-5281

Bebop music is thought to have been "born" here in the early 1940s when Thelonious Monk, Fats Waller, Charlie Parker, Dizzy Gillespie, Kenny Clarke and others were allowed to improvise by the club owner. Sessions were often after other gigs in the late hours, so they rapidly become a favorite of top jazz musicians. Legend has it that Fats Waller coined the musical term "Bop" when describing improvisational riffs by the younger musicians. The playhouse now includes a housing unit for the elderly.

Bee Gees

Sunny Isles Bridge
Miami, Florida

Each evening on the way to Criteria Studios, the Bee Gees would drive across the Sunny Isles Bridge, and the tires of their car would make a "chunka-chunka" sound as they crossed some railroad tracks. One night, Barry Gibb's wife, Linda, turned to her husband and said, "Hey, listen to that noise. It's the same every night. It's our drive talking." Barry looked at her and started to sing a song that evolved into their second number one single, "Jive Talkin'."

Big Pink

2188 Stoll Road
Saugerties, New York

This is the house where Dylan recovered from his accident and invited The Band to hang out and play with him. In addition to *The Basement Tapes*, the sessions also resulted in The Band's debut album, *Music from Big Pink*. The singles, "The Weight" and "This Wheel's on Fire" became instant classics.

Birdland

1678 Broadway Avenue (near 52nd Street), New York, New York

The original location of the club that jazz legend Charlie Parker opened in 1949 was in the basement of the building at this address. Parker's problems with drug addiction forced him to ultimately be banned from the club that bore his name, and one night he even showed up in his pajamas after having snuck out of a nearby hospital where he was attempting to detox.

Bobbysoxers

Paramount Theater
Broadway Avenue and 43rd Street, New York, New York

Bandleader and clarinetist Benny Goodman had been on a grueling coast-to-coast tour that had been mostly unsuccessful until they reached the Palomar Ballroom in Los Angeles. There, he found "his" audience, one that went completely wild over the swing sound, setting off a worldwide sensation. Goodman brought the orchestra back to New York's Paramount Theater, and just like out west, the audience danced up a frenzy in the aisles. "Bobbysoxers" had been born, and with them, the "jitterbug" dance craze.

Enter Frank Sinatra. The skinny, wavy-haired kid in the bow tie started out singing on a Major Bowes amateur radio broadcast. His career gained momentum in the Big Band era, under Henry James and Tommy Dorsey, then took off like wildfire at the Paramount Theater in New York, where he opened on December 31, 1942. "Bobbysoxers" went crazy, screaming in delight, "jitterbugging" in the aisles, fainting, and eventually spilling out into Times Square, causing such havoc that a riot squad had to be called.

The Brill Building

1619 Broadway, New York, New York

"The Brill Building sound" came out of the stretch along Broadway between 49th and 53rd Streets. The building – named after the Brill Brothers whose clothing store was first located in the street level corner and who would later buy it – contained 165 music businesses in 1962, including many of the songwriting teams who would help craft the sounds of the 1960s.

Jerry Leiber and Mike Stoler worked here, writing many of Elvis's hits, plus Phil Spector, Doc Pomus, and Mort Shuman. And of course, the famous Aldon staff hired by Don Kirshner, which included Carole King, Gerry Goffin, Neil Sedaka, Barry Mann, Cynthia Weil, and Howard Greenfield. This was the group who wrote such hits as "The Loco Motion," "One Fine Day,' "Up on the Roof," and "Will You Still Love Me Tomorrow?" Though these names have moved on, the building still houses some music companies today.

Cal Jam

Ontario Motor Speedway
Ontario Mills Shopping Center (at the intersection of Interstate 10 and
Interstate 15, approximately 40 minutes east of Los Angeles)
One Mills Circle, Ontario, California
909-484-8300

The "Cal Jam" concerts heralded in a new era of rock festival: organized, detailed, and packaged. Technically, they were slick, and the stage and lighting designs were the prototypes for today's tightly-run festivals. Cal Jam I took place on April 6, 1974 and featured the Eagles, Deep Purple, Rare Earth, Emerson, Lake & Palmer, and Black Sabbath. 200,000 fans paid $10 each and so the show grossed $2 million, at that time one of the largest gates in the history of rock and roll.

Aerosmith co-headlined California Jam II on March 18, 1978 in front of 350,000 people. The other performers at that show were Bob Welch, Dave Mason, Santana, Heart, Ted Nugent, Foreigner, Frank Marino & Mahogany Rush and Rubicon.

CBGB-OMFUG

315 Bowery at Bleeker Street, New York, New York
212-982-4052

It may stand for "Country, Bluegrass, Blues and Other Music for Uplifting Gourmandisers," but it was ground zero for some of the most influential rock and roll ever spawned. From the mid-'70s on this hole-in-the-wall club was home to such bands as Television, Blondie, the Dead Boys, the Ramones, the Talking Heads, and many other punk legends. Considered the home to NYC's underground rock scene, it's still a vital place to experience music. Many nights in the seventies, it would not be uncommon to find Debbie Harry, Patti Smith, Joey Ramone, Iggy Pop, David Johansen, or any other number of local legends holding court at the bar.

Central Avenue

Central Avenue (from Downtown to 103rd Street), Los Angeles, California

During its heyday in the 1940s, Central Avenue was to L.A. what 52nd Street was to New York: a hotbed of jazz joints, dance halls, and nightclubs. Along this sprawling avenue, one could see everyone from Charlie Parker to Duke Ellington to hundreds of other musicians, singers, and entertainers.

Though much of the area has fallen into decline, the landmark Dunbar Hotel retains much of its old glory at 4225 Central Avenue (corner of 42nd Street; 323-234-7882). Beginning in the 1920s, the Dunbar, which was specifically built for black patrons to combat racist practices of other hotels, was like a second home for many out-of-town musicians. Ellington, Basie, Billie Holiday – they all played here and they all stayed here.

Chess Records

2120 South Michigan Avenue , Chicago, Illinois
312-808-1286

This is one of the most famous addresses in rock and roll history. After settling at this two-story building in 1957, the Chess Bothers (Polish-Jewish immigrants Leonard and Phil) continued the tradition they had started 10 years ago of recording the jazz players who performed at the brothers' nightclubs. Only now they had a permanent address and a real recording studio, as opposed to the various rented storefront offices they'd been using.

Over the years, many classic records were cut at Chess. Chuck Berry recorded "Johnny B. Goode" there on February 29, 1958, and Bo Diddley, Muddy Waters, Howlin' Wolf, Willie Dixon, Ramsey Lewis, James Moody and many other blues greats recorded here.

British blues bands like the Rolling Stones and the Yardbirds treated Chess like Mecca — the Stones even cut a song called 2120 Michigan Avenue in homage. After years of being used as a dance theater, today it's been restored and tours are available.

Clapton, Eric

461 Ocean Boulevard
Highway (A1-A), Golden Beach (20 miles north of downtown Miami, Florida)

461 Ocean Boulevard was the name of Eric Clapton's 1974 "comeback" album. It's the address of the posh beach house Clapton stayed in while recording the disc nearby, and he liked the place so much, he used it as the name of the album. Though the house is on private property, you can still get a good view of it from the beach.

The Clash

The Palladium
126 East 14th Street, New York, New York
212- 473- 7171

A famous concert venue and then disco in the '80s and '90s, it was here that the famous cover of The Clash's 1980 album *London Calling* was photographed. The picture, which shows bassist Paul Simenon smashing his guitar onstage, is considered to be one of the most definitive in rock and roll.

Costello, Elvis

Holiday Inn City Center
175 East Town Street, Columbus, Ohio
614-221-3281

Elvis Costello found himself in hot water in 1979 after making racist comments about Ray Charles and James Brown. While on tour promoting his new *Armed Forces* album, Costello was at this Holiday Inn bar discussing British and American music with Stephen Stills and Bonnie Bramlett, when the remarks were made. Bramlett responded by punching Costello in the face, thereby ending the discussion. After much publicity about the incident, Costello held a press conference and apologized.

Cotton Club

644 Lenox Avenue at 142nd Street, Harlem, New York

This was the location of the most famous nightclub in Harlem, the fabled Cotton Club. The actual building was torn down in the 1950s to make way for a housing project. The posh club was home to everyone from gangsters to celebrities throughout the 1920s and into the mid-1930s, at which time the club was moved to West 48th Street after the Harlem race riots. It was bandleader Duke Ellington's home base for four years and Cab Calloway's for three, and played host to famous black artists from Louis Armstrong to Ethel Waters.

Dead Man's Curve

Sunset Boulevard near Whittier Drive, Beverly Hills, California

The story of "Dead Man's Curve," made famous in the Jan & Dean song, ironically came true near this site on April 12, 1966, when singer Jan Berry had a near-fatal car accident in his Corvette Stingray 427 that left him permanently disabled. The infamous curve originally mentioned in their hit song referred to a curve slightly west on Sunset Boulevard, near Groverton Place, just north of UCLA.

Disco Demolition Night

Comiskey Park
333 West 35th Street, Chicago, Illinois

Chicago DJ Steve Dahl is credited by many with single-handedly ending the disco era. On July 12, 1979, after several smaller anti-disco events, Dahl's "Disco Demolition" between games of a twi-night doubleheader at old Comiskey park ended up with the field completely trashed, and the White Sox forced to forfeit the second game.

The Doors

Morrison Hotel
1246 South Hope Street, Los Angeles, California

The squalid hotel depicted on the cover of the Doors' album *Morrison Hotel* is located in downtown L.A., just two blocks east of the Los Angeles Convention Center. The hotel's owner supposedly chased the Doors away when they came by to shoot the cover for the 1970 LP, but they snuck back and grabbed the shot anyway (the picture was taken by famed photographer, Henry Diltz).

The Doors' Office

8512 Santa Monica Boulevard, West Hollywood, California

This former antique store, now the Benvenuto Café, once housed The Doors' offices, rehearsal space and a makeshift recording studio. In fact, the classic album, *L.A. Woman*, was recorded here between October 1970 and February 1971 using an eight-track tape deck with Bruce Botnick co-producing with The Doors.

Dylan, Bob

Delmonico Hotel

502 Park Avenue, New York, New York
212-355-2500

This mid-town hotel actually hosted two significant Beatle events. The first was in late 1963 when their manager Brian Epstein visited Ed Sullivan (who lived in the hotel) to square away details for the Beatles first U.S. TV appearance on Sullivan's show in a few months. The next year, on August 28th, Dylan paid a visit to the group's hotel room while they were in the middle of their first U.S. tour and introduced them to pot, thus getting them high for the very first time.

Newport Folk Festival

Festival Field
Intersection of Girard Avenue and Admiral Kalbfus Road
Newport, Rhode Island

On July 25, 1965, Bob Dylan (and band) upset the folk music generation by plugging in at the Newport Folk Festival and cranking out "Maggie's Farm," "Like a Rolling Stone" and a few other choice selections. While Dylan's seminal show allegedly generated way more disgust than glee amongst the crowd, it became a turning point in his career (and the course of popular music). In one shining moment, he had fused rock and roll with protest songs. The field where the festival was held in 1965 in now the sight of the Festival Field Apartments.

Dylan, Bob

Hard Rock Cafe

279 Yonge Street, Toronto, ON
416-362-3636

The first plaque marking a rock 'n' roll historic site in Toronto was installed at the Hard Rock Cafe in January 2002. It commemorates the spot where Bob Dylan first rehearsed with Levon and the Hawks. The plaque inscription reads: "An event that *Time* magazine once called 'the most decisive moment in rock history' took place a few steps from where you are now standing. Here in the early morning of Thursday, September 16, 1965, Bob Dylan first heard Levon and the Hawks, a hard-edged Toronto rock group, later to become famous as The Band. After the show, Dylan began rehearsing with the Hawks for what turned out to be his stunning eight-month debut tour on electric instruments.

"At the time, this building was famous as the Friar's Tavern. It was one of Toronto's most popular nightclubs and Levon and the Hawks were the city's top band. One of their biggest fans was Mary Martin, a Toronto woman who in 1965 was working in New York City for Albert Grossman, Bob Dylan's manager. Mary watched as Dylan grew fed up playing folk guitar alone in front of silent, reverential crowds. She also witnessed his electric first performance at the Newport Folk Festival.

"So Mary Martin decided to play matchmaker. She knew that Dylan needed a fiery band like the Hawks to help him launch his new direction, and that the Hawks needed a star like Dylan to take them beyond the Friar's. On September 15, 1965 Dylan arrived in Toronto. For the next two nights, after hours, he rehearsed with the Hawks on a stage along the north wall – now the window side of the restaurant. One week later, their tour opened in Austin, Texas, unleashing a whole new sound. – John Goddard, Rock Historian, 2002"

Motorcycle Accident

Zena Road, south of Highway 212, Woodstock, New York

On July 29, 1966, the back wheels of Dylan's Triumph 500 locked and threw him over the handlebars, disabling him for 18 months. This near-fatal motorcycle accident that broke his neck caused him to retreat to his home in Woodstock to mend and spend time with his new family.

A few months later, The Band joined him at the rented home (called the "Big Pink") and they began recording. Many of the tapes made there were finally released eight years later as *The Basement Tapes* after being bootlegged by many fans. The supposed exact site is one mile south of Highway 212, where Zena Road sharply turns, near a rustic barn called the Old Zena Mill.

The Eagles

Beverly Hills Hotel
9641 Sunset Boulevard, Beverly Hills, California
310-276-2251

This, one of the most famous hotels in the world, served as the cover for the Eagles' Grammy-winning 1976 masterpiece, *Hotel California*. To get the shot of the "mission bell," a cherry picker was used (making it hard to imagine the angle when you stand in front of the hotel). The inside photo of the band in the hotel "lobby" was actually shot inside the Lido Apartments, located in Hollywood at 6500 Yucca Street.

Fillmore East

105 Second Avenue, New York, New York

The Fillmore East, another of promoter Bill Graham's psychedelic concert venues, hosted hundreds of memorable rock and roll events. Jimi Hendrix's Band of Gypsys played here on New Years Eve, 1969. John Lennon showed up one time to jam with Frank Zappa. The Jeff Beck Group (featuring Rod Stewart) made their American debut here in 1968, on a bill with the Grateful Dead.

But the most famous aural document from this theater may be the shows taped by The Allman Brothers on March 11-13, 1971. These legendary sets (one of which ended at 7:05 A.M.) became part of a landmark live album, the back cover of which was shot against the theater's back exterior wall. The wall is still there today, though the Fillmore is long gone.

Fillmore West

San Francisco Honda
10 South Van Ness Avenue at Market Street, San Francisco, California
415-441-2000

From 1968 to 1971, the theater at this site (originally called the Carousel Ballroom) hosted everyone from the Who to the Jefferson Airplane to Cream. Famed promoter Bill Graham took it over in 1968, renamed it the "Fillmore West," and thus created one of rock and roll's most legendary venues. Today, it's the second floor of a Honda dealership. Supposedly, there's some graffiti in the rear stairwell that's an actual artifact from the theater.

Fleetwood Mac

Sound City
15456 Cabrito Road, Van Nuys, California
818-787-3722

In late 1974 when Mick Fleetwood was looking for a studio to record the next Fleetwood Mac album, he went to Sound City on a recommendation, liked the sound, and hired engineer Keith Olsen to produce and engineer the album. In the process of hearing a demonstration of that studio's sound and Olsen's production work, Fleetwood also stumbled upon two musicians who would soon become members of the band when Bob Welch departed.

Fleetwood came down to hear what the studio sounded like and Olsen put on a song called "Frozen Love" from the Buckingham Nicks album, which had been recorded there. Fleetwood decided to hire Lindsey Buckingham and Stevie Nicks based on the experience, and within two years the "new" Fleetwood Mac had the number one album in the country. (Nirvana also recorded *Nevermind* here, and Dennis Wilson brought a singer named Charles Manson to cut demos here in the late '60s.)

Frampton, Peter

Marin Civic Center
3501 Civic Center Drive, San Rafael, California
415-479-4920

 This pretty Frank Lloyd Wright designed center has a distinctive round blue roof and sits on the north side of the Civic Center lake in San Rafael. On June 13, 1975, Peter Frampton and his band recorded a live concert here, much of which was used on *Frampton Comes Alive*, one of the largest selling albums of that decade. The Grateful Dead rented the facility for months in the '80s, using the 2,000 seat concert hall as a recording studio as they laid down the basic tracks for their 1989 release, *Built to Last*.

Freed, Alan

WJW
One Playhouse Square Building
1375 Euclid Avenue, Cleveland, Ohio

Seminal disc-jockey Alan Freed (who popularized the term "rock 'n' roll") began broadcasting his "Moondog Rock 'n' Roll Party" over WJW radio in 1951. The station's 50,000 watt power made the show's influence enormous and helped bring many early rock and roll records to a huge audience. A small plaque near the building's entrance acknowledges the history, even though the radio station is long gone.

Gold Star Recording Studios

6252 Santa Monica Boulevard, Hollywood, California

The reason Brian Wilson of the Beach Boys wanted to record here was because he knew it was where Phil Spector had created his famous "Wall of Sound" approach to recording: the dense, layered, echo-filled sound that surrounded songs like "He's a Rebel," "Be My Baby," "Baby, I Love You," and "You've Lost That Loving Feeling" to name a few. The result was *Pet Sounds*, the dynamic 1967 album that supposedly pushed the Beatles to up the ante with *Sergeant Pepper's Lonely Hearts Club Band*. Small and lacking air conditioning, the main recording studio at Gold Star sat on the southeast corner of Santa Monica and Vine, but was razed in the mid 1980s to make room for the mini-mall that's there now.

Grand Ole Opry

Ryman Auditorium
116 Fifth Avenue North, Nashville, Tennessee
615-889-3060

Opened in 1892, the famous Ryman Auditorium gained its true fame with the coming of the *Grand Ole Opry* show in 1943. After garnering a reputation as the "Mother Church of Country Music," the Opry moved in 1974 to its current home by the Gaylord Opryland Resort and Convention Center, which left the original venerable theater empty. Twenty years later, the Ryman was restored to its original grandeur and is once again a national showplace for country music. Over the years, musicians ranging from Elvis Presley, to James Brown to Patsy Cline to Sheryl Crow have performed on the Ryman stage.

Grateful Dead

710 Ashbury, San Francisco, California

This house was the headquarters of the Grateful Dead in the late 1960s. Because of its reputation for being a den of inequity, the San Francisco police came into the home in 1967 and arrested everyone in the house for marijuana possession (Dead guitarist Jerry Garcia was shopping at the time, thereby avoiding arrest). In March of 1968, the band decided to move up north to Marin County. However, they didn't go without fanfare, performing a farewell concert in front of the house from the back of a flatbed truck.

A Great Day in Harlem

17 East 126th Street, Harlem, New York

Jean Bach's documentary *A Great Day in Harlem* told the story of a day in 1958 when many of America's greatest jazz artists were gathered at 10 A.M. – an ungodly hour for musicians who had played until dawn that very morning – to this stoop for a photograph. Amazingly, many showed up, and the photograph, taken by Art Kane and featuring Dizzie Gillespie, Charles Mingus, Thelonious Monk, Marian McPartland, Art Blakey, Milt Hinton, Count Basie, Sonny Hawkins, Lester Young, and dozens of other old lions and upcoming stars assembled on and around the steps of a nondescript brownstone in Harlem, became famous the world over.

Hall and Oates

Adelphia Ballroom
1400 North 52nd Street, Philadelphia, Pennsylvania

The is where Daryl Hall first met John Oates. It happened in 1967 when both young singers were part of competing doo-wop groups. A gang fight broke out and they made their acquaintance while hiding out in the freight elevator of the theater. (They didn't go on to record together until 1972.)

Hendrix, Jimi

Café Wha?

115 Macdougal Street
Greenwich Village, New York
212-254-3630

An early Bob Dylan hangout, this is where Animals' bassist Chas Chandler first saw the unknown Jimi Hendrix play in 1966. Under Chandler's guidance, Hendrix soon moved to England, where his career began to crystallize. In addition to Hendrix, artists such as Bruce Springsteen, Bill Cosby, Richard Pryor, and many others all played here on the way up. (Mary Travers was a waitress at Cafe Wha? until she joined up with Peter Yarrow and Noel Stookey to form Peter, Paul and Mary.)

Ashbury Tobacco Center

1524 Haight Street, near Ashbury
San Francisco, California

The Hendrix song "Red House" was supposedly written about this old Victorian mansion, which at the time in the 1960s was painted red. Though he never lived here full-time, Hendrix did spend many nights here as he kept two girlfriends living on the second and third floors.

Electric Lady Studios

52 West 8th Street
New York, New York
212-677-4700

In 1968, Jimi Hendrix was looking to buy a recording studio when he found the Generation Club on West 8th Street in the heart of Greenwich Village. After shelling out the $50,000 asking price, Hendrix turned it into a recording facility, becoming the first major artist to own and operate his own studio. Sadly, Jimi died within a month after the studio opened.

In June 1997, the original distinctive curved brick facade entrance to Electric Lady Studios was demolished (the New York Landmark Society unsuccessfully attempted to halt the renovation of the building, which would have been eligible for landmark status in just three years).

Holly, Buddy

Norman Petty Studios
1313 West Seventh Street, Clovis, New Mexico

Studio tours are available year round by contacting:
Kenneth Broad
Box 926, Clovis, New Mexico
505-356-6422

The Norman Petty Studios on 7th Street is known worldwide as the place where Buddy Holly recorded the smash hit, "Peggy Sue," as well as 18 other hits in just 15 months. In his studios, Petty mixed songs for other stars, including Roy Orbison. Clovis' own Fireballs also recorded "Sugar Shack," the number one song in 1963, at Norman Petty Studios.

Hyatt on Sunset (AKA "Riot" House)

8401 Sunset Boulevard
West Hollywood, California
323-656-1234

When British bands first invaded this hotel in the 1960s, it was simply known as the Continental Hyatt House. It didn't take long before the place picked up a more appropriate nickname: the "Riot House." Led Zeppelin supposedly had the most fun at the hotel, riding Harleys down the hallways, parading groupies in and out, and tossing TVs out of windows. Room 1015 bares the distinction of being where Rolling Stone Keith Richards mooned the world, and in 1986, Guns and Roses frontman Axl Rose tossed sizzling steaks to fans below, after the fire department showed up to halt his balcony barbecue. Recently renovated, the hotel still has a sense of what makes it famous, as evidenced by the poster of a long-haired musician posted at the front desk. It says: "Be kind to this customer. He may just have sold a million records."

Jackson, Michael

Thriller Video

1345 Carroll Avenue, Glendale, California

In the 1982 music video *Thriller*, Michael Jackson is chased by ghouls through a neighborhood of old Victorian homes, and this is the main house that was used.

Pasadena Civic Auditorium

300 East Green Street, Pasadena, California
626-449-7360

On March 25, 1983, Michael Jackson, in front of his brethren Motown crowd, slid across the stage and introduced "Moonwalking" to the strains of a pre-recorded "Billie Jean" during the Motown 25th Anniversary television show. The both the live and television audience went wild at the sight of Jackson seemingly floating above the floor.

Neverland Ranch

Figueroa Mountain Road, Los Olivos, California

Directions: Neverland is located on Figueroa Mountain Road, six miles north of Los Olivos, California. Los Olivos is in the Santa Ynez Valley, 25 miles north of Santa Barbara.

You can't see beyond the guard at the gate, but within this sprawling complex is where Michael Jackson houses his zoo, amusement park, and theatre. It's from here that he broadcast his 1993 speech declaring his innocence when charges of child molestation arose.

Jazz is Born I

Congo Square (now called Armstrong Park)
Located off North Rampart Street, near the intersection of St. Philip Street
New Orleans, Louisiana

In the early 1800s, this area was known as Congo Square and was the only legal place where slaves could get together on Sunday afternoons. On those days, they would gather to play drums, gourds, banjo-like instruments, marimbas, and such European instruments as the violin, tambourine, and triangle – creating what many consider to be the origins of American Jazz music. Today, Congo Square has become Armstrong Park, a Jazz Historical Park named for legendary trumpeter Louis Armstrong, who was born in New Orleans in 1900.

Jazz is Born II

Storyville
Iberville Street between Basin Street and Claiborne Avenue
New Orleans, Louisiana

Some music experts theorize that this was the true birthplace of Jazz. For about 20 years at the turn of the century, this was New Orleans's legal red-light district, and many early jazz players were employed in this area at local clubs. All but shut down in 1917, this area can be located by looking for the Iberville Housing Project.

Jefferson Airplane

2400 Fulton Street at Willard Street North (facing the northern side of Golden Gate Park), San Francisco, California

This is where the Jefferson Airplane parked it during their hey day in the late '60s and early '70s. Many of rock's royalty paid a visit to this stately manor for what are considered some of the most legendary parties in rock and roll history.

Johnson, Robert

The Crossroads
Clarksdale, Mississippi, Intersection of Highways 61 and 49

This is the legendary crossroads where, according the myth, in the dark Mississippi night seminal blues artist Robert Johnson traded his soul to the devil for fame and guitar-playing genius.

Johnson, Robert

Gunter Hotel
205 East Houston Street, San Antonio, Texas
210-227-3241

The Blue Bonnet hotel at the southeast corner of Pecan and St. Mary's Streets was torn down in 1988. For many years, it was believed that legendary blues guitarist Robert Johnson made several landmark recordings in a studio in the building in the 1930s. However, it eventually was determined his recordings were made in the Gunter Hotel (a memorial marker in the hotel lobby commemorates the Robert Johnson sessions).

Johnson, who died at the age of 27 in 1938, recorded only twice, for a total of 29 songs. His first recordings, and the largest body of his recorded work, took place at the Gunter from November 23-27, 1936. Songs included in those sessions were "Terraplane Blues," "Cross Road Blues," "Sweet Home Chicago," and "I Believe I'll Dust My Broom." Johnson's influence is cited as primary in the musical careers of numerous artists, and he was inducted into the Rock and Roll Hall of Fame in 1986.

King, Carole

Tapestry
8815 Appian Way, Los Angeles, California

This was the house where Carole King lived while recording *Tapestry*, then one of the best-selling albums in history. The famous cover of the album was taken sitting next to one of the windows in this house.

Kiss Alive

Cobo Hall
600 Civic Center Drive, Detroit, Michigan

Several live albums were recorded here over the years, including Bob Seger's *Live Bullet*, but it was *KISS Alive* that's remembered as one of the 1970's true icons, in a city where they were adored, on a night when they truly kicked it out. As the announcer revved up the crowd before they started said, "You wanted the best and you got it—the hottest band in the land . . . Kiss!"

Led Zeppelin

Physical Graffiti

96 St. Mark's Place, New York, NY

This old brownstone served as the cover for the band's 1975 album, *Physical Graffiti*. Located in the lower right hand corner of the building is the "Physical Graffiti" used clothing store (named after the record came out). This is also the building where Keith Richards sat with a bunch of Rastafari waiting for Mick Jagger in the Rolling Stones' 1981 video, "Waiting on a Friend."

Absinthe Bar

400 Bourbon Street, New Orleans, Louisiana
504-525-8108

This famous bar, the walls of which are covered with thousands of yellowed business cards and dollar bills, was re-created in a London studio for the cover of the band's last album, 1979's *In Through the Out Door*. The actual bar had long been a Zeppelin hangout; Jimmie Page even met his wife there, and so the band wanted to pay tribute.

Sunset Sound

6650 Sunset Boulevard, Hollywood, California
323-469-1186

When musician Tutti Camarata opened his studio in 1958, his main client was Walt Disney (and many soundtracks were cut here). But once the 1960s kicked in, rock and roll took over and this unpretentious little building near the intersection of Cherokee and Sunset became enormously popular for musicians seeking a recording studio.

Led Zeppelin recorded their second and fourth albums here, the latter of which included "Stairway to Heaven." The Doors did the majority of their recording here, and the Rolling Stones cut *Beggars Banquet* here. Other famous recordings include James Taylor's "Fire and Rain," Janis Joplin's "Me and Bobby McGee," Michael Jackson's "Beat It," and hundreds of others.

Lennon, John

Astor Towers Hotel

1340 North Astor Street, Chicago, Illinois

The Beatles' last U.S. tour in 1966 had a different feel than the first tour two years earlier. Much of the mania had died down and on August 11th John Lennon created a PR nightmare during a televised press conference in this hotel. Grilled about an interview he had given a few months earlier on religion (where he had stated that the Beatles were "More popular than Jesus now"), Lennon on this day apologized for his remarks as a means of trying to quell the numerous Beatle record burnings that were taking place throughout the Bible Belt. The hotel has since been converted into an apartment building.

Fairmont The Queen Elizabeth

900 Rene Levesque Boulevard West, Montreal, Quebec, Canada H3B 4A5
514-861-3511

On May 26, 1969, newlyweds John Lennon and Yoko Ono took the corner suite rooms (1738-40-42) at the elegant Queen Elizabeth Hotel to stage their week-long "bed-in for peace." A couple of weeks before that, the couple had bedded down in the Amsterdam Hilton for their first bed-in for peace, as documented in the song, "The Ballad of John and Yoko."

On June 1st, the lovebirds ordered up some for recording equipment, and with comedian Tommy Smothers playing guitar, the song "Give Peace a Chance" was recorded. The single was released a month later. Today, couples can make their own peace in the same bed as John and Yoko in that very suite.

Doug Weston's Troubadour

9081 Santa Monica Boulevard, West Hollywood, California
310-276-1158

This legendary club has seen its share of history. The Troubadour is where Elton John performed his first show in the United States on August 25, 1970. Randy Newman started out here. And on and on. But it was also here on March 12, 1974 that a drunken, despondent, Yoko-less John Lennon made infamous headlines when, after he and (also drunk) Harry Nilsson were about to get tossed for heckling the Smothers Brothers, he taped a Kotex to his forehead. When a waitress refused to give him what he  thought was proper respect, he snapped, "Don't you know who I am?" "Yeah, you're some asshole with a Kotex on his head," was her response.

Little Richard

J & M Studios
523 Gov. Nichols Street, New Orleans, Louisiana

Legendary recording engineer Cosimo Matassa owned several recording studios around the Big Easy. In the one that was located at this site, Little Richard recorded some of the most influential records in rock and roll history: "Tutti Frutti," Lucille," and "Good Golly Miss Molly." The structure is now a condominium.

Live Aid

JFK Stadium
Broad Street (near Patterson Avenue), Philadelphia, Pennsylvania

This is where the American portion of the legendary "Live Aid" benefit concerts was held on July 13, 1985 (the London portion took place at Wembley Arena). That day saw the likes of Bob Dylan, Led Zeppelin, Mick Jagger, Neil Young, and many more come together to help raise funds to feed the world's hungry. J.F.K. Stadium, the longtime home of the Army/Navy football game, was torn down in the 1990s.

"Louie, Louie"

Northwest Recorders
415 S.W. 13th Street, Portland, Oregon

The Kingsmen had formed in Portland in 1960 and consisted of Lynn Easton on drums, Mike Mitchell on guitar, Don Gallucci on keyboards, Bob Nordby on bass, and guitar player and lead singer Jack Ely. By the time they recorded "Louie, Louie," they ranged in age from 17 to 20. On a Friday night in April, 1963, The Kingsmen performed at an outdoor concert and did a marathon version of the song. The following morning, they went to a small recording studio in Portland called Northwest Recorders to lay down the tracks. Paul Revere & The Raiders recorded the tune in the same studio the same month, but it was The Kingsmen's version that was destined for greatness. The building is no longer used as a studio, but a plaque commemorates its importance.

Lynyrd Skynyrd

Robert E. Lee High School
1200 South McDuff Avenue, Jacksonville, Florida

This was where the unpopular gym teacher Leonard Skinner taught—the hardass eventually made famous when some students changed the name of their band from "My Backyard" to "Lynyrd Skynyrd" in honor of him.

MacArthur Park

Wilshire Boulevard (near Alvarado Street)
Los Angeles, California

MacArthur Park is most famous for the song named after it: a smash hit written by Jimmy Webb and performed by Richard Harris in 1968. In 1978, a disco version by Donna Summer again hit the top of the charts. Running more than seven minutes, it is apparently about a lost love and a rendezvous in the park. It has been covered more than 50 times, including versions by Waylon Jennings, Glenn Campbell, and Liza Minelli.

MacArthur Park was originally named "Westlake Park," and built in the 1880s. It was renamed shortly after the end of World War II for General Douglas MacArthur.

Madison Square Garden

4 Pennsylvania Plaza, New York, New York
212-465-MSG

Aptly nicknamed "The World's Most Famous Arena," the Garden has over five million fans a year passing through its doors. Though the notable musical performances are too numerous to mention here, a few of the more legendary events that have graced the Garden's stage: George Harrison's Concert for Bangladesh, The MUSE Concerts, Sly Stone's wedding, Led Zeppelin's *The Song Remains the Same* concert sequences, and many of the Rolling Stones' *Gimme Shelter* concert sequences. More recently, the Garden was the site for the Paul McCartney-organized concert that benefitted firefighters in the wake of the 9/11 tragedy.

Martin, Dean/Rolling Stones

The Hollywood Palace
1735 Vine Street, Hollywood, California
213-462-3000

Opened in 1927, the Hollywood Palace is where Groucho Marx filmed his TV quiz series *You Bet Your Life*. It was also the site of the *Merv Griffin Show*, and for a TV variety show called, appropriately enough, *The Hollywood Palace* (hosted by Jimmy Durante) which showcased a weekly cavalcade of superstars. But it was also here that Dean Martin insulted the Rolling Stones on their first American national TV appearance. After the Stones played, a guy in a suit was shown bouncing on a trampoline. Martin slurred, "This is the father of the Rolling Stones. He's been trying to kill himself ever since."

Max's Kansas City

213 Park Avenue South (between 17th and 18th off Union Square)
New York, New York

"Max's Kansas City was the exact spot where Pop Art and Pop Life came together in the 1960s." So said Andy Warhol, and he should know, because he held court here for many years. From the mid '60s through the end of the '70s, this is where much of New York City's music and artistic culture developed. The house band for a time was the Velvet Underground, followed by the New York Dolls. Aerosmith was discovered here. Bruce Springsteen opened for Bob Marley here.

"Upstairs" at Max's was the place to be in the glitter-packed early '70s, hanging out with Alice Cooper, Todd Rundgren, Mick Jagger, Iggy Pop, David Bowie and the rest of the then avant-garde establishment. Today, sadly, it's a gourmet market.

Mayfield, Curtis

Wingate Field
Wintrop Street and Brooklyn Avenue
East Flatbush, Brooklyn, New York

On August 14, 1990, at an outdoor concert at Wingate Field in the East Flatbush section of Brooklyn, legendary soul artist Curtis Mayfield was struck and paralyzed from the neck down by a lighting scaffold that fell during a windstorm. He released a new album in 1996 (*New World Order*) on which he only sang given that he could no longer play guitar. Sadly, he died on December 26, 1999. Mayfield is remembered for such hits as "It's All right," "People Get Ready," and "Freddie's Dead," to name a few.

Miller, Glen

Tuxedo Junction
1728 20th Street, Birmingham, Alabama

Named for the streetcar crossing at Tuxedo Park, a black community on the west side of the city, the junction came to national fame through the 1939 hit song "Tuxedo Junction" by Birmingham composer Erskine Hawkins. The song was made popular by Glen Miller and his orchestra after Hawkins sold the rights to Miller (it was very difficult for smaller-name black artists to get radio airplay back then). Tuxedo Junction was also the name of the second floor dance hall of this, the Nixon Building, and was the social hub for Birmingham's black community in the 1920s and '30s. A historic marker documents the building's history (it's now a dental clinic).

Milli Vanilli

Le Mondrian Hotel
8440 Sunset Boulevard, West Hollywood, California
800-525-8029

This is where one of the lead "singers" for the pop duo Milli Vanilli tried to kill himself in 1991. The dreadlocked pair had won the Grammy Award for Best New Artist of 1989, but the statue was taken away from them after it was discovered that the two singers hadn't sung at all on their debut item: they had only lip-synched the songs.

One member of the duo, Rob Pilatus (from Germany), took an overdose of pills, slashed his wrists, and tried to jump out of the ninth-floor window of this hotel before the police finally stopped him. Five years later, on North Van Ness Street in Hollywood, Pilatus was arrested on charges of attempted burglary and making terrorist threats, after he first tried to steal a car and then tried to break into a man's home. His attempt failed when the victim hit Pilatus over the head with a baseball bat. On April 3, 1998, Pilatus was found dead of an apparent overdose in a Frankfurt, Germany hotel room.

Mitchell, Joni

Garden of Allah
Southwest corner of Sunset and Crescent Heights
Hollywood, California

"They paved paradise, and put up a parking lot," sang Joni Mitchell wistfully about the end of the Garden of Allah, Hollywood's famed apartment-hotel that welcomed transient show business guests from 1935–1955. It was actually a collection of private bungalows, frequented by stars such as Errol Flynn, Clark Gable, Greta Garbo, W.C. Fields, Humphrey Bogart, F. Scott Fitzgerald, the Marx Brothers, and Orson Welles.

Legend has it that Tallulah Bankhead swam naked in the pool here, and Marilyn Monroe was discovered here sipping a Coke next to that same swimming pool. Today, the site contains a modern strip-mall. Until recently, the bank at the mall had a model of the hotel complex in a glass case, but the bank changed names and the model is now gone.

Moon, Keith

Stage 43
CBS Television City
7800 Beverly Boulevard
Los Angeles, California
323-575-2458

On September 15, 1967, Keith Moon affixed explosives to his drums for the Who's appearance on the *Smothers Brothers Comedy Hour*. Tommy Smothers had seen the band in person at the recent Monterey Pop Festival and their intense performance prompted him to arrange for the Who to make their American TV debut on the Smothers Brothers' TV show, as the program prided itself on bringing renegade acts to the masses. At the end of their second song (lip-synching to a live version of "My Generation"), Moon ignited his drums, causing a ferocious explosion – which is what originally impaired guitarist Pete Townsend's hearing. Game shows use the stage today.

Monterey Pop Festival

Monterey County Fairgrounds
2004 Fairgrounds Road (off Fremont Street, near Highway 1), Monterey, California
831-372-5863

Held in Monterey, California on June 16–18, 1967, the Monterey Pop Festival was the first commercial American rock festival. Dunhill Records executive Lou Adler and John Phillips of the Mamas and the Papas organized the festival around the concept of the successful Monterey Jazz Festival and staged it at that festival's site.

Featuring the first major American appearances of Jimi Hendrix, and the Who, it also introduced Janis Joplin to a large audience and featured performances by the Jefferson Airplane, the Grateful Dead, the Byrds, Canned Heat, Buffalo Springfield, Otis Redding, Ravi Shankar, and many others.

Arguably the most famous moment of the festival, (and one of the most memorable in rock and roll history) was when Hendrix lit his guitar on fire before smashing it at the climax of "Wild Thing." The stage where the show took place has hardly changed at all since then. At the exact spot where Hendrix knelt and "sacrificed" his guitar, "Jimi Hendrix 1967" has been scrawled into the wood floor.

Interestingly, it was here that Mickey Dolenz of the Monkees (a huge commercial act at the time) decided to take the generally unknown Hendrix on the road as the Monkees opening act. Several shows into the tour however, everyone soon realized that Hendrix was not a good fit for the teenybopper audience and he left the tour.

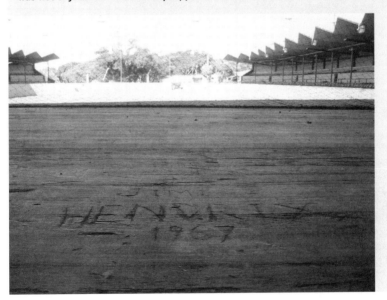

Morrison, Jim

Alta Cienega Motel
1005 N. La Cienega Avenue, West Hollywood, California
310-652-5797

Jim Morrison kept a room here from 1968–1970, as the sign on room 32 attests. Inside the tiny space, fans from all over the world have scrawled messages upon the wall. Inside the motel office, an interview with Morrison that was conducted in room 32 hangs on the wall.

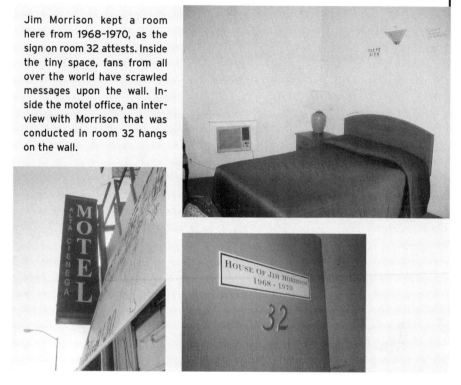

Morrison, Jim

Dinner Key Auditorium
Coconut Grove Exhibition Center
2700 South Bayshore Drive (at Pan American Way), Coconut Grove, Florida
305-579-3310

On March 1, 1969 at Miami's Dinner Key Auditorium, Jim Morrison of the Doors was arrested for allegedly exposing his penis during the show. Morrison was officially charged with lewd and lascivious behavior, indecent behavior, open profanity and public drunkenness. Found guilty in October 1970 of indecent exposure and profanity, his sentence totaled eight months hard labor and a $500 fine. The case was still on appeal when Morrison died in Paris in 1971. The auditorium still stands, but has been enveloped by the Coconut Grove Exhibition Center.

Motown

2648 West Grand Boulevard, Detroit, Michigan
313-875-2264

The Motown sound was born in this old brick house is now home to a museum. Marvin Gaye, Smokey Robinson, Diana Ross and the Supremes, Stevie Wonder, the Jackson Five — they all got their starts here under the orchestration of Motown Records svengali Berry Gordy, Jr. Today, this declared Michigan historic site looks just like it did in the early 1960s. You can see sheet music and the actual music studio equipment they used, including the piano used by all the greats. Photographs

and gold records adorn the walls, and original costumes are also on display.

MTV

Unitel Video
515 West 57th Street, New York, New York

This was where MTV was launched on August 1, 1981. Today, they've moved downtown a bit to 1515 Broadway, where their state-of-the-art, "open-faced" complex is visible from all over Times Square.

New York Dolls

Gem Spa
131 Second Avenue, New York, New York
212-995-1866

Open 24 hours every day of the year, the Gem Spa newsstand has been in business for nearly 70 years. In addition to making what many New Yorkers consider to be the world's best egg cream, this is also where the legendary New York Dolls posed for the back cover of their first album in 1973 (the record was produced by Todd Rundgren). David Johansen, Johnny Thunders and the rest of the Dolls returned for a follow-up shoot in 1977, after the original group had dissolved.

Osbourne, Ozzy

Epic Records
Century Park West and Little Santa Monica Boulevard, Los Angeles, California

In May of 1981, a drunk Ozzy Osbourne bit the head off of a live dove during a promotional visit to the Epic Records building. He was promptly banned from ever re-entering the building and proceeded to release an album under the Epic label, *The Blizzard of Oz*, that would become a triple platinum hit.

Osbourne, Ozzy

Veterans Memorial Auditorium
833 5th Avenue, Des Moines, Iowa
515-242-2946

During the 1981–82 "Blizzard of Oz" tour, rocker Ozzy Osbourne would bite the heads off of rubber bats as part of his show. Fans got into the act, and throughout the course of the tour would throw their own offerings onstage. On January 20, 1982 someone tossed a very real, very stunned bat on to the stage. Oz, thinking it was a rubber prop, chomped the head off it and thus sealed his own legend as a satanic, ritualistic animal killer. He was taken to the hospital right after the show and checked for rabies.

Pandora's Box

Sunset Boulevard and Crescent Heights, Hollywood, California

It was the tearing down of this club in 1966 that helped fuel the Sunset Strip riots. During late 1966, Pandora's Box was a center of controversy. One of the few underage clubs of its day, it became a flashpoint of the era as defiant teenagers got into fights with cops who began handing out curfew violations. These riots are what inspired the Buffalo Springfield song "For What It's Worth." The exact location of the club is the island in the middle of Sunset at Crescent Heights.

Perkins, Carl

Route 13 (between Dover and Woodside, one mile north of Woodside), Dover, Delaware

Carl Perkins was traveling on March 2, 1956 from Memphis to appear on Perry Como's TV show in New York when the car he and his band were driving struck the rear of a truck heading in the same direction. The driver of the truck was killed in the wreck and Perkins' brother Jay died later. His career never recovered from the six months he had to spend in the hospital recuperating, and his legend remains one who might have been.

Presley, Elvis

Mississippi-Alabama Fairground

Mulberry Alley off West Mains Street, Tupelo, Mississippi

This now run-down fairground is where Elvis Presley made his first public performance on October 3, 1945 after being entered in a talent contest by one of his teachers (the 10-year old Elvis sang a tune called "Old Shep" and won five dollars). Eleven years later he played the same spot, only by this time he'd become an international star and was promoting his first film, *The Reno Brothers* (later renamed *Love Me Tender.*)

Sun Studio

706 Union Avenue, Memphis, Tennessee
800-441-6249

Opened in 1950 by a local radio station engineer named Sam Phillips, some of the most legendary moments in rock and roll history were captured at this tiny Memphis studio. By 1952, Phillips had started Sun Records and two years later a nervous local teenager came in to lay down a few vocal tracks. The date was July 5th, 1954.

"It was just an audition," remembers Scotty Moore, the country guitarist brought in to back a green Elvis Presley for his Sun Records tryout. Near the end of the day, Presley broke into an obscure blues tune, "That's All Right," and history was made. Eventually, Phillips sold his discovery's contract to RCA for $40,000, a huge sum at the time.

A few years before Elvis, a local DJ named Ike Turner produced a session at Sun with teenager Jackie Brenston. Their 1951 version of "Rocket 88," is considered by many to be the first genuine rock and roll record. As well, Jerry Lee Lewis recorded "Great Balls of Fire" and "Whole Lotta Shakin' Goin' On" at Sun.

The studio was restored with Sam Phillip's help, and in 1987 opened its doors as both a tourist attraction and a working recording studio. Ringo Starr, Def Leppard, John Fogerty, Tom Petty, Paul Simon, Bonnie Raitt, U2, and Matchbox 20 are only some of the music greats who have come to record at Sun Studio since it reopened.

Overton Shell

1928 Poplar Avenue, Memphis, Tennessee

On July 30, 1954, Elvis gave his first professional (paid) performance on this stage, opening for Slim Whitman and Billy Walker. Since 1936, the Overton Shell has been an important Memphis landmark, and in 1982 it was named the Raoul Wallenberg Shell after a Swedish diplomat responsible for saving thousands of Jews from Nazi death camps.

Presley, Elvis

RCA Nashville

1525 McGavock Street, Nashville, Tennessee

When Elvis Presley signed with RCA in 1955, this was their main Nashville studio (though many more would soon be opened). On January 10, 1956, Elvis came in for his first RCA sessions and recorded some of his most formative singles, including: "Heartbreak Hotel," "I Got a Woman," and "Money Honey." Today, it's a production studio for The Nashville Network.

RCA Studios

55 East 24th Street, New York, New York

It now houses classrooms, but in 1956 you could find RCA's Studio "A" in this building, and it was here that Elvis Presley cut three of his most timeless singles, "Hound Dog," "Don't Be Cruel," and "Blue Suede Shoes."

Presley, Elvis and Frank Sinatra

Fountainbleau Hotel
4441 Collins Avenue, Miami Beach, Florida
305-538-2000

Though more of a Rat Pack haunt than a rock and roll hangout, it was from this hotel's Grand Ballroom that Elvis dueted with Frank Sinatra (on one of Frank's many TV specials) in a very famous TV appearance in 1960 immediately after returning from the army. They sang "Witchcraft" and "Love Me Tender" and part of the performance can be seen in the movie *This is Elvis*.

Market Square Arena

300 East Market Street, Indianapolis, Indiana

Elvis Presley gave his last concert at Market Square Arena on June 26, 1977. Twenty-five years later, a commemorative plaque was placed here (the marker is in a gravel parking lot where the arena stood before being demolished). A time capsule encased within holds Presley memorabilia, including a scarf of Presley's and a bootlegged recording of one of his last shows. A bronze plaque reading "Ladies and Gentlemen, Elvis has left the building" sits atop a stone column, just as Elvis' show announcer Al Dvorin would say at the end of each of Presley's shows.

Rolling Stones

Swing Auditorium

G Street (just south of Rialto, next to the railroad tracks)
San Bernardino, California

The Rolling Stones gave their debut American concert on July 5, 1964 at the Swing Auditorium, in San Bernardino, California. They played a total of 11 songs to 4,400 fans. On September 11, 1981, an airplane crashed into the Swing Auditorium, killing the pilot and his passenger. The building was so damaged that remaining parts of the structure had to be demolished. Over the years, everyone from Jimi Hendrix to the Grateful Dead to Led Zeppelin played at the Swing.

Fort Harrison Hotel

210 South Fort Harrison Avenue
Clearwater, Florida

The Rolling Stones had just played to 3,000 teenagers at Jack Russell Stadium in May, 1965. They performed only four songs before the crowd turned rowdy and the police stepped in, ending the show. That night, Keith Richards awoke in his room at the Jack Tar Harrison Hotel (today it's the Fort Harrison) with "Satisfaction's" opening guitar riff in his head. He grabbed his guitar, got the notes on tape and went back to sleep. The next day, he woke and worked with Mick Jagger on the rest of the song by the hotel pool. Today, the building is owned by the Church of Scientology.

Rolling Stones

Muscle Shoals Recording Studios

3614 Jackson Highway
Shefield, Alabama

In the 1970 film *Gimme Shelter*, the Rolling Stones are seen recording "Brown Sugar" and "Wild Horses" in this legendary southern recording studio. The first big record that was recorded here was R. B. Greaves' "Take a Letter, Maria," in 1967. After that, artists including the Allman Brothers, Rod Stewart, Cher, Linda Ronstadt, and Paul Simon all cut some of their biggest hits here. The building is now used to sell used refrigerators and stoves.

Theodore Francis Green State Airport

Warwick, Rhode Island

On July 19, 1972, Mick Jagger and Keith Richards and three members of the Rolling Stones entourage were arrested in Warwick, Rhode Island on charges of assault and obstructing police. The five were involved in a scuffle with a photographer as they made their way through the small airport. They pleaded guilty and were released, but the incident caused a four-hour delay of their concert in Boston that night (which, by many accounts, was one of the greatest shows they've ever played).

One Fifth Avenue

New York, New York

On May 1, 1975, there was a press conference scheduled to announce the Stones "Tour of the Americas" at the restaurant called Feathers of Fifth Avenue. Professor Irwin Corey, the famous American comedian was the M.C. Instead, a flat bed truck with the band on top playing "Brown Sugar" came down Fifth Avenue, stopping in front of the hotel. It was so exciting that everybody ran out into the street to watch. The Stones just carried on down the road, tossing out leaflets with tour dates. When they finished the song, they just pulled away in their truck, turned the corner, jumped into limos, and were gone.

Saturday Night Fever

Criteria Studios
1755 NE 149th Street
Miami, Florida

This Miami studio has recorded many classic songs, like James Brown's "I Feel Good," Derek & the Dominoes' "Layla," and Brook Benton's "Rainy Night in Georgia." But it was the Bee Gee's *Saturday Night Fever*, also recorded here, that became one of the biggest selling records in history.

The Sex Pistols

Great Southeast Music Hall and Emporium
3871 Peachtree Road, NE
Brookhaven, Georgia

It's no longer there, but this one-time shopping center punk club near Atlanta is where the Sex Pistols played their first American show of their first (and only) American tour on January 5, 1978. It's now the site of the Lindbergh Plaza Shopping Center. The band stayed at the nearby Squire Inn, now called the La Quinta Inn at 2115 Piedmont.

Soulsville, USA

STAX Records
870 East McLemore Avenue, Memphis, Tennessee
901-946-2535

Stax Records is critical in American music history as it is one of the most popular soul music record labels ever formed – second only to Motown in sales and influence but first in gritty, raw, stripped-down soul music. In 15 years, Stax placed over 167 hit songs in the top 100 on the pop charts and an astounding 243 hits in the top 100 R & B charts.

Stax launched the careers of major pop soul stars Otis Redding, Sam & Dave, Carla & Rufus Thomas, Booker T. & the MGs, and '70s soul superstar Isaac Hayes, and Stax songs have become part of the pop music vernacular. "Green Onions," "Sittin' on the Dock of the Bay," "Soul Man," "I'll Take You There," "Hold On, I'm Comin'" and "Theme from Shaft" are classic radio staples that are instantly recognizable by music fans and casual listeners alike. Though the original building is gone, STAX has been rebuilt on its original site and is set to re-open in 2003 as a museum/recording studio.

Springsteen, Bruce

"E" Street

Belmar, New Jersey (just south of Asbury Park, along the Jersey Shore)

This is the road that gave Springsteen his band's name. A one way street running for just a few blocks east of Highway 71 (the main route in and out of town), it's where David Sancious's (an early keyboard player in The E Street Band) mom lived.

Harvard Square Theater

10 Church Street
Cambridge, Massachusetts

In 1974, Boston area rock music critic Jon Landau reviewed a concert at the Harvard Square Theater for *The Real Paper*. In his piece, Landau started by bemoaning the lack of passion and soul in the current music scene, and how he had become bored with something that, at one time, had been so vital and relevant. But then he got to writing about the concert, in which a skinny, scruffy, 20-something beach rat from Asbury Park, New Jersey gave him reason to believe. Landau's words crackle and resonate even today:

"But tonight there is someone I can write of the way I used to write, without reservations of any kind. Last Thursday, at the Harvard Square Theatre, I saw my rock'n'roll past flash before my eyes. And I saw something else: I saw rock and roll future and its name is Bruce Springsteen. And on a night when I needed to feel young, he made me feel like I was hearing music for the very first time."

Rolling Stone magazine picked-up Landau's quote of seeing the future of rock and roll and the legend of "The Boss" was born. Landau went on to become Springsteen's manager and co-producer; today, the site is a movie theater.

The Record Plant

321 West 44th Street, New York, New York

This recording studio is a virtual rock and roll museum, having been the site where Springsteen cut *Born to Run* and *Darkness of the Edge of Town*, and also where Hendrix recorded *Electric Ladyland* in 1968. The night John Lennon was murdered in 1980, he had just left a mixing session from this studio.

Stone Pony

913 Ocean Avenue, Asbury Park, New Jersey
732-502-0600

A rock and roll landmark for years, this is the local Jersey bar where Bruce Springsteen's "Glory Days" video was shot. Back in the early '70s, Springsteen played here frequently, as did Southside Johnny and other locals.

The Sunset Grill

7439 Sunset Blvd, Hollywood, California

Subject of Don Henley's "Sunset Grill" from his *Building the Perfect Beast* album. When the tune came out, the Sunset Grill's owner, Joe Frolich, had no idea he and his establishment had been immortalized. After customers started telling him that he and his restaurant were being sung about by the ex-Eagle, Joe's wife, Eva, finally recognized Henley at the Grill one day. By that time, tourists had already started gawking and pulling up to take snapshots. Henley was quoted back then as saying the song was an indictment not of Southern California, but of urban sprawl in general and the changing nature of American cityscapes.

The T.A.M.I Show

Santa Monica Civic Auditorium
1855 Main Street, Santa Monica, California
310-393-9961

Filmed in a single day (October 29, 1964), this rarely seen concert film represents one of rock and roll's seminal concert events – one of the first major "package" performances which fused together all of music's most primal forces of the day. Featuring outstanding performances by James Brown (featuring two go-go dancers named Teri Garr and Toni Basil), Marvin Gaye, Chuck Berry, the Beach Boys, the Rolling Stones, the Supremes, Jan and Dean, and

Smokey Robinson and the Miracles, the concert was documented by television cameras and kinescoped onto film by director Steve Binder. The title stood for "Teenage Awards Music International" and the show had a huge influence on how other directors (such as D.A. Pennebaker at Monterey Pop) would soon document rock and roll on film.

US Festival

Glen Helen Regional Park, San Bernardino, California

This was the site for the massive 1982 and 1983 festivals put on by Apple Computer's Steve Wozniak. The shows featured dozens of acts, including U2, the Clash, the Talking Heads, the Grateful Dead, the Police, the B52s, Ozzy Osbourne, Van Halen, the Stray Cats, Stevie Nicks, and David Bowie. The park is located just off I-15 about an hour east of Los Angeles, and is a great place for fishing, camping, hiking, and more.

U2

Corner of 7th Street and Main Street, Los Angeles, California

This is the L.A. rooftop where U2 taped the music video for the song "Where the Streets Have No Name" in 1987. They actually performed on the roof of a row of stores located right at the corner of 7th Street & Main Street, near the Skid Row section of downtown, before the cops broke it up.

Valley Girl

Sherman Oaks Galleria
Ventura and Sepulveda Boulevards (northwest corner), Sherman Oaks, California

Though it's hard to peg who came up with the actual term "Valley girl," for sure the phrase gained widespread recognition in 1982 with the release of the Frank Zappa novelty hit, "Valley Girl." The minor rap mocked the speech and attitudes of rich teenage girls in Southern California, particularly the San Fernando Valley (where Zappa's daughter Moon Unit used to observe the obnoxious brats). In fact, that's Moon Unit herself dueting with her father on the song. Of course, the Galleria (now an office/shopping complex) was prominently featured in the tune.

Watkins Glen

Route 16 and Meade's Hill Road, Watkins Glen, New York

On July 28, 1973, the largest rock and roll concert ever presented was held at the Raceway in Watkins Glen, New York. Over 600,000 people attended the single day affair. It was estimated that 12 hours before the show was scheduled to begin, traffic had been blocked for over 100 miles. And Watkins Glen was simply a presentation of three enduring rock & roll bands – the Grateful Dead, the Band, and the Allman Brothers.

The day before the concert, all three bands played short one to two hour sets for the 150,000 people that had already arrived. Then, on the day of the concert, the Dead played for five hours, the Band for three hours, and the Allman Brothers for four hours. To close the show, everyone got on stage for a 90-minute jam.

Wattstax Concert

Los Angeles Memorial Coliseum
3911 South Figueroa Street, Los Angeles, California

Wattstax was a memorable August 1972 concert held at the Los Angeles Memorial Coliseum. Its purpose was to benefit the neighborhood of Watts some seven years after the Watts riots, and the concert drew an overwhelmingly African-American crowd of 100,000 and turned into a memorable black-pride event.

A documentary was filmed of the show and remains one of the great (if rarely-seen concert films). The show (hosted by Richard Pryor) featured R&B legend Rufus Thomas, the Bar-Kays, the Dramatics, the Emotions, Isaac Hayes, Albert King, Little Milton, Mel and Tim, the Staple Singers, Johnny Taylor, Carla Thomas, Kim Weston, and others.

Wilson, Jackie

Latin Casino
2235 Marlton Pike
Cherry Hill, New Jersey

Specializing in Vegas-style floor shows, this onetime nightclub hosted everyone from Sinatra to Diana Ross. On September 25, 1975, while onstage at the Latin Casino, Jackie Wilson had the heart attack (with brain damage occurring) that eventually led to his death in 1984. The Latin Casino was torn down soon after and it's now the site of a car manufacturer's office building.

The Who

Flint Holiday Inn (now a Days Inn)
2207 West Bristol Road
Flint, Michigan
313-239-4681

On August 23, 1967, Who drummer Keith Moon celebrated his 20th birthday. That night, the band had opened for the Herman's Hermits at Atwood Stadium, a Flint high school football field. Afterwards, everyone returned to the hotel to celebrate Moon's birthday and the rest is rock and roll history. Moon emptied fire extinguishers, jumped naked into the motel's pool, threw food all over the place, and finally drove a Lincoln Continental into the same pool.

After spending the night at a dentist (who couldn't repair Moon's newly broken teeth — due to the amount of booze in his system he couldn't administer anesthesia), Moon joined his band in leaving Flint the next day. The tab for the "party" came to almost $40,000. And it's the last time the band was ever allowed to stay at a Holiday Inn.

The Who

Riverfront Coliseum (now U.S. Bank Arena)
100 Broadway
Cincinnati, Ohio

Eleven people tragically died here at a 1979 Who concert here during the band's first tour after Keith Moon's death some three months earlier. The fans were trampled in a stampede that developed when they were trying to reach unreserved, "festival" seating. An episode of the TV show *WKRP in Cincinnati* later made the incident a focal point of one of its shows.

Winterland

2000 Post Street (at Steiner)
San Francisco, California

On Thanksgiving Day in 1976 (and all through the night), the Band held its farewell concert at the venue where it had played its first live concert — Winterland in San Francisco. Joining them that night were Joni Mitchell, Bob Dylan, Van Morrison, Neil Young, Eric Clapton, and others. The concert and other festivities were filmed by Martin Scorsese and released a year and a half later as *The Last Waltz*.

There's not a trace of the historic venue that hosted this landmark show, nor the hundreds of others that took place there — including many of the selections used on *Frampton Comes Alive*, recorded on June 13th, 1975, and the last performance ever given by the Sex Pistols in 1978. At the Post Street entrance to the apartment complex at the site however, you will find a Winterland Photo exhibit, paying homage to what once happened at the location. Winterland closed on New Year's Eve 1978 with a show starring the New Riders of the Purple Sage, the Blues Brothers, and the Grateful Dead.

Woodstock

Hurd and West Shore Roads, outside Bethel, New York

Directions: Drive north on Hurd Road off 17B. To get to 17B, drive west from the New York State Thruway on Highway 17. The turn for 17B comes up just as you pass through Monticello. Once you get into the town of Bethel, look for the Bethel County Store – the Hurd Road turnoff is a quarter-mile past the store (look for a white farmhouse on the south side of the road at the intersection). Drive up Hurd Road until you hit West Shore Road and you'll be able to locate the marker.

A concrete marker sits at the spot where the stage stood for the original, legendary Woodstock "Music and Art Fair," three days of peace and love that took place on August 15-17, 1969 at Max Yasgur's farm. This seminal event was documented both on film and record. Among the performers were: the Band, Creedence Clearwater Revival, Crosby, Stills, & Nash, the Grateful Dead, Jimi Hendrix, Jefferson Airplane, Janis Joplin, Santana, Sly & The Family Stone, the Who, and Neil Young (Young performed a few songs with Crosby, Stills, & Nash and later joined the group). Woodstock festivals in the 1990s were held in the nearby town of Saugerties on the Winston Farm at the intersection of Routes 212 and 32.

We Are the World

A&M Studios (now Henson Productions)
1416 North La Brea Boulevard
Hollywood, California

The concept for "We Are the World" came from a group of British artists known as "Band Aid" who had gotten together in late 1984 to record a song called "Do They Know It's Christmas?" Given that song's success, singer Harry Belafonte got together Lionel Ritchie, Michael Jackson, and producer Quincy Jones to come up with an American anthem.

Jackson and Ritchie spent just two hours writing the song, which they wanted to record right after the American Music Awards. Immediately after the award show, 45 artists arrived here to record. The result was 21 lead vocal performances from the likes of Paul Simon, Billy Joel, Tina Turner, Huey Lewis, Bruce Springsteen, Bob Dylan, Daryl Hall, and many more. The song went on to sell 7.5 million copies in the U.S. alone., and raise more than $50 million.

Channel Surfing

Academy Awards

Dorothy Chandler Pavilion
135 North Grand Avenue, Los Angeles, California
213-972-7211

"The only laugh that man will ever get in his life is by stripping . . . and showing his shortcomings." So quipped host David Niven at the 46th Oscars on April 2, 1974. The suave host was preparing to introduce Elizabeth Taylor, who would be announcing the Best Picture Winner. All of a sudden, a completely nude man ran out from the wings behind Niven, flashed a peace sign and ran off. "Well, ladies and gentlemen, that was almost bound to happen," Niven explained, referencing the streaking fad that had recently become popular. Then, he tossed out one of the smoothest ad-libs of all-time.

All in the Family

89-70 Cooper Avenue, Queens, New York

The private residence shown as the Bunker's home is actually located at 89-70 Cooper Avenue in the Glendale section of Queens. The Cumberbatches, a black family, later moved into this home on the 1994 CBS spin-off series *704 Hauser Street*. Actor Carroll O'Connor, who played the role of Archie Bunker, supposedly came up with the name of the address for the Bunker household (704 Hauser Street) while commuting to the studio one day. Driving along Hauser Boulevard (just a few blocks east of CBS TV City), O'Connor noticed the name and thought it had the feeling of a Queens neighborhood, where the Bunkers were supposed to live.

The Andy Griffith Show

Franklin Canyon Lake
2600 Franklin Canyon Drive, Beverly Hills, California

Can you hear the song being whistled? In the opening credits of *The Andy Griffith Show*, Andy Griffith and Ron Howard are seen walking with their fishing gear toward an idyllic lake, located one might imagine, near Mount Pilot or Mayberry, North Carolina. However, it's Franklin Canyon Lake in Los Angeles, a beautiful wooded area that was chosen because of its tall pine and redwood trees.

This location was heavily used in the 1960s for such TV shows as *The Andy Griffith Show*, *Combat*, *Star Trek*, and *How the West Was Won*, but was also utilized by film companies: one scene from *On Golden Pond* was shot at a small pond next to the reservoir. There are actually two bodies of water here: a duck pond and the reservoir. The reservoir is where Opie tosses the rock. As well, two album covers were shot here: Simon and Garfunkel's *Sounds of Silence* and the Rolling Stone's *Big Hits (High Tide and Green Grass)*.

Batman

380 South San Rafel Avenue
Pasadena, California

Wayne Manor was the home of Bruce Wayne, Dick Grayson, Aunt Harriet and Alfred the butler. Though the famous basement was shot on a set at the studio, the exterior footage was filmed here. The house was also used as a convent in the 1991 movie *Dead Again*. Unfortunately, you cannot see the house from the street.

Batman

Los Angeles, California

Directions: About a quarter mile walk from the north end of Bronson Avenue (Canyon Drive) on the southwest side of Griffith Park.

The "Bat Cave" in the *Batman* TV series (and the first two *Batman* movies) is located in Griffith Park. Known as the Bronson Caves, it has been used in numerous science fiction, horror, and western movies.

Baywatch

Temescal Canyon Road and Pacific Coast Highway, Pacific Palisades, California

David Hasselhoff and his bevy of red-suited beauties were stationed in between Santa Monica and Malibu, near where Temesecal Canyon Road meets Pacific Coast Highway. Look for Will Rogers State Beach and its lifeguard tower. After several seasons shooting here in Southern California, the show was moved to Hawaii.

Benson

1365 South Oakland Avenue, Pasadena, California

This home was used as the exterior of the Governor's Mansion in the 1970's sitcom *Benson* starring Robert Guillaume.

The Beverly Hillbillies

750 Bel Air Road, Beverly Hills, California

Jed and Granny Clampett were supposed to live at the fictional address of 518 Crestview Drive in Beverly Hills. But in fact, this is the huge mansion built in 1935 by millionaire Lynn Atkinson that was used each week on *The Beverly Hillbillies*. Unfortunately, the home has been remodeled, so you won't probably will not recognize it – if you can even see it over the giant wall that's been erected.

Beverly Hills 90210

Torrance High School
2200 West Carson Street, Torrance, California

The exterior scenes of this TV show were not shot in Beverly Hills, but at Torrance High in Torrance, a pleasant, middle-class community about 30 minutes from Beverly Hills.

Bonanza

100 Ponderosa Ranch Road
Incline Village (Lake Tahoe), Nevada
775-831-0691

Remember the opening of *Bonanza*, the classic, long-running western TV show? An aged map pinpointed the Ponderosa's location, then burned away. And just where was the beautiful Ponderosa located? Here in Lake Tahoe, where the show's actual filming location is now a western theme park. *Bonanza* aired for 14 Seasons from 1959-1973 and become one of television's most popular programs of all-time. This show, shot in color to help promote and sell color televisions for RCA, was eventually seen in 86 Countries and translated into 12 languages. Today, visitors can experience the legacy of the unforgettable Cartwright characters as well as the spirit of the early pioneers who struggled so hard to make it in the American west.

The Brady Bunch

11222 Dilling Street (on the south side of the street)
Studio City, California

Though Mike, Carol, and the kids lived at 4222 Clinton Way on the show, this is the actual house. Sure, some trees have grown over and the owners put up a fence to keep tourists off the property, but other than that, it looks just as it did in the early 1970s. Note: Given how the show's interior was designed to be two levels, the *Brady* producers temporarily installed a fake window on the left side of the roof to make the ranch-style home appear to have second story.

Charlie's Angels

189 North Robertson Boulevard
Beverly Hills, California

From 1976 to 1981, this was the building used as the exterior of "Townsend Investigations," the agency where the nation's three most gorgeous detectives were employed. Today, the small brick building houses a vacuum cleaner store.

Cheers

Bull & Finch Pub
84 Beacon Street
Boston, Massachusetts
617-227-9605

The place "where everybody knows your name" was based upon this bar/restaurant in Boston's Back Bay. Three producers, Jim Burrows, and Glen and Les Charles, were looking to create a new sitcom based on an American neighborhood bar. One of them suggested going to Boston, where sports and politics have always been hot issues in the local watering holes. During their search, the producers dropped into the Bull & Finch. After they took a few hundred pictures and gave them to a set designer, they filmed a pilot and sold the show, which they named *Cheers*, to NBC.

The show premiered on September 30, 1982, and became one of the top-rated programs in TV history. All of the actors have been to the Bull & Finch Pub, either for filming or stopping by informally when they visit Boston. The pub itself was created in 1969 by a Canadian architect, who built it in England and transported it to Boston, where it was carefully reconstructed piece by piece. Today, it remains an international attraction, thanks to the characters of Sam, Norm, Diane, Carla, Cliff, Frasier, and the rest of the gang.

The Cosby Show

10 St. Lukes Street
Greenwich Village, New York

The Cosby Show was a breakthrough for African-American families, as it portrayed an upper class Brooklyn family of professionals. The number one show from 1985-1988, in 8 years it never dropped below the top 20. During its original run, *The Cosby Show* won numerous honors, including several Emmys, Young Artist Awards, Directors Guild prizes, Viewers for Quality Television Awards, PGA Golden Laurels, and Humanitas Prizes, in addition to multiple Golden Globe Award nominations. This is the building that was used for the exterior of the house on the show.

Dallas

Southfork Ranch
Event and Conference Center
3700 Hogge Drive, Parker, Texas
972-442-7800

Tour guides now squire visitors through the "Ewing" mansion and 41-acre estate, pointing out memorabilia from the show: the gun that shot J.R., Lucy's wedding dress, saddles used by the stars, etc.

Diff'rent Strokes

NW corner of 79th and Park Avenue
New York, New York

Diff'rent Strokes ran on TV from 1978 through 1986. It took place in New York and centered around the wealthy Philip Drummond (played by Conrad Bain), a widower with a daughter, Kimberly. He was also quite wealthy and lived in the penthouse of a luxurious apartment building, pictured here.

The show's premise came from the fact that Drummond's black housekeeper died, and on her deathbed requested that he take care of her two sons, Arnold and Willis Jackson; obviously, Drummond honored her request. The show's child stars – Gary Coleman, Todd Bridges, and Dana Plato – all experienced difficult times after the show ended, particularly Plato, who is believed by authorities to have committed suicide in 1999.

Dynasty

1145 Arden Road, Pasadena, California

The exteriors of the Carrington mansion from this catty 1980s TV series were shot at this private Pasadena residence.

Emergency!

Station 127
2049 East 223rd Street (just east of Wilmington Avenue), Carson, California

This popular 1970s show featured storylines around the Los Angeles County Fire Department's "Station 51" and its paramedics. This is the actual fire station used in that series, and it has since been named "The Robert A. Cinader Memorial" station in honor of the television producer who created the TV show. A large plaque on the outside wall is dedicated in his name.

Fantasy Island

Los Angeles State and County Arboretum
301 North Baldwin Avenue, Arcadia, California
626-821-3222

Over 100 movies and television shows have been filmed at this 127-acre property. One of its most recognizable features is the Queen Anne cottage used in the opening sequences of the show *Fantasy Island*, which starred Ricardo Montalban as Mr. Roarke and the diminutive Herve Villechaize as Tattoo. It's located beside the lagoon in the historical area of the park. Interestingly, the seaplane which brought guests to the island had to be lowered into the water by crane.

Friends

97 Bedford Street (corner of Bedford & Grove), Greenwich Village, New York

This is the exterior of the building where the six New Yorkers live in *Friends*, the hit show created in 1994 by David Crane and Marta Kauffman.

General Hospital

County USC Hospital
1200 North State Street, East Los Angeles, California

In the long-running soap opera *General Hospital*, fans know that the seventh floor of "Port Charles Hospital" is where most of the action is centered. Though those scenes are shot at ABC Television Center Studios in Hollywood, this is the hospital exterior that is used.

Gilligan's Island

Alamitos Bay Marina on Enna Drive, Long Beach, California

This is where the opening shot of *Gilligan's Island* was filmed, as *The Minnow* left port for her "Three hour tour." Portable palm trees were brought in for the shoot to simulate Hawaii, and today it is rumored that the original *Minnow* boat is still docked within this Marina.

Gilligan's Island

Coconut Island, Oahu, Hawaii

This is the island seen at the beginning of the opening sequence of *Gilligan's Island*. Coconut Island, located in Kaneohe Bay on the northeast shore of Oahu, is just 25 acres across. However, far from a remote isle for castaways, it boasts cabins, a beach cabana, a swimming lagoon, and a boathouse. Over the years, the island has hosted luminaries such as Presidents Harry Truman and Lyndon Johnson.

Happy Days

565 North Cahuenga Avenue, Los Angeles, California

The house used as the exterior of the "Cunningham" home in the long-running (1974-1984) TV series *Happy Days*, is located here on North Cahuenga Avenue. The show began as a vignette on the TV series *Love American Style* and was such a hit that producers decided to turn it into a series. *Happy* also spawned the shows *Laverne & Shirley*, *Mork & Mindy* and *Joanie Loves Chachi*.

Hawaii Five-O

Iolani Palace
Corner of South and Richards Streets, Honolulu, Hawaii
808-522-0832

This served as Steve McGarret's (played by Jack Lord) headquarters in the wildly popular island cop show, *Hawaii Five-O*. On the air from 1968 to 1980, it remains the longest running police show in TV history. This grand building was once the palace of King Kalakaua, then a legislature and courts building. Today, it houses a local museum.

I Love Lucy

Hollywood Center Studios
1040 Las Palmas Avenue, Hollywood, California

Built in 1919 as the Jasper Studio, the current Hollywood Center Studios has witnessed a lot of Hollywood history. Shirley Temple made her film debut here, as did Jean Harlow in the Howard Hughes silent movie, *Hell's Angels*. But it was on Sound Stage 2 in 1951 that Lucille Ball and husband Desi Arnaz shot the pilot (and the next two seasons) of *I Love Lucy*. They insisted on filming the series in front of a live audience with three cameras (a first) and the show stayed in the top ten for nine seasons.

The Jeffersons

185 East 85th Street
New York, New York

When they "moved on up," this is where George
and Weezie landed – "a deluxe apartment in the
sky." It was used primarily in the opening credits.
The Jeffersons was one of television's longest
running and most watched sitcoms. Starting as
a spin-off from *All in the Family*, *The Jeffersons*
debuted in September 1975, and ran in prime
time for 10 years.

Kojak

35th Street & 9th Avenue
New York, New York

This was the exterior used as the headquarters
for *Kojak*, the popular cop series about the lol-
lypop-sucking detective. Lieutenant Theo Kojak,
of course, was played by Telly Savalas; his supporting cast included Dan Frazer, his brother
George Savalas, and Kevin Dobson. The show
ran from 1973-78. The character of Lieutenant
Theo Kojak, a dedicated, hard-nosed New York
cop, first appeared in a 1973 made-for-television
film titled *The Marcus-Nelson Murders*.

L.A. Law

444 Flower Street
Los Angeles, California

This is the office tower seen on the television show, *L.A.
Law*, which ran from 1986-1994. Among the cast of this
taut, realistic drama series were Harry Hamlin, Susan Dey,
Jill Eikenberry, Corbin Bernsen, and Jimmy Smits. Both
critically acclaimed and Emmy award-winning, *L.A. Law*
focused not just on legal battles inside the courtroom, but
also on the struggles and conflicts the lawyers faced in their
personal lives. Located in downtown Los Angeles, this
office tower is right across the street from the famous
Bonaventure Hotel at the southeast corner of 4th & Flower.

Leave It to Beaver

1727 Buckingham Road, Los Angeles, California

The exterior shots for the Cleaver residence on the popular *Leave it to Beaver*—which ran on television from 1957–1963 –

where shot at this home on Buckingham Road. An identical copy of the home's stone and wood rambler facade was built on the show's back lot on Colonial Street, located on the Upper Lot at Universal City. The Cleaver's house was also used in the 1956 Universal film *Never Say Goodbye* starring Rock Hudson.

The Lone Ranger

Iverson Ranch
Redmesa Drive, Chatsworth, California

Directions: Exit the 118 freeway at Topanga Canyon Boulevard and turn left, passing under the freeway. Turn right at Santa Susanna Pass Road. At Redmesa Drive, turn right and head up the hill. Park just before you come to the first condominiums. To your right is the "Lone Ranger Rock."

This huge, craggy stone was familiar to virtually every kid who watched television in the 1950s and 1960s. It's the spot where the Lone Ranger's horse, Silver, reared up in the opening sequence of the show. Today, the area is surrounded by apartments.

The Love Boat

The Pacific Princess Ocean Liner
San Pedro, California

The hit comedy that became a prime-time commercial for the cruise industry was filmed predominantly on the real luxury liner. The original show was shot chiefly aboard the Pacific Princess and the Island Princess. The 1990's version was shot aboard the Sun Princess. These Princess "fun ships" dock regularly at the cruise terminal just beneath the Vincent Thomas Bridge in San Pedro, California. For more information on the status of the ships used for the TV show and how you can book passage on one, contact Princess Cruises at 1-800-PRINCESS.

The Mary Tyler Moore Show

The Nicollet Mall Pedestrian Shopping Area
Seventh Street and Nicollet Mall
Minneapolis, Minnesota

You can hear Sonny Curtis singing "You're gonna make it after all . . ." and then you picture the image, one of the most enduring in television history: Mary Tyler Moore flinging her tam into the air with that big carefree smile on her face. Today, a bronze statue capturing Moore in mid-toss can be found near the exact site where Mary originally twirled in the opening montage from *The Mary Tyler Moore Show*.

In the opening scenes, Moore is actually *in* the intersection when she tosses her tam. The southwest corner of Seventh Street and Nicollet Mall, a pedestrian walkway, in front of the Marshall Field's department store (known as Dayton's when Moore threw her hat) was chosen for the statue.

Mary Tyler Moore
Who can turn the world on with her smile?

Presented by the people at TV LAND

The Mary Tyler Moore Show

1204 Kenwood Parkway, Minneapolis, Minnesota

This Victorian house was the exterior of Mary Richard's house (before she moved to the apartment building in season number five). This was the place that also supposedly housed Phyllis and Rhoda, though from the outside it doesn't seem nearly big enough to be an "apartment" house. Nevertheless, it remains one of TV's most recognizable landmarks.

MASH

Malibu Creek State Park
1925 Las Virgenes Road
Calabasas, California
818-880-0367

This is where the opening scenes from the television show *MASH* were filmed, where the choppers landed at the army hospital and unloaded wounded soldiers, and where base camp was for the duration of filming in the 1970s until the memorable final episode. It was also used in the film, *MASH*. During that final episode there was a forest fire, and the entire set burnt down, so they simply wrote it into the script.

At one time this was the 20th Century Fox movie ranch. Over the years, many films were shot here, including *Planet of the Apes* and the original *Frankenstein.* But it is because of the 4077th that many make the 2 1/3 mile hike from the parking area at Malibu Creek State Park. It's a beautiful, not-too-grueling hike to the site, where you'll find a couple of gutted vehicles from the show, remnants from the helicopter landing pad, and lots of memories.

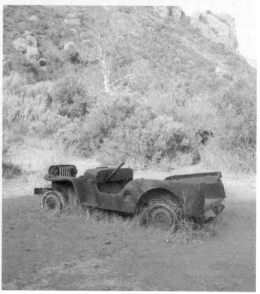

Medical Center

U.C.L.A. Medical Center (South end of U.C.L.A. campus)
Westwood Boulevard, Westwood, California

Chad Everett played Dr. Joe Gannon on the popular TV series *Medical Center* from 1969–1976. While on the show it was called "University Medical Center," this building that was shown each week is actually the U.C.L.A. Medical Center.

Melrose Place

4616 Greenwood Place
Los Angeles, California

The main apartment building where the characters lived, loved, and fought is in the Los Feliz area of Los Angeles, at 4616 Greenwood Place. The ad agency was at 5750 Wilshire Boulevard. The hangout bar called "Shooters" is actually a small restaurant called "Fellini's," and is located at 6810 Melrose Avenue.

Mork and Mindy

1619 Pine Street (just a few blocks from the Boulder Mall)
Boulder, Colorado

This was the exterior for the house used in the late '70s and early '80s for the popular *Mork and Mindy* TV program. The show, featuring Robin Williams and Pam Dawber, focused on an alien who lands in Boulder, Colorado. *Mork and Mindy* was a spin-off from a 1978 episode of *Happy Days,* in which an alien from the planet Ork landed on Earth and attempted to kidnap Richie Cunningham.

The Munsters

Universal Studios Hollywood
100 Universal City Plaza
Universal City, California
800-777-1000

The house from *The Munsters* (address in the show, 1313 Mockingbird Lane) is one of the most memorable in TV history. And it has an interesting history itself. When *The Munsters* finished production in 1966, Universal continued to use the house, though it was stripped of its gate, landscaping and some of the building adornments.

By late 1970s it had been painted yellow and was even featured in the short-lived NBC series, *Shirley,* starring Shirley Jones. Then Universal converted the house into a Cape Cod-style structure for use as a neighboring house to Jessica Fletcher's abode on *Murder, She Wrote* by removing the building's remaining gothic touches (a wraparound porch was added, as well). The house remains on the lot today in that state, though it's been painted gray.

Murder She Wrote

Blair House Inn
45110 Little Lake Street
P.O. Box 1608, Mendocino, California
800-699-9296

Murder She Wrote fans will recognize this gracious 1888 Victorian residence as the home of TV sleuth Jessica Fletcher (Angela Lansbury). Located in charming Mendocino Village, Blair House Inn is renowned for stunning ocean views, cozy featherbeds, serene atmosphere, and remarkable construction of clearheart redwood.

Newhart

The Waybury Inn
457 East Main Street, Historic East Middlebury, Vermont
800-348-1810

Chosen by a Hollywood set designer as the quintessential New England inn, the Waybury Inn earned a place in TV history thanks to the popular sitcom. Although only its exterior appeared on the show, the 1810 country inn (called Stratford on *Newhart*) now displays star-autographed photos and props from the show, and it sells T-shirts that say "Stratford Inn."

Northern Exposure

Roslyn Cafe
Roslyn, Washington

This was the first TV show to shoot entirely on location in (central) Washington, although the real-life Roslyn (population during filming: 875) was supposed to be the fictional Cicely, Alaska. You can't miss the whimsical mural featuring a camel painted outside the Roslyn Cafe (in the show, a woman named Roslyn was said to be a co-founder of Cicely).

The Odd Couple

1049 Park Avenue
New York, New York

"On November 13th, Felix Unger was asked to remove himself from his place of residence. That request came from his wife. . . ." For TV viewers, this was the location where Felix arrived, "The home of his childhood friend, Oscar Madison. Sometime earlier, Madison's wife had thrown him out, requesting that he never return." The apartment was used both in the show's opening sequence as well as for various establishing shots. The brilliant ABC series ran from 1970–1974.

The Ozzie and Harriet Show

1822 Camino Palmero Drive
Hollywood, California

On their classic TV sitcom, the Nelsons (Ozzie, Harriet, Ricky, and David Nelson) lived at the fictitious address of 822 Sycamore Road. But you can find the actual house located above Hollywood Boulevard, one half a mile east of Graumann's Chinese Theatre. The family, who played themselves on the air, ran on TV for 14 years in prime time, producing a mind-boggling 435 episodes.

The Rockford Files

28128 Pacific Coast Highway
Malibu, California

29 Cove Road was the fictional address of Jim Rockford's beach side trailer in the *Rockford Files*. It was really parked on the beach behind the Sandcastle restaurant at Paradise Cove off of Pacific Coast Highway, north of downtown Malibu.

Partridge Family

Warner Bros. Studio Ranch
3701 West Oak Street, Burbank, California

The Partridge home façade was located on the 40-acre back lot of this Warner Bros. ranch. It often doubled as the residence of the Kravitzs on the *Bewitched*. The Partridge home eventually met its end when it was bombed during the filming of the movie *Lethal Weapon*. The adjacent garage where the Partridge Family rehearsed their music still exists.

Also at the Warner Bros. ranch was the main house from *Bewitched*. The Stephen's residence is still visible on the lot at the corner of North Kenwood and West Streets. Thankfully, it barely survived an episode of the sitcom *Home Improvement* when Tim Taylor set it on fire.

Petticoat Junction

Railtown 1897 State Historic Park
5th and Reservoir Streets
Jamestown, California (south of Sonora on California Highway 49)
209-984-3953

Petticoat Junction was one of a number of successful rural comedies to emerge in the 1960s. First seen in September of 1963, *Petticoat Junction* centered around Kate Bradley, who ran the Shady Rest Hotel, located in the farming valley of Hooterville. Kate's three beautiful daughters, Billie Jo, Bobbie Jo, and Betty Jo were seen in the opening sequence of each show flipping their petticoats over the rim of a giant tower, located here at this charming park.

Many other TV shows and movies were shot here, and Petticoat Junction's Engine No. 3 is also on display in the roundhouse. Trains run seasonally; call ahead for schedules.

Peyton Place

Gilmanton, New Hampshire
603-267-6700

In the 1950s, the tiny town of Gilmanton was made reluctantly famous, or infamous, thanks to the late Grace Metalious, author of the notorious book *Peyton Place*. The novel, supposedly based on this rural community where the author lived, touched off the largest scandal in the area's history. It contained salacious tales of overt sex and adultery, hot stuff in 1956, and went on to sell over a million copies (as well as spawning a successful TV series and two movies). Metalious died at age 39 from liver damage brought on by too much drinking. Today, the town still has no formal acknowledgement of what brought them so much international attention.

Rivera, Geraldo

Basement of the Lexington Hotel Chicago
2135 South Michigan Avenue, Chicago, Illinois

In 1986, a nationally broadcast television special "The Mystery of Al Capone's Vault" was hosted by Geraldo Rivera – and it became the highest rated television special in history. Unfortunately, Rivera was unable to discover anything in the vaults, though he did fire a submachine gun into the walls of the second floor gymnasium where Capone's bodyguards used to work out.

When Al Capone moved into the Lexington Hotel in 1928, he rented the entire fourth floor and most of the third. He lived in #430, a six-room suite, and was living here in 1931 when he was convicted of tax evasion. The hotel was torn down in 1997.

Saturday Night Live

8-H Saturday Night Live
30 Rockefeller Plaza, New York, New York
212-664-3056

"Live, from New York, it's Saturday Night!" was first yelled by Chevy Chase on October 11, 1975. The show was called *NBC's Saturday Night* because the name *Saturday Night Live* was already taken by Howard Cosell's show on ABC. Further mocking his show, the cast was dubbed the "Not-Ready-For-Prime-Time Players" after Cosell's own "Prime-Time Players."

George Carlin hosted the first show. The musical guests (there were two that night) were Janice Ian and Billy Preston. Andy Kaufman also made an appearance, mouthing the words to the Mighty Mouse theme. The first ever sketch was called "The Wolverines," and it involved writer Michael O'Donoghue teaching nonsense English phrases to John Belushi (playing an Eastern European immigrant).

Seinfeld

Tom's Restaurant ("Monks")

2880 Broadway at 112th Street
New York, New York
212- 864-6137

The famous "Monk's" is actually Tom's Restaurant. This diner made pervious history by being the subject of Suzanne Vega's hit song, "Tom's Diner." While the interior looks nothing like it did on the show, there is Seinfeld memorabilia on the wall.

The Westway Diner

614 9th Avenue (between 44th and 43rd Streets)
New York, New York
212-582-7661

This diner may very well be the inspiration behind Monk's, rather than Tom's Restaurant. It is at this establishment that Larry David and Jerry Seinfeld came up with the idea for a show about nothing.

Soup Kitchen International

259A West 55th Street
(north side of the street
between 8th Avenue and Broadway)
New York, New York
212-757-7730

This is the home of the infamous "Soup Nazi."

Pendant Plaza

600 Madison Ave
(southwest corner of Madison and 55th Street)
New York, New York

As most Seinfeld fans should know, this is the publishing company where Elaine worked for much of the show.

Superman

Los Angeles City Hall
200 North Spring Street
Los Angeles, California

"Faster than a speeding bullet! More powerful that a locomotive! Able to leap tall buildings at a single bound! Look! Up in the sky! It's a bird! It's a plane! It's . . . Superman!" This famous building served as *The Daily Planet* building in the *Adventures of Superman* TV series starring the man of steel, George Reeves. The show premiered in 1951 (starting in black and white) and ran through 1957 (it was produced in color from 1954-57.) This building's image was also on Joe Friday's police badge in the series *Dragnet*.

77 Sunset Strip

8524 Sunset Boulevard
West Hollywood, California

Remember the old TV series *77 Sunset Strip*? If you do, you'll no doubt remember "Dino's Lodge." While it was indeed an actual building, it was torn down years ago. Return to the address today and you'll find that a plaque has been laid into the sidewalk, marking the spot made famous on the show, which starred Byron Keith, Edd Byrnes, and Efrem Zimbalist, Jr. among others.

The Tonight Show

Hudson Theatre
145 West 44th Street
New York, New York
212-789-7583

This legendary theatre has changed owner-ship many times and each new owner has added to its colorful history. The CBS Radio Playhouse broadcast from here in the 1930s and '40s. In 1950, NBC turned the theatre into a television studio. On September 27, 1956 the first nationwide broadcast of *The Tonight Show* starring Steve Allen came from the Hudson Theatre. Barbara Streisand made her television debut on the *Jack Paar Show*, also broadcast from the Hudson.

Saved from demolition by public outcry, it became part of the Macklowe Hotel in 1990. The Hudson Theatre was granted landmark status for both its interior and exterior fea-tures in 1987. Now called the Millennium Broadway, Millennium Conference Center, Restaurant Charlotte, and Hudson Theatre, it is fully restored and renovated with the tech-nical capabilities of a production studio.

The White Shadow

North Hollywood High
5321 Colfax Avenue
North Hollywood, California

Notre Dame High School
13645 Riverside Drive
Sherman Oaks, California

From 1978-1981, TV's *The White Shadow* (Ken Howard) coached basketball at "Carver High School," supposedly a gritty, inner-city environment. In real life, the exterior scenes were shot at these two very suburban high schools in the San Fernando Valley (North Hollywood High was used primarily for the establishing exterior shots). The show reached deep beyond basketball, using the team as a framework to feature stories cen-tered around drug problems, teenage crime, personal conflict, and the dangers of growing up in a tough neighborhood.

Play Ball!

Aaron, Hank

Fulton County Stadium
Lakewood Station
Atlanta, Georgia

Who can forget the sight of Aaron rounding the bases on April 8, 1974 in Atlanta, while those goofball fans chased him near shortstop and were pushed away by the new home-run king himself? Aaron hit the record-setting homerun – the 715th of his career (Babe Ruth had 714) – off of the Dodgers' lefthander Al Downing in the fourth inning of the Braves' home opener against Los Angeles. After the ball left Aaron's bat, Dodger centerfielder Jimmy Wynn and leftfielder Bill Buckner made a run for it, with Buckner even climbing the wall. Nevertheless, the ball made it into the Braves' bullpen after striking a billboard that said, "Think of it as money."

The ball was rounded up by Braves reliever Tom House, who quickly ran it in to Aaron at homeplate. The blast resulted in a game-delaying celebration, in which Aaron spoke to the crowd and hugged his dad. Aaron would go on to rack up 755 homers in his career, still the Major League record. The ballpark has since been torn down, but part of the retaining wall remains.

Ali, Muhammad

St. Dominick's Arena (now called the Central Maine Civic Center)
190 Birch Street, Lewiston, Maine
207-783-2009

On May 25, 1965, in a small community arena in Lewiston, Maine, the rematch took place between Cassius Clay (who by now had changed his name to Muhammad Ali) and former champion Sonny Liston. The bout had originally been scheduled for November 16, 1964, but several days before the fight it was discovered that Ali had a hernia. Due to the operation, the fight had to be postponed seven months.

Despite the buzz surrounding the match, only 2,434 people (about half-capacity) found their way to St. Dominick's Arena on fight night. The bout lasted just over a minute and a half; Ali threw only six punches before Liston went down. Liston was hit by a so-called "phantom-punch" that many of the spectators had not even seen. Seeing Liston on the canvas, Ali refused to go to the neutral corner but stood over Liston yelling: "Get up and fight, sucker!" That image of a scowling Ali has become one of sports' most famous snapshots.

Baseball

Elysian Fields
11th and Washington Streets, Hoboken, New Jersey

Frank Sinatra's birthplace is also the place where the first recorded baseball game was played on June 19, 1846 when Alexander Cartwright's Knickerbockers lost to the New York Baseball Club by a score of 23 to 1. The game was held at the Elysian Fields, in Hoboken, New Jersey. A plaque at 11th and Washington Streets in Hoboken commemorates the game.

Basketball

782 State Street, Springfield, Massachusetts
413-788-1444

Dr. James Naismith invented basketball on a cold, autumn day in 1891. He was the physical education instructor at the International YMCA Training School (now Springfield College) at Springfield, Massachusetts. Baseball had just finished up, and football was still a few weeks away. The athletes needed a sport to keep them in superb condition, and since it was too cold to train outside, Naismith had to think up a new indoor activity.

He remembered a game he played as a child called "Duck on a Rock." Changing a few rules around, he came out with the sport "Basketball." It was played with two peach baskets and a soccer ball, and 12 of the 13 rules Naismith created are still basic to the game. Today, a McDonald's near campus occupies the exact site of the "Naismith Gym." Inside are photos and some information describing the location's history.

Black Sox Courthouse

54 West Hubbard Street, Chicago, Illinois

"Say it ain't so, Joe" was supposedly uttered by a devastated kid as the disgraced Joe Jackson entered this one-time courthouse. It became known as the "Black Sox" scandal when several members of the Chicago White Sox conspired to lose the 1919 World Series to the Cincinnati Red Stockings. Despite their acquittal, Baseball Commissioner Judge Landis permanently banned all of those players from the game. Jackson, one of the greatest players of all-time, had a series batting average of .375 that year and played error-free defense. However, he still received the same lifetime banishment from Judge Landis which is what keeps him from the Hall of Fame. This building was the site of many other legendary trials, including the Leopold and Loeb murder case.

Chamberlain, Wilt

Hersheypark Arena
100 West Hershey Park Drive, Hershey, Pennsylvania
717-534-3911

It's arguably the NBA's most unbreakable record: 100 points in a single game, set by Philadelphia Warrior Wilt Chamberlain on March 2, 1962. The Warriors trained in Hershey and thus returned each season to play several games there for local fans. On this wintry night before just over 4,000 people (about half the gym's capacity), Chamberlain did the unthinkable in this arena that still stands in the world's chocolate capitol. The final score was Philadelphia over the New York Knicks, 169–147. The next night when these two teams played each other in New York, Chamberlain was "held" to just 54 points.

Cobb, Ty

Hilltop Park
Broadway (between West 165th and 168th Streets), New York, New York

This was the event that sealed the Georgia Peach's reputation as perhaps the biggest jerk in baseball history. On May 15, 1912, the Tigers were in New York to play the Yankees. A fan named Claude Lueker, who had lost one hand and three fingers on the other in a printing press accident, was heckling Cobb. The two traded insults for a couple of innings. After one exchange, Cobb charged into the grandstand and proceeded to beat and stomp Lueker. When somebody said he has no hands, Cobb shouted, "I don't care if he has no feet."

Lueker was pummeled by Cobb, who himself was suspended by league president Ban Johnson. In Detroit's next game against Philadelphia, Cobb suited up. The umpires told Cobb to leave so he did. But so did the rest of the Tigers. Cobb's suspension was eventually reduced to 10 days. The Columbia Presbyterian Hospital now occupies the site.

Decker, Mary

Los Angeles Memorial Coliseum
3911 South Figueroa Street
Los Angeles, California

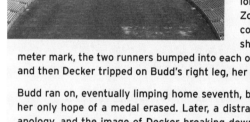

Mary Decker had hoped to run both the 1,500 and 3,000 meters at the Los Angeles Olympics in 1984, but withdrew from the 1,500 because the events overlapped. So her hopes were staked on the longer race, in which her rivals included Zola Budd, the diminutive South African controversially granted British citizenship earlier in the year. At the 1,700-meter mark, the two runners bumped into each other twice in the space of a few strides and then Decker tripped on Budd's right leg, her spikes digging deeply into Budd's heel.

Budd ran on, eventually limping home seventh, but Decker fell forward onto the infield, her only hope of a medal erased. Later, a distraught Decker refused to accept Budd's apology, and the image of Decker breaking down became synonymous with the event. Since the 1984 Olympics, the running track has been removed from the Coliseum.

Dempsey, Tom

Tulane Stadium
Aron Student Residences at Stadium Place
(intersection of McAlister Drive and Willow Street)
Tulane University
New Orleans, Louisiana
504-865-5724

On November 8, 1970, New Orleans Saints' placekicker Tom Dempsey, prepared to kick a 63-yard field goal in the closing seconds of a game against the Detroit Lions. If he made it, it would be the longest field goal in NFL history. The Lions were up 17 to 16 and so Dempsey was the Saints' last chance. Adding to the drama was the fact that  Dempsey's kicking foot was deformed to the point that he only had half a foot. Incredibly, Dempsey put it through the goalposts, making history and winning the game for the Saints. The images of the kick remain some of the most memorable in NFL history.

To date, the record stands as the longest, though Denver's Jason Elam tied the record in 1998. Tulane Stadium was the home field of the New Orleans Saints and the Sugar Bowl, as well as playing host to three Super Bowls. Torn down in 1980, there is not a single piece of the stadium remaining. However, three plaques that used to be on the stadium's walls remain, now placed at what once was the northeast corner of the stadium.

Dempsey, Jack/Tunney, Gene

Soldier Field
425 East McFetridge Drive, Chicago, Illinois
312- 747-1285

Dempsey vs. Tunney II at Soldier Field in Chicago produced a gate of $2.65 million, a record that stood for 50 years. A hugely-hyped rematch (Jack Dempsey had lost the first fight), the fight did not disappoint. In the seventh, Dempsey caught Gene Tunney with a long right and followed up with a left hook to the chin. For the first time in their two contests, Tunney was on his back foot and soon he was on the canvas, dropping hard after a four-punch flurry to his head.

Thus began boxing's fabled "long count." Dempsey – who would later ask what a neutral corner was – failed to back away from Tunney as the then-new rule dictated. Referee Dave Barry took several seconds to convince him to do so, but only after half-pushing Dempsey in the right direction did Barry turn back to Tunney and begin his count. He reached nine before a shaken (but clearly lucid) Tunney regained his feet.

Afterwards, Tunney would insist that he could have gotten up earlier. Either way, he managed to stave off Dempsey for the rest of the round and recovered to box his way to another points victory. He would retire unbeaten as a heavyweight, a record only Rocky Marciano has duplicated.

Flutie, Doug

The Orange Bowl
1501 N.W. 3rd Street
Miami, Florida

Doug Flutie, the 5-foot-9 Boston College quarterback already was considered a lock for the Heisman Trophy when, on November 23, 1984, he led the Eagles against Miami in the Orange Bowl (the annual game was moved to Pro Player Stadium in 1996). The Hurricanes led the Eagles 45-41, having gone ahead with 28 seconds remaining. But Flutie made the most of those remaining seconds.

Two passes and 22 seconds later, the ball was a couple of yards beyond midfield; time for just one more play. Flutie dropped back, scrambled, then launched the ball. Three receivers and three defenders were bunched together as they arrived at the goal line. Receiver Gerard Phelan drifted back a couple of yards away from them as the ball sailed toward the pack. Defensive backs Darrell Fullington and Reggie Sutton leaped to deflect the ball – which sailed over their fingertips and into Phelan's arms. Touchdown, making it Boston College 47, Miami 45 in one of football's wildest finishes.

Football

Recreation Park
Intersection of Grant and Pennsylvania Avenues, Pittsburgh, Pennsylvania

Pro football began in 1892 in Pittsburgh, Pennsylvania when former Yale star William "Pudge" Heffelfinger was paid $500 to play in a single game for the Allegheny Athletic Association on November 12th. The field was located near the former site of Three Rivers Stadium.

Gaedel, Eddie

Sportsman's Park
Area bounded by Dodier Street, Spring Street, Sullivan Avenue, and Grand Avenue
St. Louis, Missouri

One of the most publicized stunts in baseball history happened on August 18, 1951 when 3-foot 7-inch tall, 65-pound Eddie Gaedel, wearing a Browns uniform with the number 1/8, pinch hit in the first inning for Frank Saucier. Legendary Browns owner Bill Veeck had instructed the diminutive Brownie to crouch low, and not swing his toy-like bat. Due to the tiny strike zone, he walked in his only plate appearance. Sportsman's Park no longer stands, but the field (part of the Herbert Hoover Boy's and Girl's Club on North Grand Avenue) is still there.

Gathers, Hank

Gersten Pavilion
Loyola Marymount University
7900 Loyola Boulevard, Los Angeles, California
310-338-2700

As a junior the previous season, Loyola Marymount forward Hank Gathers was the NCAA's leading scorer and rebounder. But early in the 1990 season, he blacked out during a game. Doctors cleared him to play again, placing him on medication to regulate his arrhythmia – an erratic heartbeat.

On March 4, 1990, while playing against Portland in the semifinals of the West Coast Conference tournament played at Loyola, the 6-foot-7 Gathers slammed home a dunk, enthusiastically high fived a teammate and trotted back to midcourt. Suddenly, he put his hands on his knees and crumpled to the floor. Going into convulsions, he rolled over and got to his hands and knees before collapsing again. Despite efforts to revive him, he was pronounced dead at the hospital. Hank Gathers was just 23, and the chilling images of Gathers collapsing were shown for days following the tragedy.

Gretzky, Wayne

The Forum
3900 West Manchester Boulevard, Inglewood, California
310-419-3100

On March 23, 1994, Wayne Gretzky (who already had broken Gordie Howe's record for most points in NHL history), passed his hero once again. This time, it was for most goals scored in a career. Against the Vancouver Canucks on the power play, Gretzky tipped a pass into the net for his 802nd goal, putting him one up on Howe as the NHL's all-time leading goal scorer. Gretzky scored his 802 goals in just 1,117 games, while it took Howe 1,767 games to notch 801.

At a center-ice ceremony honoring the Los Angeles Kings center, NHL commissioner Gary Bettman gave Gretzky a book with a score sheet of every game in which he scored a goal. The Forum, once home to both the Kings and Lakers (before the building of Staples Center) is now used only sporadically.

Harris, Franco

Three Rivers Stadium
300 Stadium Circle, Pittsburgh, Pennsylvania

The "Immaculate Reception" refers to Franco Harris' miraculous 60-yard touchdown catch that gave the Pittsburgh Steelers a 13-7 victory over the Oakland Raiders in the 1972 AFC Divisional Playoffs. Down 7-6, with just over a minute left, the Steelers' Terry Bradshaw fired a pass downfield to halfback John Fuqua, who was nailed hard by Raiders defender Jack Tatum just as the ball arrived. It hit one of the players and bounced in the air and, luckily for the Steelers, into the hands of rookie running back Franco Harris.

After his "immaculate reception," Harris ran 42 yards to score with 5 seconds left, giving the Steelers an improbably 13-7 victory. It's still one of the most miraculous finish in the history of sports. The stadium has since been demolished.

Hayes, Woody

Memorial Stadium
Jacksonville University, Jacksonville, Florida

Woody Hayes, the legendary Ohio State coach, led the Buckeyes to three national championships while going 205-61-10 from 1951 to 1978. But his career ended ugly. Clemson led Ohio State 17-15 in the Gator Bowl, when Clemson's Charlie Bauman intercepted a pass with two minutes left. As he was run out-of-bounds on the Ohio State sideline, Hayes took a swing at him. With a huge TV audience watching and the subsequent photos that followed of the incident, Hayes' coaching career was over.

Irving, Julius

McNichols Arena
1635 Bryant Street, Denver, Colorado
303-640-7300

At the 9th ABA All-Star Game, on January 27, 1976, during halftime, the era of the Slam Dunk contest was ushered in to our culture. And Julius Irving, "Dr. J," created and perfected the mother of all dunks – his famous court-length, take-off-from-the-foul-line-and-throw-it-down showstopper. While the contest has certainly lost some of its luster over the years, this circus-like highlight is what set the entire slam dunk-as-entertainment train in motion. The arena has since been demolished.

Johnson, Magic/Larry Bird

Special Events Center at the University of Utah (now the Huntsman Center)
University of Utah
1825 East South Campus Drive Front, Salt Lake City, Utah

The NCAA tournament, which began the decade with a 25-team field, had expanded to include 40 teams by 1979, and the championship game featured Indiana State and Michigan State. Leading unbeaten Indiana State was Larry Bird (fifth-year senior, Player of the Year and already a first round draft pick of the Boston Celtics). The Spartans were led by Magic Johnson, just a sophomore, but a six foot, nine inch point guard – unheard of at the time.

Michigan State won the game by 11 as Magic outscored Bird, 24–19 in the most watched NCAA game in history. A year later, Bird was the NBA's Rookie of the Year in the NBA and Magic, who entered the 1979 draft as an underclassman, helped lead the Los Angeles Lakers to the world championship.

Jordan, Michael

Delta Center
301 West South Temple
Salt Lake City, Utah
801-325-2000

This was Bob Costas' call: "Here comes Chicago–17 seconds, 17 seconds from game 7 or from championship number 6. Jordan – open – Chicago with the lead!" That shot over Byron Russell, at that point the "last shot" of Jordan's remarkable career, gave the Bulls a victory over the Utah Jazz, and the Bulls' sixth NBA championship in eight years. The image of Jordan canning the shot is still one of the most enduring in the NBA. Since then, the actual piece of floor was taken up, auctioned off, placed in pieces of collectible cards, etc.

King, Billie Jean/Bobby Riggs

Houston Astrodome
8400 Kirby Drive
Houston, Texas

On September 20, 1973, Billie Jean King raised women's tennis to new heights with her "Battle of the Sexes" victory over the outspoken chauvinist Bobby Riggs. Riggs, the 55-year-old hustler who had challenged King to a best three sets out of five match, had vowed there was no way a woman could beat him. And if King did, he promised to jump off a bridge somewhere in California – that never happened. King rolled to an easy 6-4, 6-3, 6-3 straight sets victory, and Riggs was so tired, he could barely speak.

It happened in front of the largest crowd ever to watch a tennis match (30,472), with a television audience estimated at 40 million, and with viewers tuned in via satellite in 36 foreign countries. The Houston Astrodome was the world's first air-conditioned, domed, all-purpose stadium. Constructed in the early 1960s, it was the home of the Houston Astros from 1965-1999.

Knievel, Evel

Snake River Canyon, Twin Falls, Idaho
203-733-3974

Directions: A mile north of town on US-93, south of the I-84 freeway. The jump site can be seen from the Twin Falls Visitors Center at the south end of the Perrine Bridge.

This is the site of Evel Knievel's ill-fated attempt to jump the Snake River Canyon on a rocket-powered motorcycle on September 8, 1974. Although the rockets did not perform as required, the daredevil jumper still floated by parachute to safety.

There's a large parking area and a visitor center at the south foot of the delicate Perrine Memorial Bridge, and it's well worth stopping to see the remains of his launch pad (a triangular pile of dirt, on private property a mile or so east of the bridge) or the stone monument that calls him "Robert 'Evel' Knievel – Explorer, Motorcyclist, Daredevil."

Knight, Bobby

Assembly Hall at Indiana University
1001 East 17th Street
Bloomington, Indiana
866-IUSPORT

On February 23, 1985, Knight's Hoosiers were playing the Purdue Boilermakers at home. While Purdue's Steve Reid was attempting to shoot free throws, the notorious hothead Knight tossed a chair across the court, nearly hitting the people in the wheelchair section across the way. Knight was ejected from the game and suspended for one game by Big Ten Commissioner Wayne Duke. Knight issued a statement apologizing for the incident, but the image of the toss came to define the coach's always intense, sometimes violent tendencies he's showed through much of his career.

Also at Assembly Hall, in 1997, Bobby Knight was caught on videotape choking Hoosier player Neil Reed during a practice. Though there had been other accusations of physical abuse against Knight over the years, the tape seemed to back up the player's charge that Knight had in fact grabbed him around the neck, forcing his head to snap back. This incident was instrumental in helping to spark a zero tolerance policy that Indiana's Board of Trustees eventually imposed on Knight. It also resulted in a $30,000 fine and a three game suspension – which many fans felt was a light punishment given the evidence. Neil Reed left Indiana in 1997.

After 29 years with Indiana University, three national championships, and 763 victories, Bobby Knight was fired in September 2000, for violating the school's no tolerance policy. Currently he is the head basketball coach at Texas Tech University.

Laettner, Christian

Philadelphia Spectrum
601 South Broad Street, Philadelphia, Pennsylvania
215-389-9558

On March 28th, 1992, at the NCAA East Regional men's basketball final, Kentucky had just taken a one-point lead on Sean Woods' bank shot with two seconds left. After a timeout, an unguarded Grant Hill threw a risky, baseball-style pass some 80 feet to Christian Laettner (who was set up near the foul line) who, stunningly, dribbled, faked and spun before releasing what became one of the most miraculous shots in college hoops history. Duke won that game 104-103, and a week later won their second consecutive National Championship in Minneapolis.

Maravich, Pete

First Church Of the Nazarene of Pasadena
3700 East Sierra Madre Boulevard, Pasadena, California
626-351-9631

On January 5, 1988, basketball great "Pistol Pete" Maravich joined Dr. James Dobson's 7:00 A.M. basketball scrimmage at this church gymnasium. Moments after telling Dr. Dobson he felt great, Pete collapsed, went into seizure and died of congenital heart failure. Just 40 years old, the scrappy, former NBA All-Star was famous for his droopy socks and mop-top hairdo. In college, Maravich averaged 44.2 points a game at LSU, leading the nation in scoring three times, then played 10 years in the NBA, where he was the top scorer in 1977.

Mazeroski, Bill

Forbes Field
230 South Bouquet Street (at the intersection of Sennott and Bouquet)
Pittsburgh, Pennsylvania

Bill Mazeroski was the first player to end a World Series with a home run, and the image of his shot clearing both the head of Yogi Berra and the red brick outfield wall at old Forbes Field is one of baseball's best (as is the sequence of Mazeroski then rounding the bases and getting mobbed at homeplate).

In the 1960 Fall Classic, the Yankees had rallied with two runs in the top of the 9th to tie the game 9-9. Mazeroski led off the 9th and hit a 1-0 slider over the left field wall to give Pittsburgh a 10-9 victory and a World Series title. Today, Forbes Field is gone, but you can still cross homeplate where Mazeroski got mobbed. It sits encased in plastic near its original location in a hallway of the University of Pittsburgh.

"THIS MARKS THE SPOT WHERE BILL MAZEROSKI'S HOME RUN BALL CLEARED THE LEFT CENTER FIELD WALL OF FORBES FIELD ON OCTOBER 13, 1960, THEREBY WINNING THE WORLD SERIES CHAMPIONSHIP FOR THE PITTSBURGH PIRATES. THE HISTORIC HIT CAME IN THE NINTH INNING OF THE SEVENTH GAME, TO BEAT THE NEW YORK YANKEES BY A SCORE OF 10-9."

Miracle on Ice

Olympic Regional Development Authority
218 Main Street
Lake Placid, New York
518-523-1655

"Do you believe in Miracles?" It's thought by many to be the greatest moment in sports history, one that may have even helped end the Cold War. All thanks to the rag-tag group of college players that shocked the world by beating the heavily favored Russians before going on to win the gold medal at the 1980 Winter Games in Lake Placid. Today at the rink, a museum can be found which honors both the 1980 and the 1932 Games that were both played here.

Munson, Thurman

Akron-Canton Airport
5400 Lauby Road NW
North Canton, Ohio

On August 2, 1979, Thurman Munson, superstar catcher for the New York Yankees, died in a plane crash. The 32-year old was practicing takeoffs and landings in his new twin engine Cessna Citation jet at the Akron-Canton airport. Something went wrong, causing the jet to clip a tree and fall short of the runway on a landing attempt. The plane then burst into flames, killing Munson who was trapped inside, and injuring two other companions. The entire Yankee team attended his funeral in Canton, Ohio.

Namath, Joe

The Miami Touchdown Club
3785 N.W. 82nd Avenue, Suite 111
Miami, Florida
305-477-1815

The Jets were given little chance of winning Super Bowl III against the Baltimore Colts in 1969. Writers and bookmakers alike all predicted a blowout for the Colts. But none of this fazed Jet Quarterback Joe Namath. In fact, at a Super Bowl week awards dinner at this private club, Namath stunned both experts and fans with his now famous boast: "The Jets will win on Sunday, I guarantee you." True to his words, on Super Bowl Sunday, "Broadway Joe" completed 17 of 28 passes for 206 yards and the inspired Jets made big defensive plays to stun the Colts 16-7, completing one of the biggest upsets in sports history.

The Polo Grounds

155th Street and 8th Avenue
New York, New York

Home of three teams for more than a half a century, the Polo Grounds was one of baseball and football's most hallowed parks. It stood in the area known as Coogan's Bluff from 1911 until 1964 and hosted many memorable moments. It was the home of the Yankees in the early 1920s and the New York Giants home field until the team moved to San Francisco in 1957. The New York Mets played there from 1962-63. Today, a plaque marks the site where home plate used to sit. Here are just a few of the memorable—both tragic and heroic—events that took place at this hallowed stadium:

Chapman, Ray

Ray Chapman is the only modern major leaguer to have died as a direct result of being hit by a pitch. It happened here on August 16, 1920, when Chapman, crowding the plate as usual, was struck in the temple by a pitch from fiery Yankee submarine baller Carl Mays. The much-loved Chapman (who was able to walk off the field) was taken to St. Lawrence hospital in New York City, but he never regained consciousness and died 12 hours later.

Interestingly, Chapman was replaced at shortstop by rookie Joe Sewell, who was about to embark upon a Hall of Fame career. Cleveland Indian players wore black arm bands the rest of the season, and manager Tris Speaker rallied his crestfallen men to win the first World Championship in club history, taking the World Series from the Brooklyn Dodgers.

Football's "Sneaker Game"

The night before the December 9, 1934 NFL Championship game, freezing rain all but turned the Polo Grounds into a skating rink. At half time, with his team trailing 10-3, Giants coach Steve Owen sent his the equipment manager, Abe Cohen, in search of better footwear for the team.

Cohen returned with sneakers for the entire team, which greatly improved their traction on the icy field. In the second half, the Giants exploded behind halfback Ed Downowski, who ran for a touchdown and threw for another. The 8-5 Giants then upset the previously undefeated Bears, ending the Bears' championship streak at two in one of the strangest games in NFL history.

The Polo Grounds

Hubbell, Carl

On July 10, 1934, New York Giant's pitcher (and future Hall of Famer) Carl Hubbell did what seemed like the impossible at the second Baseball All-Star Game. After allowing a single and a walk, Hubbell struck out Babe Ruth, who went down looking. Then he fanned Lou Gehrig who went swinging. Hubbell ended the inning by striking out Jimmie Foxx, normally a first baseman but playing third in this game because of Gehrig's presence at first. Next inning, Hubbell struck out Al Simmons and Joe Cronin, making it five future Hall of Famers to go down on strikeouts consecutively.

Mays, Willie

It's generally regarded as "The greatest catch of all-time." With the score tied 2-2 in the first game of the 1954 World Series, Cleveland Indians' slugger Vic Wertz drove a ball deep into straight-away center. New York Giants' centerfielder Willie Mays ran straight back, catching the ball over his head while in a full-speed stride, turned and threw to home from 440 feet away keeping the runner from scoring. Don Liddle, the pitcher who had entered the game to face Wertz, was removed before the next batter. As he came into the dugout he jokingly flipped his mitt to a teammate and said, "Well, I got my guy." Today a basketball court sits at the exact location where Mays hauled in the ball.

Ruth, Babe

On May 6, 1915, Red Sox pitcher Babe Ruth clobbered his very first Major League home run, off the Yankees Jack Warhop in the third inning at the Polo Grounds. Ruth had two other hits but lost the game in the 13th, 4-3, as the Red Sox commit four errors behind him.

Thomson, Bobby

One of the most dramatic homeruns in baseball history (if not *the* most dramatic), happened on October 3, 1951. Bobby Thomson's three-run home run off Brooklyn Dodger pitcher Ralph Branca clinched the pennant for the Giants and broke the heart of the borough of Brooklyn in one sudden instant. It happened in the first inning of the final game of a three-game playoff; the Giants and Dodgers had wound up the season in a tie for first.

As memorable as the homerun was, the call of the Giant's announcer Russ Hodges screaming "The Giants win the pennant, the Giants win the pennant!" lives on as well.

Riegels, Roy

Rose Bowl
1001 Rose Bowl Drive
Pasadena, California
626- 577-3100

This is what legendary announcer Graham McNamee screamed as he broadcast the 1929 Rose Bowl game between Georgia Tech and California. "Am I crazy? Am I crazy? Am I crazy? Am I crazy?" What was he seeing? Roy Riegels of the California Bears had snagged a football fumbled by Georgia Tech. He caught it on the first bounce, got spun around and, seeing daylight, sprinted toward the goal line 64 yards away. However, he was headed the wrong way!

Teammate Benny Lom chased Riegels half the length of the field, shouting at him to turn around. It wasn't until he had almost crossed the goal line, with Lom pulling at him, that Riegels understood and tried to reverse direction. But it was too late. Georgia Tech gang-tackled him at the one-yard line.

Robinson, Jackie

Ebbets Field
Area bounded by Sullivan Place, Bedford Avenue, Montgomery Street, and McKeever Place.
Brooklyn, New York

April 15, 1947, was the day that Jackie Robinson played his first game for the Brooklyn Dodgers, the first time a black man had appeared in a Major League baseball game. He went hitless, but did score the winning run.

That season, the 28-year-old rookie played first base, the only position open on the Dodgers (he would move back to second base the next year). The new position was easy compared to all he had to endure – taunting and a near rebellion by some of his teammates, black cats thrown on the field, and many other threats. Despite the pressure, he kept his temper under control.

One poignant moment at this first game happened when Dodgers' shortstop Pee Wee Reese, a native of Louisville, draped an arm over Robinson's shoulder, a quiet expression of support that spoke volumes.

Rose, Pete

Riverfront Stadium
100 Riverfront Stadium, Cincinnati, Ohio

Ironically, the night before the July 14, 1970 baseball All Star Game, Pete Rose had dinner with friend Sam McDowell and catcher Ray Fosse (over at Rose's house). The next night, Rose again had Fosse for dinner, figuratively speaking. In the 12th inning, Rose scored the National League's winning run on Jim Hickman's single to center. But as the aggressively running Rose hit home plate, he crashed into Fosse with a football shoulder block, crushing the catcher.

Despite the broken shoulder he suffered in the famous incident, Fosse went on to catch for the 1973-75 pennant-winning A's. However, injuries took their toll on him and forced an early retirement. He later became an Oakland executive and broadcaster. Riverfront Stadium, later re-named Cinergy Field, was demolished in 2003.

Ruth, Babe

Wrigley Field
1060 West Addison Street, Chicago, Illinois
773-404-2827

Did he or didn't he? Baseball's most greatly debated legend was born when New York Yankee Babe Ruth faced Chicago Cubs pitcher Charlie Root at Wrigley Field on October 1, 1932, in the fifth inning of the third game of the World Series. Some believe that the "Sultan of Swat" boldly pointed to centerfield to indicate that on the next pitch he would hit a home run. Others say Ruth was merely chiding the Cubs bench in answer to their taunting of him.

Well, we know that he hit the homerun, but newspaper reports and eyewitness accounts of the day differ as to whether Ruth really "called his shot." The pitcher, Root, never gave the legend any credence. Ruth, however, would for years offer varying accounts of his own dramatic feat. Today, Wrigley Field remains the home to the Chicago Cubs.

Trevino, Lee

Cog Hill Golf & Country Club (Dubsdread Course)
12294 Archer Avenue, Lemont, Illinois
630-257-5872

At the 1975 Western Open, golfers Lee Trevino, Jerry Heard, and Bobby Nichols were all struck by lightning. All three men survived, and Trevino went on to win the 1984 PGA Championship and have a record-setting career on the Senior PGA Tour. But this one incident prompted brand new safety standards in weather preparedness at PGA events.

Tyson, Mike/Evander Holyfield

MGM Grand Hotel
3799 Las Vegas Boulevard, South Las Vegas, Nevada
800-929-1111

On June 28, 1997, during Holyfield-Tyson II, with 40 seconds left in the third round, Evander Holyfield stepped away from Mike Tyson and began jumping up and down. The replay clearly (and graphically) showed that Tyson had bitten a chunk out of Holyfield's right ear.

Tyson was warned that another foul would cost him the bout. A few seconds later, Tyson spit his mouth guard out and bit Holyfield's *left* ear. Then the fight was stopped and Tyson was disqualified. He attempted to charge Holyfield's corner, but succeeded only in punching one of the security guards. Fortunately, the chunk of ear was found and taken to a hospital, where it was sewn back onto Holyfield.

Washington, Kermit/Rudy Tomjanovich

The Forum
3900 West Manchester Boulevard, Inglewood, California
310-419-3100

On December 9, 1977, during a game between the Houston Rockets and the Los Angeles Lakers, Rocket all-star Rudy Tomjanovich was rushing to help his teammate Kevin Kunnert, who was in the midst of a tangle first with Kareem Abdul-Jabbar and then with Kermit Washington. Tomjanovich ran up right behind Washington, who turned and delivered a nearly fatal right-hand punch to Tomjanovich's face, knocking him to the floor. The punch remains one of the most horrifying video clips in sports (or any) history.

Tomjanovich had five operations, and missed the remainder of the season, while Washington served a 60-day suspension. Neither player's careers were ever the same, though Tomjanovich went on to a successful coaching career. Washington's term as a player ended in disgrace soon after the punch.

Weissmuller, Johnny

Payne-Whitney Gymnasium, Yale University
20 Tower Parkway, New Haven, Connecticut

On March 6, 1923, Johnny Weissmuller (who would later gain fame as "Tarzan") became the first swimmer to break five minutes for 440 yards. Weissmuller, representing the Illinois Athletic Club, finished in 4:57, clipping 11 seconds off his own world record of 5:08. The record was the 47th set by the great swimmer.

Yankee Stadium

**161st Street and River Avenue
Bronx, New York
718-293-4300**

The Yankees legendary home since 1923, this venerable stadium obviously has hosted some landmark moments. It was nicknamed "The House That Ruth Built" in honor of Babe Ruth, whose huge drawing power all but guaranteed huge crowds when the ballpark opened. Prior to playing here, the Yankees played just across the Harlem River at the Polo Grounds, sharing it with the New York Giants.

Gehrig, Lou

It's one of the most famous speeches in American history, let alone baseball history. Gehrig, who was stricken with the devastating disease that would one day bare his name, addressed the 4th of July crowd in 1939 as they honored his courage, his talents, and the many examples he had set for the youth of America. "Fans, for the past two weeks you have been reading about the bad break I got. Yet today, I consider myself the luckiest man on the face of the earth. . . ."

Larsen, Don

Who can forget the image of catcher Yogi Berra jumping into the arms of pitcher Don Larsen after Larsen completed the impossible—a perfect game in the 1956 World Series? Ironically, in the second game of the Series, Larsen had been chased out in the second inning. But game five was different. Larsen faced Sal Maglie of the Dodgers in a historic pitching duel. Larsen set down 27 Dodgers in a row to get a 2-0 win for the Yankees—the only perfect game to ever be thrown in a World Series.

Dale Mitchell was the last batter to face Larsen, going down on a called strike three. Mitchell thought the ball was outside, but it didn't matter—that was the ump's call and the game was over. As soon as the strike was called, catcher Yogi Berra ran on the field and jumped into Larsen's arms as the celebration began.

Yankee Stadium

Louis, Joe/Max Schmeling

On June 22, 1948, as the winds of war began to swirl, American boxer Joe Louis owned the heavyweight title and was prepared to defend it in a rematch with his old German nemesis, Max Schmeling. Given that Schmeling was a follower of German leader Adolf Hitler, the fight contained an extra layer of drama – a Schmeling victory would fuel the German fire of "white superiority" since Louis was an African-American. However, Louis decimated the German in a one-round TKO.

Maris, Roger

It was October 1, 1961, the season finale between the Yankees and Red Sox. Roger Maris had 60 home runs and was tied with Babe Ruth for the single-season home run mark. The Yankees had already clinched the AL pennant, so the only drama left was to see whether Maris would snag the record. In the fourth, Maris hit a 2-0 fastball off Tracy Stallard, the Boston starter, into the right field seats to become  baseball's single-season home run king. Interestingly, Yankee Stadium was one-third full– only 23,154 fans turned out to see if Maris could break Ruth's mark. Baseball Commissioner Ford Frick became a legend due to the infamous "asterisk" placed after the record. It was his belief that the record had to be broken in the same amount of games as Babe Ruth, which in 1927 was 154. Since it took Maris 162, the records were listed separately in the record book– one for each type of season.

NFL Championship Game, December 28, 1958

The matchup was the New York Giants and the Baltimore Colts. With a 14-3 lead in the 3rd quarter, the Colts had the ball on the Giants' 1-yard line and seemed to coasting toward a championship victory. But the Giants made a determined goal-line stand, got the ball on their own 5-yard line, and drove downfield for a touchdown make it 14-10.

In the 4th quarter, Frank Gifford caught a touchdown pass to give the Giants a 17-14 lead. But legendary Colts quarterback Johnny Unitas marched his team downfield to get within field goal range. With just seven seconds left, the Colts tied the game with a field goal to force the first post-season overtime in NFL history.

In the extra period, the Giants were forced to punt and Unitas went to work. Leading the Colts 80 yards into the Giant's zone, this set up the famous one-yard touchdown plunge from Colt's fullback Alan "The Horse" Ameche, ending what many still call "the greatest game ever played."

Pop Culture Landmarks by State

Acknowledgments

Many individuals and organizations have been so generous with their time, information, and materials, that it would probably take another book to thank them all. So collectively and with much gratitude, I offer a heartfelt "thank you."

In particular, I'd like to acknowledge my publisher and editor (and now friend), Jeffrey Goldman, for his humor, professionalism, and good judgment. Thank you, Jeffrey. Also, to Ken Niles for his smart design and ingenious cover idea for this book. To Dave Lugin, for his enthusiastic interest in the book and great suggestions. Hank Donat, the brains behind the terrific MisterSF.com has been a wealth of Bay Area information and a good supporter.

The resources of both the National Parks Service and the Library of Congress are invaluable and I encourage everyone to take advantage of all they have to offer. To the collective mailing list who receives (and many times responds to) my chrisepting.com updates, thanks for all of your interaction.

To my wife, Jean; son, Charlie; daughter, Claire; my Mom, sisters Margaret and Lee, Ciro, Billy, Linda and Luca: thank you, gang, for helping to make every day historic.

In memory of my grandmother, Margaret Gallo, and my father, Lawrence Epting. And finally, thank you to David McAleer. He's a cousin, he's a friend, he's like the brother I never had. You're the best, kid.

Chris Epting

Photo Credits

© Bettmann/CORBIS, p. 16, p. 28 bottom, p. 34, p. 107 middle right, p. 109 top, p. 149 upper right, p. 284 bottom

Dan Tobias, p. 17

Central Methodist Church, p. 21 top

Oatman Hotel, p. 22 bottom

The Punxsutawney Spirit, p. 23 top

Louis' Lunch, p. 23 bottom

Ivy Green, Birthplace of Helen Keller, p. 27

Cathedral of Saint Matthew the Apostle, p. 28 top

Ed Jackson, p. 29 top

Harland Sanders Café and Museum, p. 30 top

Hidalgo Chamber of Commerce, p. 30 bottom

David McAleer, p. 32, p. 35, p. 44 top/bottom, p. 93, p. 98, p. 100 bottom, p. 114, p. 127 top, p. 189, p. 220 top, p. 223 top, p. 226 top, p. 230 bottom, p. 233 bottom, p. 234, p. 239 top, p. 243 bottom, p. 266 bottom, p. 270 top and middle, p. 276, p. 279, p. 281, p. 285 top, p. 286 bottom

The International Mother's Day Shrine, p. 36 top

Point Pleasant Chamber of Commerce, p. 36 bottom

UFO Museum and Research Center, p. 37 top and middle

Wabash Chamber of Commerce, p. 40 top

© 2002 Dan Kuja, p. 40 bottom

Courtesy Betsy Ross/Historic Philadelphia, Inc. (2003 Historic Philadelphia, Inc.), p. 43 top

The Boston Insider at www.TheInsider.com, p. 43 bottom

Philip Greenspun, p. 45 bottom

National Park Service, p. 46 top, p. 47 top and bottom, p. 50 top and bottom, p. 58, p. 66 top, p. 67, p. 69 top, p. 70 top, p. 74 bottom, p. 75 bottom, p. 76, p. 112, p. 182 bottom, p. 207 top

Wesley Treat, p. 51, bottom, p. 188 bottom

Golden Spike National Historic Site, p. 53

Marshall Gold Discovery State Historic Park, p. 54 top

Brooke Huntsinger and Todd Olsen, p. 54 bottom, p. 95 bottom, p. 122 bottom, p. 225 top, p. 285 bottom

Public Affairs Office, Naval Air Engineering Station Lakehurst, p. 56 top and bottom, p. 57 top and bottom

Johnstown Flood National Memorial, p. 60 top

Sylvia J. Capper, p. 60 bottom

Images of American Political History, p. 61, p. 63, p. 97 middle and bottom, p. 99 top and bottom, p. 117 left

Gary Harwood, Copyright Kent State University, p. 62, top, bottom left, and bottom right; p. 108

Lewis and Clark National Historic Trail, p. 65

William P. Wattles, Ph.D., p. 68

USGS/Cascades Volcano Observatory, p. 69, bottom

Rosa Parks Library and Museum, p. 72 top

Pony Express Museum, p. 74, top and middle

Scopes Trial Museum and Rhea County Courthouse, p. 77

Independence Seaport Museum, p. 79 top

Library of Congress, p. 80, p. 84 bottom three, p. 111 top, middle, and bottom; p. 121 top and bottom

The Curry Pilot, p. 81

Trinity Site, White Sands Missile Range, p. 82 and 83

Courtesy F. Lawrence McFall, p. 84 top

Edwards Air Force Base, p. 85

Gibsland Museum, p. 90 top

Lizzie Borden Bed and Breakfast Museum, p. 90 bottom

Fort Sumner state Park, p. 100 top

Hank Donat, p. 101 top and middle, p. 233 top, p. 259 bottom

Old Style Saloon No. 10, p. 103 top and bottom

Dick Tinder, p. 104 top and bottom

Books Available From Santa Monica Press

Blues for Bird
by Martin Gray
288 pages $16.95

The Book of Good Habits
*Simple and Creative Ways
to Enrich Your Life*
by Dirk Mathison
224 pages $9.95

The Butt Hello
*and other ways my cats
drive me crazy*
by Ted Meyer
96 pages $9.95

Café Nation
*Coffee Folklore, Magick,
and Divination*
by Sandra Mizumoto Posey
224 pages $9.95

**Discovering the History
of Your House**
and Your Neighborhood
by Betsy J. Green
288 pages $14.95

Exploring Our Lives
*A Writing Handbook for
Senior Adults*
by Francis E. Kazemek
288 pages $14.95

Footsteps in the Fog
Alfred Hitchcock's San Francisco
by Jeff Kraft and
Aaron Leventhal
240 pages $24.95

**Free Stuff & Good Deals
for Folks over 50, 2nd Ed.**
by Linda Bowman
240 pages $12.95

**Jackson Pollock: Memories
Arrested in Space**
by Martin Gray
192 pages $14.95

James Dean Died Here
*The Locations of America's
Pop Culture Landmarks*
by Chris Epting
312 pages $16.95

**How to Find Your Family
Roots and Write Your
Family History**
by William Latham and
Cindy Higgins
288 pages $14.95

How to Speak Shakespeare
by Cal Pritner and
Louis Colaianni
144 pages $16.95

**How to Win Lotteries,
Sweepstakes, and Contests
in the 21st Century**
by Steve "America's
Sweepstakes King" Ledoux
224 pages $14.95

The Keystone Kid
Tales of Early Hollywood
by Coy Watson, Jr.
312 pages $24.95

Letter Writing Made Easy!
*Featuring Sample Letters for
Hundreds of Common
Occasions*
by Margaret McCarthy
224 pages $12.95

**Letter Writing Made Easy!
Volume 2**
*Featuring More Sample
Letters for Hundreds of
Common Occasions*
by Margaret McCarthy
224 pages $12.95

**Nancy Shavick's Tarot
Universe**
by Nancy Shavick
336 pages $15.95

Offbeat Food
*Adventures in an
Omnivorous World*
by Alan Ridenour
240 pages $19.95

Offbeat Golf
*A Swingin' Guide to a
Worldwide Obsession*
by Bob Loeffelbein
192 pages $17.95

Offbeat Marijuana
*The Life and Times of the
World's Grooviest Plant*
by Saul Rubin
240 pages $19.95

Offbeat Museums
*The Collections and Curators
of America's Most Unusual
Museums*
by Saul Rubin
240 pages $19.95

Past Imperfect
*How Tracing Your Family
Medical History Can Save
Your Life*
by Carol Daus
240 pages $12.95

A Prayer for Burma
by Kenneth Wong
216 pages $14.95

Quack!
*Tales of Medical Fraud from
the Museum of Questionable
Medical Devices*
by Bob McCoy
240 pages $19.95

Redneck Haiku
by Mary K. Witte
112 pages $9.95

**The Seven Sacred Rites
of Menarche**
*The Spiritual Journey of the
Adolescent Girl*
by Kristi Meisenbach Boylan
160 pages $11.95

**The Seven Sacred Rites
of Menopause**
*The Spiritual Journey to
the Wise-Woman Years*
by Kristi Meisenbach Boylan
144 pages $11.95

Silent Echoes
*Discovering Early Hollywood
Through the Films of Buster
Keaton*
by John Bengtson
240 pages $24.95

Tiki Road Trip
*A Guide to Tiki Culture in
North America*
by James Teitelbaum
288 pages $16.95

What's Buggin' You?
*Michael Bohdan's Guide to
Home Pest Control*
by Michael Bohdan
256 pages $12.95

Order Form 1-800-784-9553

	Quantity	Amount

Blues for Bird (epic poem about Charlie Parker) ($16.95)

The Book of Good Habits ($9.95)

The Butt Hello . . . and Other Ways My Cats Drive Me Crazy ($9.95)

Café Nation: Coffee Folklore, Magick and Divination ($9.95)

Discovering the History of Your House. . . ($14.95)

Exploring Our Lives: A Writing Handbook for Senior Adults ($14.95)

Footsteps in the Fog: Alfred Hitchcock's San Francisco ($24.95)

Free Stuff & Good Deals for Folks over 50, 2nd Ed. ($12.95)

Jackson Pollock: Memories Arrested in Space ($14.95)

James Dean Died Here: America's Pop Culture Landmarks ($16.95)

How to Find Your Family Roots . . . ($14.95)

How to Speak Shakespeare ($16.95)

How to Win Lotteries, Sweepstakes, and Contests . . . ($14.95)

The Keystone Kid: Tales of Early Hollywood ($24.95)

Letter Writing Made Easy! ($12.95)

Letter Writing Made Easy! Volume 2 ($12.95)

Nancy Shavick's Tarot Universe ($15.95)

Offbeat Food ($19.95)

Offbeat Golf ($17.95)

Offbeat Marijuana ($19.95)

Offbeat Museums ($19.95)

Past Imperfect: Tracing Your Family Medical History ($12.95)

A Prayer for Burma ($14.95)

Quack! Tales of Medical Fraud ($19.95)

Redneck Haiku ($9.95)

The Seven Sacred Rites of Menarche ($11.95)

The Seven Sacred Rites of Menopause ($11.95)

Silent Echoes: Early Hollywood Through Buster Keaton ($24.95)

Tiki Road Trip ($16.95)

What's Buggin' You?: A Guide to Home Pest Control ($12.95)

Shipping & Handling:	Subtotal _____
1 book – $3.00	CA residents add 8.25% sales tax _____
Each additional book is $ .50	Shipping and Handling (see left) _____
	TOTAL _____

Name_____

Address_____

City_____ State_____ Zip_____

❑ Visa ❑ MasterCard   Card No.:_____

Exp. Date_____ Signature_____

❑ Enclosed is my check or money order payable to:

Santa Monica Press LLC
P.O. Box 1076
Santa Monica, CA 90406

SANTA MONICA PRESS

www.santamonicapress.com 1-800-784-9553